MAGICAL CRITICISM

MAGICAL CRITICISM

The Recourse of Savage Philosophy

CHRISTOPHER BRACKEN

THE UNIVERSITY OF CHICAGO PRESS

CHICAGO AND LONDON

CHRISTOPHER BRACKEN is associate professor of English at the University of Alberta and author of *The Potlatch Papers: A Colonial Case History.*

The University of Chicago Press, Chicago 60637
The University of Chicago Press, Ltd., London
© 2007 by The University of Chicago
All rights reserved. Published 2007
Printed in the United States of America

16 15 14 13 12 11 10 09 08 07   1 2 3 4 5
ISBN-13: 978-0-226-06990-6 (cloth)
ISBN-13: 978-0-226-06991-3 (paper)
ISBN-10: 0-226-06990-7 (cloth)
ISBN-10: 0-226-06991-5 (paper)

Library of Congress Cataloging-in-Publication Data

Bracken, Christopher.
   Magical criticism : the recourse of savage philosophy / Christopher Bracken.
      p.   cm.
   Includes bibliographical references and index.
   ISBN-13: 978-0-226-06990-6 (cloth : alk. paper)
   ISBN-10: 0-226-06990-7 (cloth : alk. paper)
   ISBN-13: 978-0-226-06991-3 (pbk. : alk. paper)
   ISBN-10: 0-226-06991-5 (pbk. : alk. paper)
   1. Semiotics.   2. Magical thinking.   3. Philosophy and civilization.
4. Ethnophilosophy—History.   I. Title.
   B840.B67   2007
   301.01—dc22

                                                   2006038722

♾ The paper used in this publication meets the minimum requirements of the American National Standard for Information Sciences—Permanence of Paper for Printed Library Materials, ANSI Z39.48-1992.

It is by a long, long road that I choose to go back to primitive life. What I need first is condemnation by my race.

—Jean Genet, *The Thief's Journal*

CONTENTS

ACKNOWLEDGMENTS

Duncan Greenlaw, Karen Engle, Cheryl Suzack, and Cody McCarroll did excellent work as my research assistants; they have since gone on to higher tasks. Cheryl Suzack, Cody McCarroll, Karlyn Koh, and Karyn Ball read drafts of the manuscript. Karyn Ball vocally supported the project for many years in many conversations. I thank the readers for the University of Chicago Press for their suggestions and enthusiasm—which came at just the right time. Chapter 4 is loosely adapted from "The Language of Things: Walter Benjamin's Primitive Thought," in *Semiotica* 138.1/4 (2002): 321–49. The support of the Social Sciences and Humanities Research Council of Canada is gratefully acknowledged.

What Are Savages For?

We Savages

It is this world, our own, which in its way has become savage again.
—*Jean Baudrillard, "The Precession of Simulacra"*

This book convokes forbidden possibilities of discourse. Approach it, therefore, as a "path" to "something unapproachable." The project came to me during a seminar on Sigmund Freud and Jacques Lacan at the Kootenay School of Writing, then located at the back of a gallery in the downtown east side of Vancouver. A dismal obsession with Lacan's account of the naysaying father compelled me to revisit Freud's *Totem and Taboo* one damp afternoon. I had read it while preparing my dissertation but grew obsessed, on rereading, with Freud's insistence that savage philosophers regard signs as vehicles for the transmission of forces, as if the elaboration of a discourse were enough to effect changes in the nondiscursive world. But you can say anything about discourse as long as you are discoursing about savages.

Freud's review of "savage philosophy" imports a word into the language of psychoanalysis—"taboo." He says it comes from Polynesia and connotes something both "sacred" and "forbidden."[1] Taboo is not a thing. Being taboo is a condition. Whatever is taboo is "unapproachable," for it is said to be charged with "a peculiar magical power" (18, 20). Freud calls this energy *mana*. It passes back and forth between the animate and inanimate worlds. He cites the *Encyclopaedia Britannica*: "Persons or things which are regarded as taboo may be compared to objects charged with electricity; they are the seat of a tremendous power which is transmissible by contact, and may be liberated with destructive effect if the organisms which provoke its discharge are too weak to resist it" (20). Mana is energy in motion. The rulers of a society carry it. So do their possessions. More importantly, it can be transmitted by the utterance of names, for it is a fundamental premise of savage philosophy that signs have a "real" and "physical" connection with things.[2] Freud's authorities insist, however, that only "the savage" would take such a possibility seriously. In the 1922 edition of *The Golden Bough*, J. G. Frazer attributes the mana theory to a failure of discernment: "Unable to discriminate clearly between words and things," he concludes, "the savage commonly fancies that the link between a name and the person or thing denominated by it is not a mere arbitrary and ideal association, but a real and substantial bond which unites the two."[3] To affirm that signs have mana breaks a taboo. It transgresses the limits of what civilized scholars can reasonably say about acts of discourse. This prohibition remains in effect today.

Freud explains that when desire encounters a prohibition it cannot otherwise circumvent, it retreats to the unconscious, where it remains active but escapes detection. The prohibition meanwhile remains "noisily conscious."[4] We are compelled to avoid certain acts and to repeat certain others, but we no longer understand why, until finally the burden of avoiding what we want to do dictates everything that we allow ourselves to do (26–30). Desire, however, is energy. As long as it is held in "tension," it seeks out every available means of discharge. So it takes the detour of the sign. Forbidden to satisfy itself directly, it turns its energies onto "substitute objects" and aims. The savage philosopher is one such substitute, an avenue for the pursuit of forbidden objects of scholarly desire. We scholars speak of "the savage" in order to speak of something else. What is it? And what are the limits of the prohibition against it?

One school of authors keeps coming back to the hypothesis that discourse is not an instrument for the communication of thought but an occasion for the deployment of forces. Together they share a desire for words with mana. Such a desire, to use Freud's language, is taboo. To indulge it does not harm you directly. Instead, like all things taboo, it cuts you off from the academic community (22). When you break a prohibition, you are as dangerous as the forbidden deeds you have done or the words you have uttered, for you tempt others to imitate your transgression (32). If, though, you project your desire for transgression onto the figure of the savage philosopher, then you can safely entertain, for research purposes only, of course, the most extravagant hypotheses about the relation between signs and things. Do you seriously suggest that images are alive or that acts of discourse have physical effects? No, you are just repeating what savage philosophers think. Nothing you say can be too far-fetched, no hypothesis too improbable, as long as you are sketching a portrait of premodern thought. Still, a prohibition is only as strong as the desire it forbids, because it is fed by the energy it represses. The more loudly scholars censure savage philosophers for positing a real, physical connection between signs and objects, the stronger is the desire to commit the same radical error.

Freud points out that "taboo" and "mana" belong to a larger "world-picture" that anthropologists of an earlier generation called animism (64–65). Savage philosophers believe that a host of "spiritual beings" causes changes in nature and that "similar spirits"—or "souls"—dwell in human bodies and make them move (75–76). Animism, Freud speculates, was born of the "practical" need to master natural and social events. It therefore includes, as one of its branches, a set of instructions for influencing the actions of people, animals, and things. "These instructions," he says, "go by the names of 'sorcery' [*Zauberei*] and 'magic' [*Magie*]" (78).[5] Sorcery aims to control events by controlling the spirits who cause them. Magic bypasses the spirit world and aims instead to control events by means of "special procedures" (78). Echoing Frazer, Freud classes them into two great genres. Techniques of imitative magic operate on the principle of similarity. They assume that like produces like. If you want to harm someone, make "an effigy" of him, for whatever is done to the copy happens to the "detested original" (79). Techniques of contagious magic operate on the principle of contiguity. They assume that objects that were once in contact continue to act on each other at a distance. If you want to influence someone, speak her name, for it remains connected to her even when uttered in her absence (81).

In a celebrated 1956 essay, Roman Jakobson notes that the two genres of magic mimic the two fundamental rules for the formation of discourses. These rules govern the selection of signs from a code (vocabulary) and the combination of signs into utterances (syntax).[6] Selection, like imitative magic, obeys the principle of similarity. It substitutes one sign for another. "'Did you say *pig* or *fig*?' said the Cat." Combination, like contagious magic, obeys the rule of contiguity. It sets one sign beside another: "'I said *pig*,' replied Alice" (97). Jakobson assimilates the rule of selection to the trope of metaphor, which substitutes one sign for another on the basis of resemblance ("my flame" for "my love") and the rule of combination to the trope of metonymy, which substitutes one sign for another on the basis of contiguity ("crown" for "sovereign") (109–10). For the linguist, metaphor and metonymy are relations between signs; for the magician, though, they are relations between things. The theory of magic works on the premise that physical forces can be deployed by discursive means.

Yet Jakobson is only repeating an argument that E. B. Tylor had made almost a century earlier. The first principle of magic, according to Tylor, consists of "mistaking an ideal for a real connexion."[7] Frazer mimics him: "the order on which magic reckons is merely an extension, by false analogy, of the order in which ideas present themselves to our minds."[8] Freud mimics them both, arguing that magical thought is the "projection outwards of internal perceptions."[9] Projection, he adds, is "a primitive mechanism" (64), which explains why "primitive man," as Freud pictures "him," would rather think about things than do them, satisfying his desires in fantasy instead of taking the steps required to satisfy them in reality. If primitive thought inclines toward magic, it is because the savage philosopher over-values psychical processes and undervalues physical ones: "Things become less important than ideas of things" (85). Ironically, Freud and his authorities are guilty of the very error they project onto their "picture" of the savage philosopher. They value the sign over the thing itself. When they speak of savage philosophy, therefore, they are speaking of their own discourse.

Consider a remark made by another of Freud's authorities, Darwin's country neighbor John Lubbock, in his preface to *The Origin of Civilisation*, published in 1870. Lubbock notes that anthropology not only describes the social practices that exist today but reconstructs those that existed in pre-history: "a knowledge of modern savages and their modes of life enables us more accurately to picture, and more vividly to conceive, the manners and customs of our ancestors in bygone ages."[10] To understand is to picture forth. The project of anthropological discourse is to make a projection. In repeating what we already know about "savages," we conjure up what we could not otherwise know about ourselves. The savage is a living sign, and what that sign stands for is "us," but earlier. "The sign," observes Derrida, "is deferred presence."[11] The savage, says Lubbock—and Freud agrees—is the deferred presence of "our ancestors."[12] Lubbock paints a picture of something that does not exist and then mistakes it for something that does. That, according to Tylor, is what savages do. But Tylor repeats Lubbock's mistake a year later in *Primitive Culture*: "the European," he says, "may find among the Greenlanders or Maoris many a trait for reconstructing the picture of his own primitive ancestors."[13] Tylor, like Lubbock, invites his reader to regard the verbal "picture" of a contemporary society as if it were the living presence of a prehistoric society. His discourse does not just paint an image but makes it real.

In his 1893 lectures on industrial evolution, Karl Bücher confesses that anthropology's "picture" of savagery unhinges the opposition between mimesis, a discourse that imitates, and poiesis, a discourse that invents. "The picture of primitive man that we make for ourselves must be not an imaginary one," he insists. "Its lines must all be drawn from reality."[14] But the desire for living images involves the scholar in a paradox he cannot untangle. He instructs us to "make" a "picture" even as he warns us not to make it up. Then he makes a slip, for he concedes that "primitive man" does not exist *until* we picture him forth. "Great as is the number of primitive peoples that have gradually come within our ken," Bücher explains, "none of them stands any longer at the lowest stage of savagery" (3). First he calls us to make an imitation, and then he affirms there is no model for us to imitate. We have to invent one instead. And invention is a two-step procedure. First we borrow traits from various incompatible sources, and then we combine them into a type, indeed a stereotype: "The collection of these characteristics and their combination into a typical picture," Bücher therefore concludes, "must, however, be our first task" (6). The resulting collage does not portray any savage in particular—"We must, however, abandon the attempt to exemplify the primitive condition by any definite people" (6)—but the savage in general. This generic savage is the sort of sign that comes before its referent, a copy that precedes its original.

Lubbock, Tylor, and Bücher all make a similar promise. They commit themselves to composing a portrait that reflects "our" origins back to us. Students of rhetoric have a term for the picture that is painted in words and addresses its audience from within the borders of a text.[15] It is called *ekphrasis:* the trope of the speaking picture. But the portrait of the savage philosopher is a peculiar kind of *ekphrasis.* It is a picture that speaks about the art of picturing forth. Hence it is the self-portrait of the discourse that paints it.

What does this picture have to tell us today? Savage philosophy asserts that discourse has a real, physical connection with its world, but the connection is not, or not simply, one of representation. Signs do more than stand for things when things cannot make themselves present. They take part in the realization of objects, processes, and even worlds. What is more, they are irruptive, for they expend a surplus of living, self-actualizing energy in a scarcity of time. It will not be long, though, before a prohibition finds its voice. "You are going too far," it will say. "These 'savage philosophers,' as you call them, are guilty of crimes against reality. Don't you see that it is not just logically but morally wrong to say that ideas—or 'signs' as you call them—have the same value as things? Besides, what does this speaking portrait have to say to us now? Who even uses the word 'savage' anymore? Why don't you read something new?" The curious fact, however, is that we scholars are not yet done with our savages. Indeed we continue to multiply them, projecting them onto new surfaces and discovering new avenues for their deployment. We may never be done with them. If we want to understand how we keep bringing them back, then it is necessary to study the philosophy that scholars have long displaced onto the savage world-picture. Only a savage philosopher would entertain the possibility that the emergence of beings is bound up with the formation of discourses. Only a savage philosopher, therefore, is properly equipped to explain how we scholars invent our savages.

Error

> My Dionysus ideal . . . the force in all life that *wills* error; error as the precondition even of thought.—*Nietzsche,* The Will to Power

Why do I insist on the scandalous word "savage"? This is a book about the racialization of ideas. For centuries, but with particular intensity in the later nineteenth century, scholars in the so-called Western tradition have taken it for granted that some concepts are not just culturally but *racially* superior to others. Do not pretend, then, that the philosophy of language is not a racial project. Prejudice is at work not only in the application but in the production of categories of thought. "When we do philosophy," says Wittgenstein, "we are like savages [*die Wilde*], primitive people."[16] Philosophers are comparable to "savages," in his view, because they pay too much attention to what words mean and think too little about how they are used. Tylor affirms the opposite. Savage philosophers, by his account, are too preoccupied with how words are used and pay too little attention to what they mean. It does not matter who is right. The point is that a difference between races has been projected onto an enduring scholarly debate about the relation between signs and things.

Nietzsche remarks in 1887 that the "first," most primitive, way to produce a category of thought is value coding. "Fixing prices, setting values, working out equivalents, exchanging—this preoccupied man's first thoughts to such a degree," he says, "that in a certain sense it *constitutes* thought."[17] Concepts do not have value because they correspond to things. They have value because they can be compared to other concepts. And some are worth more than others. Value coding is not just an economic art but a moral one. Nietzsche discovers the origin of conscience, for example, in the relationship between debtor and creditor. The debtor promises to pay the seller later for goods received today. A debtor who failed to repay a creditor was the first wrongdoer. Guilt is knowledge of a debt unpaid.

Tylor conceives of savage philosophers as wrongdoers in this moral-economic sense. When they treat signs as if they were things, they traffic in counterfeit coin. Hence they incur a debt they can never repay. The only people they cheat, however, are themselves. They give up what is worth more, the thing in itself, in return for what is worth less, a sign. This is not only a logical error but an economic one. To trade reality on par with ideality is not just bad faith. It is bad business. And Tylor is certainly not the only scholar who thinks so. Consider another, older example. Writing of his voyage to Quebec in 1608, Samuel de Champlain remarks that it is a fundamental principle among "the savages" of Canada "that all the dreams that they have are true." Only the "Divell," however, would cause mortals to confuse the recollection of images from sleep with the perception of objects by waking consciousness.[18] Champlain concludes that his savages have been led astray by "diabolical visions." The principle of magical thought, mistaking an ideal for a real connection, is therefore a sin.

Why are relations between signs less valuable than relations between things? And why, moreover, is it morally wrong to equate them? Nietzsche observes that artists perceive no opposition between representation and reality, but only greater and lesser intensities of illusion, so "what forces us," he asks, "to suppose that there is an essential opposition of 'true' and 'false'? Is it not sufficient to assume degrees of apparentness [*Scheinbarkeit*] and, as it were, lighter and darker shadows and shades of appearance [*Scheins*]—different 'values' [*valeurs*] to use the language of painters? Why couldn't the world *that concerns us* be a fiction [*eine Fiktion*]?"[19] What "forces" us is the prohibition against savage philosophy. We do not want it on our conscience. For Nietzsche, however, mistaking an ideal for a real connection is not an error that can be corrected by further study. It is the very "precondition" of study. "Whatever philosophical standpoint one may adopt today," he warns, "from every point of view the *erroneousness* of the world in which we think we live is the surest and firmest fact that we can lay eyes on." The system of values that scholars so strenuously defend against the errors of savage philosophy is itself the product of another, no less erroneous logic.

So in 1888 he proposes a drastic experiment. "Let us abolish the real world: and to be able to do this," he adds, "we first have to abolish the supreme value hitherto, morality."[20] Why does the abolition of reality depend on the abolition of morality? The real is what is good. The most real, the *ens realissimum*, is the greatest good.[21] Reality is a moral project. Undermine morality, therefore, and reality collapses along with it. Why would anyone want to abolish the good? Suppose it could be shown that the production of the highest of goods requires the perpetration of the greatest of wrongs?

We would have to conclude, as Nietzsche puts it, "that even morality is immoral." Morality itself would compel us to investigate its immorality. That was Nietzsche's unfinished project, his highest "task," and this book aims, in a limited way, to complete it. What exactly is immoral about morality? The greatest good, reality, has value only when opposed to the most "diabolical" evil, ideality. This, according to Nietzsche, was the premise of "Platonism." But the inheritors of Platonism, like Lubbock and Tylor and Bücher, go farther still. Reality, for them, is not just worth more than ideality but racially and culturally superior to it. If we acknowledge this paradoxical "truth" about "reality," then morality itself requires us to renounce the highest of goods. Morality itself declares morality immoral. And for the most moral of reasons.

But what happens afterward? What, above all, takes reality's place? Oddly, Herbert Spencer points toward an answer, though it is one he does not endorse for it entails the recourse of savage philosophy. "Distinguishing but confusedly between semblance and reality," he argues, "the savage thinks that the representation of a thing partakes of the properties of the thing."[22] His picture of the savage philosopher indicates that being participates in being-said. The savage sign does not represent its object. It activates it. It takes part in things instead of taking their place. Spencer dismisses the participation theory as a characteristically savage error, the racially inferior product of a racially inferior mind. Nietzsche, Spencer's contemporary and critic, comes to its defense. The errors of the savage philosophers supply the foundation for a new science, for "only on this now solid, granite foundation of ignorance," Nietzsche affirms, "could knowledge rise so far."[23] Thus the question is no longer "Which errors are to be avoided?" but rather "Which offer the most advantages?"

"Enough," someone may object, "the scholars of the Tylor school, like the savages who haunted their late-Victorian daydreams, belong to a bygone age. They have nothing to say to us now. We share neither their prejudices nor their projects. Let them join Champlain in the mists of history." The hard fact, though, is that these specters haunt us still. Indeed we are rather addicted to them. The philosophy that the Tylor school used to project onto the living portrait of our past is coming back to meet us from our future. The "bygone age" will soon be ours again. Do not take my word for it though. Consider what transpires in Salman Rushdie's *Fury*. The action of this 2001 novel reproduces the Tylor school's premises almost point for point because, as it turns out, Rushdie's characters "distinguish but confusedly" between signs and things. They have forgotten, or perhaps never knew, that reality is worth more than representation. There is, however, one exception. The novel is narrated from the point of view of Malik Solanka, a retired professor of history who laments that today signs are considered more valuable than things-in-themselves. His world has gone savage in the traditional sense. And he rages at it. "Something was amiss with the world," the novel tells us, "he no longer knew how to reconcile himself to an increasingly phony (he loathed, in this context, the otherwise excellent word 'virtual') reality."[24] Ironically, no one has done more to abolish reality than Solanka himself. He is, despite himself, a postmodern Prometheus. In fact it has made him rich. He resigned from Cambridge to design and manufacture puppets for British television. His most celebrated invention is Little Brain. She is a journalist-doll who began her career interviewing great-thinker dolls—or "big brains"—on a show called *Brain Street*, a *Sesame Street* for intellectuals. "In its origin," he remembers, "the doll was not a thing in itself but a representation": not a person but the three-dimensional image of one (73). Then, to his alarm, she became a star and took on a life of her own, passing from the inanimate to the animate world as if there were no border between them. Her fans routinely—and knowingly—make the mistake of seeing her as a living, breathing person. When she published her autobiography, they received it as a work of nonfiction. "Little Brain, they argued, was no longer a simulacrum. She was a phenomenon. The fairy's wand had touched her, and she was real" (98). Her fans know perfectly well how to tell puppets from people, but they behave as if they perceive no difference between them. Solanka has sparked a regression from "civilized thought" to "savage philosophy."

Nietzsche observes that philosophers traditionally respond with "blind rage" when the world deceives them into mistaking signs for things themselves.[25] Solanka's response is blind fury. One day he sits down in a Manhattan café and becomes lost in his own thoughts. Before he knows what is happening, the manager is standing at his table and asking him to leave. She informs him he has been yelling obscenities. He has no memory of it. What provokes his fugue? The answer is that the café is a "simulacrum" of "a Viennese *Kaffeehaus*" (44–46). He rages because a copy has usurped the place of the original. He reserves his deepest rage, though, for the simulacrum that he has foisted on the world. He moves from London to New York to escape Little Brain, but as soon as he settles into his sublet Manhattan apartment, he finds her staring back at him from the face of Mila, a woman who lives down the street. She has spent most of her life modeling herself in the image of Solanka's doll-child. He suspects they have even traded souls:

"Now the doll was the original, the woman the representation" (74). Mila personifies the characteristic error of the savage philosopher: she has traded reality for ideality and become a "living doll."

Solanka muses that the substitution of signs for things marks the onset of "a new cycle of Time." It is as if he is witnessing a radical and decisive break between his own time and times past. The new, he concludes, does not develop out of the old. It irrupts into being ex nihilo, forcing history to start over from the beginning. "This was how everything had begun: boom" (116). There is nothing new, however, about Solanka's definition of his new time. His hypothesis about the present recycles Jean Baudrillard's well-known definition of "hyperreality"—an odd mistake for the historian of ideas to make. Baudrillard says that the postmodern age substitutes "signs of the real for the real itself."[26] That, however, is the basic principle of magical thought. When Solanka echoes Baudrillard, he says of his own time what scholars of another time used to say of savage philosophy. Postmodernism is the recourse of premodernism; the history of the present bears prehistory's characteristic trait. The "new cycle" that happens for the first time by happening again is not a beginning, therefore, but a displacement. A caller to a radio talk-show alerts the reader to "ever'thin" that is old about the new: "Where I'm sittin' the future plain ain't arrive. Ever'thin look the same. I mean the exact same shinola goin' down all over."[27] But Solanka does not hear him. He is not ready to acknowledge that he has carried forward the old prejudice against "savage philosophy" into the "new cycle of Time."

Poetic Logic

It necessarily follows that all first peoples were poets.—*Giambattista Vico*, The New Science

Toward the end of *The Golden Bough*, Frazer repeats the commonplace that the development of thought starts with magic, takes a detour through religion, and ends in science. The magician discovers an order in nature but fails to gain control over natural events. The priest assumes that higher beings govern nature and persuades them to serve human ends. The scientist makes explicit what the magician only "implicitly assumed": that events conform to inhuman yet predictable laws. What comes after science? "The exact same shinola." Frazer's history of ideas follows a circular course. It is, to borrow Giambattista Vico's term, a *ricorso*. After science, comes magic. "Brighter stars," Frazer predicts, "will rise on some voyager of the future—some great Ulysses of the realms of thought—than shine on us. The dreams of magic may one day be the waking realities of science."[28] Magic confuses representation with reality. Science finds correspondences between them. Magical science will make representation into reality. Signs will no longer stand for things but actualize them.

Yet the past that is coming back from the future in Frazer's conclusions had already come to pass in Charles Sanders Peirce's Cambridge Conferences lectures, which he delivered in 1898 on the fringes of Harvard University. Frazer situates magic on the very ground where Peirce establishes the new field of "semiotic," a general science of signs. Peirce maintains that signs are "really active" in things. That, for Frazer, is savage philosophy. "That," for Peirce, "is the principle of scholastic realism."[29] The sign is a racial and cultural problem for Frazer; a logical and historical one for Peirce. Where Frazer finds the characteristic trait of the savage philosopher, Peirce discovers the persistence of medieval thought. The savage philosopher inherits the arguments of the scholastic philosopher. How did this exchange of identities come about?

Theodor Adorno and Max Horkheimer point to an answer in their 1944 essay "The Concept of Enlightenment." "The Enlightenment," they argue, "opposed as superstition the claim that truth is predicable of universals. It asserted that in the authority of universal concepts, there was still discernible fear of the demonic spirits which men sought to portray in magic rituals, hoping thus to influence nature. From now on, matter would at last be mastered without any illusion of ruling or inherent powers."[30] The operative phrase here is "universal concepts." Frazer and Peirce entertain very different opinions about them. Frazer is an extreme nominalist; Peirce, an extreme realist. Nominalism and realism, moreover, were the two sides in the scholastic debate about universals, one of the more celebrated episodes in the history of philosophy. Peirce says the debate hinged on the following question: "Are universals real?" The nominalist answered in the negative; the realist, in the affirmative. By the time Peirce revived the debate, the "nominalist tendency," taking root in the emergent disciplines of sociology and cultural anthropology, has racialized the realist position. What used to be a scholastic notion has been transformed into the stereotypical error of the savage philosopher, another trait in the speaking portrait of prehistoric humanity. Henceforth there would be only one realism, and it would be a characteristically savage one, the bad intellectual habit of an underdeveloped mind. The realist in the era of imperialism thinks as savages do, and what savages do, above all, is confuse signs with things.

This is not the place for a review of scholasticism. Nor is it necessary. What matters is what "realism" means to Peirce. In a lecture delivered at

Harvard in 1903, he holds up a stone and predicts "with confidence" that if he lets it go, it will drop to the floor. His concern is not whether the stone will fall, which is hardly in doubt, but our assumption that it will. Why do we trust in the regularity of events? We predict the stone's fall because we assume a general principle is "active" in its descent. This principle is gravitation. Peirce conceives of it as a sign: "the general proposition that all solid bodies fall in the absence of any upward forces or pressure, this formula, I say, is of the nature of a representation. Our nominalistic friends would be the last to dispute that," he adds. "They will go so far as to say it is a *mere* representation,—the word *mere* meaning that to be represented and really to be are two very different things" (181). For the nominalist, a sign "merely" stands for a fact. Peirce counters that the sign produces a fact. His name for the act of realization is "interpretation." It does not determine what a sign means. It is the event in which a sign actualizes itself. "This interpretation," Peirce explains elsewhere, "involves a power of the symbol to cause a real fact," and he stresses that it would be "futile" to construct a model of the universe that did not account for "the power of representations [that is, of signs] to cause real facts."[31] This sounds like savage philosophy. How can a sign cause a fact? When the stone falls, the idea of gravitation passes from potentiality to actuality. The fall shows gravitation in the act of interpreting itself. It is the self-realization of a living sign. "Now it is proper to say, that a general principle that is operative in the real world is of the essential nature of a representation and of a symbol because its *modus operandi* is the same as that by which *words* produce physical effects. Nobody," he cautions his Harvard audience, "can deny that words do produce such effects."[32] A "representation" is as much a part of nature as any other "reality" is. Indeed representation is reality's principle of change: the force that sets events in motion and brings objects into emergence.

Peirce calls a sign that is capable of realizing itself "a living general." Animate things, such as animals and plants, contain an intrinsic source of change and stability.[33] They not only grow but grow into the forms that are already their own. The acorn, to borrow Hegel's example, contains the oak tree. The living sign shares in this natural capacity for self-production. It is a potentiality that grows out of itself, toward itself, and so enters into actuality. It is reality in act: reality in the act of becoming what it represents itself to be.

What Peirce advocates is not just a scholastic but an animist realism. By the standards of a nominalist and imperialist era, he is a decidedly savage realist. The concepts his contemporaries ascribe to savage philosophers supply the postulates that the emerging natural sciences require. "I hear you say," he concedes, "'This smacks too much of an anthropomorphic conception.' I reply that every scientific explanation of a natural phenomenon is a hypothesis that there is something in nature to which the human reason is analogous."[34] Nature is intelligible because it is intelligent. Its intelligence, moreover, lies in its capacity to pass purposively from representation to reality. Peirce's universe is structured like a discourse. But it is more like a poem than a work of description, for poetry is the kind of discourse that has the capacity to create a world, whereas a description can only imitate the world that poetry creates: "the Universe as an argument is necessarily a great work of art, a great poem,—for every fine argument is a poem and a symphony,—just as every true poem is a sound argument" (194). A "true" poem actualizes the world by animating it. The order of events grows out of the "living" forces of signs.

Peirce was certainly not the first philosopher to discover a living language in nature. Indeed he belongs to something of a tradition. Herder argues in his 1772 "Treatise on the Origin of Language" that humans learned to speak as soon as they perceived that nature was speaking to them. They made signs for things by imitating the signs that things were already making by themselves: "The sound had to designate the thing, just as the thing gave the sound."[35] Language was immanent in nature, and because nature was action, language was a form of action too. "Since the whole of nature resounds," Herder argues, "there is nothing more natural for a sensuous human being than that *it lives, it speaks, it acts*" (101). The first signs did not stand for natural objects. They resonated with nature's life. The "force" that compelled humans to enter into discourse "came from nature's hand no otherwise than *living*" (127). Herder, like Peirce, affirms that an utterance made of living signs is a poem: "what was this first language but a collection of elements of poetry? Imitation of resounding, acting, stirring nature" (103). If today poetry tends to personify inanimate things, it is because poetic discourse is a survival of nature's living, self-actualizing language. Wherever people continue to live in the so-called state of nature, the sign is living still: "With the savages of North America, for example, everything is still alive: each thing has its genius, its spirit. And that it was just the same with the Greeks and the Easterners is shown by their oldest vocabulary and grammar—they are, as the whole of nature was to the inventor, a pantheon!, a realm of living, acting beings" (101). When nature granted language to humankind, it entrusted us with a share of its own life force. The savage sign harbors it even now. Savagery is the living reservoir of living language.

These selections from Peirce and Herder indicate that for a long time the philosophy of language endowed savages and poets with a trait in common. Savages were made in the image of the first people, and the first people were made in the image of the poet. Savage philosophers are poets who have survived into the age of positivism. The eighteenth-century notion of poetic logic is the precursor, and indeed the prototype, of the nineteenth-century notion of savage realism, which in turn supplies the prototype for the late twentieth-century notion of hyperreality. No matter what we scholars call it, we seem unable to do without it. The hypotheses of savage philosophy cannot be proven. Nor can they be disproven. The desire for them fuels the prohibition against them. So they keep coming back, like the ghosts the magician convokes.

Savage realism poses a problem not only for the study of philosophy, then, but for the history of ideas. How can the same hypotheses be repeated, and remain valid, in different historical contexts, albeit under different headings? The third, 1744 edition of Vico's *New Science* at once exemplifies the problem and points to a solution. Vico proposes that the history of the nations that do not enjoy divine revelation follows a single ideal and eternal course (*corso*), and, when it reaches its end, it circles around and performs a recourse (*ricorso*), initiating "a new cycle and a new recycle."[36] History's *ricorso* consists of three ages—an age of gods, of heroes, and of men—which prefigure Frazer's three stages of intellectual development: magic, science, and religion. The age of gods displays magical thought's characteristic traits. It began for the first time, says Vico, after the Flood. The sons of Noah renounced his religion and cast off the bonds of society. Men wandered alone through the forests, pursuing women and fleeing predators, until they returned to the condition of beasts. Then fear drove them into hiding and, under the direction of providence, they reestablished the law of marriage, taking a first step back toward social life (§13). The people of this first age— Vico calls them "aborigines" and "first nations"—were "poets," and they "spoke in poetic characters" (§§34, 370). Their thought was poetic because it was governed by a law of personification. "The most sublime labor of poetry," Vico explains, "is to give sense and passion to insensate things" (§186). The first poets projected human features onto inhuman objects and processes, making "of all nature a vast animate body which feels passions and affections" (§377). They made the same error in the eighteenth century that savage philosophers would make in the nineteenth: "they gave the things they wondered at substantial being after their own ideas" (§375). They personified the causes of events, for example, by molding gods in the human image, as "the American Indians" still do, Vico adds, "who call gods all the things that surpass their small understanding" (§375).[37]

If you compare Vico's portrait of poetic logic with Tylor's account of magical thought and Freud's theory of projection, you find "the exact same shinola goin' down" in three linguistic and historical contexts. The poet, the savage, and the neurotic personify the same moral error. They are guilty of mistaking connections between signs ("ideas") for connections between things ("substantial being"). Each is the *ricorso* of the others. What is the basis of their resemblance? All three practice the illogical logic of prosopopoeia: the trope that confers life, face, and voice on what lacks them. Vico classifies prosopopoeia as a species of metaphor, "most praised when it gives sense and passion to insensate things" (§404). Metaphorical animation affirms that the inanimate world both is and is not alive. Yet to misstate things is the first, necessary step toward redescribing them. The self-destruction of meaning makes way for an innovation in reference. Metaphor does not tell things as they are. It conjures up things that are not yet, "obliterating the logical and established frontiers of language," Paul Ricoeur argues, "in order to bring to light new resemblances the previous classifications kept us from seeing."[38] Abolishing a sign's "everyday reference" prepares it to refer to things still unknown.

Magical Criticism

> But true poetic language should be organically alive.—*Novalis, "Miscellaneous Observations"*

Adorno remarks in a 1934 letter to Walter Benjamin that the archaic is what survives in the present of an era that never happened in the past. The Enlightenment "produces" it as the reserve of "everything" that modernity projects beyond its limits, just as the forbidden possibilities of realism are displaced onto the living portrait of the prehistoric philosopher:

> I have come to realize that just as the modern is the most ancient, so too the archaic itself is a function of the new: it is thus first produced historically as the archaic, and to that extent is dialectical in character and not "pre-historical," but rather the exact opposite. For it is precisely nothing but the site of everything whose voice has fallen silent because of history: something which can only be measured in terms of that historical rhythm which alone "produces" it as a kind of primal history.[39]

The Enlightenment posited the archaic as the negation of the modern in order to posit the modern as the negation of the archaic. The one does not follow the other. The two pass into each other, and each bears the trace of the other. The modern is therefore archaic; the archaic is modern. The "myths" that "fell victim to the Enlightenment," Adorno explains a decade later, with Horkheimer, "were its own products."[40]

Benjamin proposes an archaic technique of interpreting modern art in a fragment dating from the same period. He calls this technique "magical criticism" and defines it in opposition to literary history: "Magical criticism [magische Kritik] as a manifestation of the highest stage of criticism. Opposite it on the same plane is the scholarly (literary-historical) treatise."[41] What relation does he discover between magic and criticism? Magic assumes that living forces are really operative in acts of discourse. Criticism, after Kant, assumes that cognition takes part in the construction of its object, looking behind "what is given in consciousness to the creative capacity which, working harmoniously and unconscious of itself, produces the whole form of the world in us."[42] In his 1919 doctoral dissertation, published as The Concept of Criticism in German Romanticism, Benjamin argues that for the early Romantics, who were thoroughly versed in Kant's thought, "the concept of criticism [Kritik] had acquired . . . an almost magical meaning [magische Bedeutung] . . . the term explicitly connoted not the sense of a merely discerning, unproductive state of mind; rather, for the Romantics and for speculative philosophy, the term 'critical' meant objectively productive, creative out of thoughtful deliberation."[43] In yoking the concepts of magic and criticism together, Benjamin ventures the possibility that a living consciousness animates the work of art. On this hypothesis, cognition not only produces the work but inhabits the work it produces.

Novalis had already outlined a "magical idealism" in a series of fragments written in the late 1790s. One of them is titled "MAGIC." Beside the title is a phrase in parentheses: "(mystical theory of language)." What does Novalis mean by "mystical"? He offers this hint: "Sympathy of the sign with the signified. One of the basic ideas of cabbalism."[44] Paradoxically, he bases his magical idealism on the conventionally realist premise that the sign takes part in its object. "The proof of realism is idealism," he explains in another fragment, "and conversely" (§32). A sign that has "sympathy" with an object is a "soul." He conceives of it as an idea capable of assuming a material form: "If you could not make a thought into an independent soul which would separate itself from you—and would now be extraneous—something that is occurring in the outside world, then do the reverse with outside things—and transform them into thoughts. Both operations are idealistic. Whoever has them both perfectly in his power is the magical idealist" (§17). The soul-sign makes a fold between cognition and its object: "The seat of the soul is the point where the inner and the outer worlds touch. Wherever they penetrate each other—it is there at every point of penetration."[45] To make an idea real, however, requires genius, which for Novalis is an innate aptitude for magic: "genius is the ability to treat imaginary objects like real ones," he says, "and to deal with them as if they were real as well" (§22). An artist who possesses this "ability" is at once a "magician" and a "poet" and is bound by the injunction that governs both magical thought and poetic logic: "Every word is a word to conjure with."[46]

Benjamin suggests that a properly "magical" criticism does not decipher the meaning of the artwork. Instead it brings it back to life. Interpretation is therefore animation. Reading is resurrection. The "soul" of the work slumbers until the critic arrives to awaken it. Magical criticism does not reflect *on* a work but provokes "the unfolding" of reflection *in* a work: "criticism," Benjamin speculates, is "an experiment on the artwork, one through which the latter's own reflection is awakened, through which it is brought to consciousness and to knowledge of itself."[47] Magical criticism actualizes the work's own self-conscious, self-reflective life force: "The subject of reflection is, at bottom, the artistic entity itself" (151). Benjamin's "modern," animist hermeneutics is the recourse of Vico's first, "archaic" poetics. But what compels him to revive the convention that links art with animism? "In the work of art," Adorno and Horkheimer remark, "that duplication still occurs by which the thing appeared as spiritual, as the expression of *mana*. This constitutes its aura."[48]

The Nutritive Life of Signs

> This appears mystical and mysterious simply because we insist on remaining blind to what is plain, that there can be no reality which has not the life of a symbol.—*Charles Sanders Peirce, "New Elements"*

Benjamin speaks of the artwork as if it were a living, self-conscious subject. Is this another case of projection? Has he made the characteristically "savage" error of mistaking the life of the critic for the life of the work? Ask instead, "What is life?" Benjamin's account of Romanticism revives Schelling's hypothesis that even "mere organized matter" harbors life, though "a life of a more restricted kind."[49] Schelling concedes that this is an "old" idea but notes that it persists "right up to the present day." One of its oldest sources is book 2 of Aristotle's *Physics*, for it is there, according to Martin Heidegger, that "Aristotle gives the interpretation of φύσις [*phûsis*] that sustains and guides all succeeding interpretations of the essence of 'nature.'"[50] According to Aristotle, every natural being, whether it is an animal

or a plant or one of the four elements, contains its own internal source of
change and stability. Change is a motion from something potential to something actual, while stability is a motion that has become actually what it
was potentially.[51] A natural being, as it grows, assumes the form that was
already its own. It contains the principle of its own production. In contrast,
the source of the production of an artifact, such as a bed or a cloak, lies outside it, in the skill (technê) of the artisan (33/192b). Human skill, moreover,
comes in two sorts. There is a skill that "imitates nature" and a skill that
"completes what nature is incapable of completing" (51/199a). Both operate
by representation (mimêsis). The first imitates what already is; the second
projects an image of what is not yet, modeling a form for what cannot give
form to itself. One copies things; the other finishes them. "There are thus,"
concludes Philippe Lacoue-Labarthe, "two forms of mimesis." The first,
"restricted," mimesis generates the "reproduction, the copy." The second,
"general," mimesis compensates for a "deficiency" in nature, an "incapacity to do everything, organize everything, make everything its work."[52]
Restricted mimesis stands for reality; general mimesis takes part in the realization of a still unfinished reality.

The savage philosopher combines the two forms of mimesis and in doing so folds the order of nature onto the order of representation. Each side
of the fold possesses the other's characteristic trait. Savage nature acts by
representation; savage representation grows out of itself, as if it were a natural being. Peirce's 1894 essay "What Is a Sign?" supplies an example. The
universe, he argues, "lives and moves" only in signs. Life, for Peirce as for
Aristotle, is a motion from something potential toward something actual.
Peirce calls this motion interpretation. The sign does not stand for an object. It determines an interpretant toward an object. The interpretant, however, is itself a sign. It does not stand for the object on another sign's behalf.
Rather it makes the object more definite. Signs therefore participate in the
definition—that is, the actualization—of objects. They grow toward objects
by growing into interpretants. "Symbols grow," Peirce flatly states. "They
come into being by development out of other signs."[53] They contain an
intrinsic source of change and stability, just as plants and animals do. This
is not a radical notion, nor is it something particularly new. Peirce merely
reanimates a dormant possibility of Aristotle's thought, releasing the sign
from restricted mimesis and restoring it to general mimesis, so that representation is once more nature's intrinsic principle of change and stability.
"The complex whole may be called a symbol," Peirce cryptically remarks,
"for its symbolic, living character is the prevailing one" (10). A "symbol" is
the kind of sign that grows into its object.

Heidegger arrives at the fold between representation and reality by way of Friedrich Hölderlin's poem "Bread and Wine." In his 1958 lecture "The Nature of Language," he pays particular attention to the verse that ends stanza 5: "Now for it words like flowers leaping alive he must find."[54] Hölderlin's simile, "words, like flowers" (*Worte, wie Blumen*), displaces the capacity for self-production from nature (*phûsis*) to human skill (*technê*), specifically to poetic skill. The poet's task is to find words that share the self-actualizing energy of natural beings. Poetry is not the imitation but the completion of nature, its blossoming. "Language is the flower of the mouth," Heidegger remarks. "In language the earth blossoms toward the bloom of the sky."[55] No longer does discourse belong exclusively to skill, nor does the flower belong exclusively to nature. Rather each assumes the attributes of the other. Discourse is nature's intrinsic principle of change. Nature grows only in signs. The essence of language is "saying," and it is saying that "moves all things" (99). Words unfold like flowers; flowers unfold like words. Hölderlin's simile opens the possibility that discourse has "the source of its being" in nature and nature its source of motion in discourse (100). "When the word is called the mouth's flower and its blossom," Heidegger concludes, "we hear the sound of language rising like the earth" (101).

Poets and savages find these flowers blooming all around them. They have inherited the thankless task of embodying the possibility of general mimesis after the historical triumph of restricted mimesis. Seen from Spencer's perspective, they are guilty of the lowest form of error; seen from Heidegger's, they are devoted to the highest task of thought. We cannot dispense with them without losing touch with what they personify. Perhaps it is time to de-racialize this possibility, time for scholars to learn to live with general mimesis instead of projecting it elsewhere.

"Mexico"

In a word, we believe that there are living forces in what is called poetry.
—*Antonin Artaud, "The Theater and Cruelty"*

Benjamin never completed his project for a magical criticism. He did not have to. It was already going on without him. Magical criticism is like a ghost that comes back as fast as we conjure it away. Antonin Artaud took it up in the 1930s in protest against the division of art from life, representation from reality, "as if there were culture on one side and life on the other."[56] Art, for Artaud, is the exercise of life. It is life in action. Conventionally, it is the magician's role to convoke the forces of life. But like Vico before him, Artaud assigns that role to the poet. Or, more accurately, he folds poetry overtop of magic, as if to acknowledge the old kinship between them. "There is a movement today," he says, "to identify the poetry of the poets with that internal magic force which provides a path for life and makes it possible to act upon life." [57] This "movement" has its source in "Mexico," which for Artaud is not a place but the spatial analogue of general mimesis. It is where general mimesis goes after it is displaced from Europe: "the Mexicans seek contact with the *Manas,* forces latent in every form, unreleased by contemplation of the forms for themselves, but springing to life by magic identification with these forms." [58] These "forces" cross back and forth between representation ("the mental") and nature ("the physical"), for they are "neither physical nor mental but may assume either a mental or a physical aspect according to the sense in which one wants to utilize them." [59] Such signs do not imitate things; they act on them.

What Artaud says is happening "today" in "Mexico" seems to keep happening day after day in one place after another. The fold between poetry and magic marks the onset of a "new cycle" and the recourse of the same old "shinola." Since the eighteenth century, scholars have repeatedly identified the poet with the magician. To explain the persistent recourse of magical criticism, however, it is necessary to put it to work. Do not just talk about it, says Artaud, but do it. This book therefore has two aims. The first is to record a neglected episode in the history of ideas. The principles of magical criticism concern us so intimately that even now we have difficulty seeing them clearly, as if they were still too close to come into focus. Each of the five ensuing chapters details how magical criticism recurs in the works of two major post-Enlightenment authors: Smith and Freud in chapter 1, Nietzsche and Tylor in chapter 2, Proust and Peirce in chapter 3, Marx and Benjamin in chapter 4, Hegel and Spencer in chapter 5. This book's second aim, though, is to reactivate magical criticism for contemporary purposes. If the discourse about savage philosophy offers a portrait of how "our own" discourse works, then what does it show us about discourses active in the world today? Rushdie reminds us that we are not done with our savages, but only a conventionally savage theory of discourse can explain how we continue to conjure them up. The chapters that follow treat three cases of discursive conjuration from three historical contexts. Chapter 1 examines an episode from the Canada of the 1890s; chapter 3, an episode from New Zealand in the 1840s; and chapter 5, an episode from Canada in the 1990s. All three indicate that the discourse about savage philosophy tends to recur against the current of historical change. Some force compels it to repeat itself to excess, even though repetition is what it says that savages do. Hence it is the sort of discourse that does what it states, a very magical discourse.

I have adapted the sardonic title of this introduction from an English translation of Heidegger's more pious essay, "What Are Poets For?" Poets, answers Heidegger, are those who "dare" language.[60] Those who dare language, he adds, are "more daring." They risk more. Indeed they risk to excess. They venture the possibility that discourse is more than a tool for bringing objects before consciousness, more than a "handle" for asserting humanity's dominance over nature, more than an instrument of rational calculation (133). "The essence of language is neither exhausted in reference," he cautions, "nor is it only a matter of signs and ciphers."[61] Language, for those who dare revert to savage philosophy, is the incalculable event of a being's emergence into being, "so that only the very thing that is sung comes to presence" (238). Savage philosophers are those who dare traffic in signs that grow into things.

What are savages for? There is no such thing as a savage society, nor has there ever been. Savage philosophers are the outgrowths of discourse, and they dare us to think more by daring to enrich signs with a principle of change. They speak from within nature in a language that grows of itself, toward itself, as everything natural does. After the Enlightenment, scholars could not acknowledge such a possibility. Nor could they do without it. So they keep calling it back in a form that can be condemned without compunction.

CHAPTER ONE

Discourse Is Now

To write history thus means to *cite* history. It belongs to the concept of citation, however, that the historical object in each case is torn from its context.—*Walter Benjamin*, The Arcades Project

Economy of time, to this all economy ultimately reduces itself.—*Karl Marx*, Grundrisse

Economies of Race

Charles Alexander Eastman recalls that in the fall of 1874 he left his father's home near Flandreau, South Dakota, and set out on foot to enroll in the residential school in Santee, Nebraska. Two days later he arrived hungry and tired at a sod farmhouse, where he was met by a white settler. Eastman offered the man a contract: "I had some money that my father had given me—I hardly knew the different denominations; so I showed the man *all* of it, and showed by signs that he might take what he pleased if only he would let me have something to eat, and a *little* food to carry with me."[1] The settler invites him inside to eat at the family table. After supper Eastman proposes another, more modest transaction: "I got up and held out to the farmer *nearly all* the money I had. I did not care whether he took it *all* or not" (36–37, emphasis added). The settler declines and invites Eastman to spend the night indoors. The astonished scholar chooses to sleep in the yard instead. Negotiations resume in the morning: "After breakfast I once more offered my money, but was refused" (39). Far more is at stake in these dealings than money. After the settler declines three times to trade hospitality for cash, Eastman decides to trade one "life" for another. "I was glad," he remembers. "Then and there I loved civilization and renounced

my wild life" (39). When he left his father's house three days earlier, he conceived of civilization and wildness as two incompatible economies. Civilization accumulates wealth. Wildness gives it away. By the time he leaves
the settler's house, he has concluded that both economies are governed by
the injunction to give. The "Indian" who offers "all" for "little" discovers
his own mirror image in the settler who accepts "little" for "all." He trades
wildness for civilization because he mistakes civilization for wildness: "no
Indian will break the law of hospitality," he explains, "unless he has lost all
the trails of his people" (38–39). Only later does he realize his mistake.

He explains that when his family was in exile in Canada, his father used
to tell him that people come in two sorts. White people accumulate the
products of labor and keep strict accounts, tallying not only things but time
itself: "here is a race which has learned to weigh and measure everything,"
the father tells the son, "time and labor and the results of labor, and has
learned to accumulate and preserve both wealth and the records of experience for future generations" (8). "Race" is an economy, and "all economy,"
as Marx foresaw in the fall of 1857, "ultimately reduces itself" to "economy
of time." In white time, one now follows another in a future-oriented series:
the now-just-passing advances into the now-just-past before the onset of
the now-to-come. Future-oriented time, moreover, is anticipatory. It is the
time of a forward-looking race. Being white, the father teaches, means being
ahead of yourself. White folks are inclined to "accumulate and preserve"
rather than spend and look forward to "results" too vast to be accomplished
in a day. They project themselves onto the horizon of their possibilities.
Later Eastman's residential-school teacher informs him that "the industries
of the white man" obey the twin principles of "thrift and forethought" (47).
Thrift defers present enjoyment for future gain. Forethought sees past sav-
ings coming back to the present from the future.

What defines the other sort? When Eastman travels to New England to
study for admission to medical school, he discovers that what his father assumed were differences in "race" can instead be explained by differences in
class and education. "I found Yankees of the uneducated class very Indian-
like in their views and habits," he confesses, "a people of strong character, plain-spoken, and opinionated." There is one difference, though, that
he continues to attribute to race alone. "I observed that the students of the
academy and their parents were very frugal and saving. Nothing could have
been more instructive to me," he remembers, "as we Indians are inclined to
be improvident. I had been accustomed to broad, fertile prairies, and liberal
ways. Here they seemed to count their barrels of potatoes and apples before they were grown" (66–67). The other sort—those he contrasts with the

"frugal"—are "Indians" like himself. They are an "improvident" race, he says, because they lack the art of anticipation. They are "accustomed" to spend "all" in the present and to save "little" for the future. They do not project themselves onto possibilities. Instead they live in the now.

The two sorts of races personify two incompatible modes of time. Future-oriented time, which fosters education, industry, and frugality, is the temporal mode of civilization. Now-time, which incites instantaneous and improvident acts of expenditure, is the mode of "wild life" or savagery. The future-oriented sort add one moment to another, just as they add new labor to "old things." They regard the future as the horizon of accumulation—for example, of "wealth and records." The present-oriented sort, in contrast, spend "all" they have in the present and expect "little" in return. They have no relation to the future. Hence they are poor in thrift and foresight. Every day is the same day for them. Hence they are today what they have always been. Although history is going forward, they stay where they already are. "What is the great difference between these people and my own?" Eastman asks. "Is it not that the one keeps the old things and continually adds to them new improvements, while the other is too well contented with the old, and will not change his ways nor seek to improve them?" (64).

The Tale of the Two Sorts

Eastman's narrative of his passage from "wild life" to "civilization" belongs to a genre constantly on the move from one context to another. It therefore exceeds the trajectory of future-oriented temporality. No matter how often it is repeated, the tale of the two sorts happens now only, as if for the first and last time. Marx suggests it is the sort of story that takes history's place. Political economists recite it to draw attention away from the events that propelled the western European nations, especially England, from the "feudal exploitation" of the late Middle Ages to the "capitalist exploitation" of the mid-nineteenth century.[2] Capitalist exploitation prevails wherever a society has been divided into a class that owns the means of production and a class that owns only its own capacity to work. But how was the division into classes achieved? Circling back over his earlier analysis, Marx takes up the search for the origin of the "capital-relation" in chapter 26 of *Capital*, volume 1: "The Secret of Primitive Accumulation." "We have seen how money is transformed into capital," he begins, "how surplus-value is made through capital, and how more capital is made from surplus-value. But the accumulation of capital presupposes surplus-value; surplus-value presupposes capitalist production; capitalist production presupposes the availability of considerable masses of capital and labor-power in the hands of commodity producers" (873). So far capital appears to have a magical capacity to add value to itself. Marx calls it self-valorizing value, as if to suggest that it contains an intrinsic principle of growth. Yet it grows only so long as it extracts surplus value from the worker's body.

Value is the labor that the worker fixes in the products of work, and labor in turn is an expenditure of the body's life force. Marx calls it the soul. Wherever the capitalist mode of production prevails, the worker's soul can be bought and sold like any other commodity. The value of labor power, which is paid in wages, is equal to the value of the commodities, principally food, clothing, and shelter, that the worker consumes in order to reproduce the body's forces and to rear the next generation of workers. Labor power, however, is a commodity like no other. The quantity of labor fixed in the products the worker makes is greater than the quantity fixed in the products the worker consumes. Thus the labor process extracts more value from the worker's body than the worker receives in wages. The difference between the two quantities is surplus value. Why do workers sell their labor power for less than it is worth? The answer is that they do not own their own means and materials of production. Hence they cannot work for themselves, as free peasant proprietors did in the fifteenth century. The more pressing question, then, is not Why do workers let themselves be exploited? but How did the working class lose ownership of the means of production? And how did the capitalists thereby become capitalists?

"The whole movement," Marx observes, "seems to turn around in a never-ending circle, which we can only get out of by assuming a primitive accumulation (the 'previous accumulation' of Adam Smith) which precedes capitalist accumulation; an accumulation which is not the result of the capitalist mode of production but its point of departure."[3] Smith argues in *The Wealth of Nations* that a nation consists of "two sorts" of people: the sort that saves and the sort that spends. The first sort are frugal and future-oriented. They accumulate stock, invest it in means of production, and, by observing the division of labor, add value to value. The second sort are improvident and present-oriented. They squander what they have on means of enjoyment rather than means of employment. Whether people own their own means of production therefore depends, according to Smith, on their moral character. Marx accuses him of inventing a nursery tale (*Kinderfibel*) better suited for pacifying restless children than for understanding the forces that propel historical change (874/742). Yet even now the political economists continue to repeat it as if it were a verifiable fact. "This primitive accumulation plays approximately the same role in political economy," Marx concludes, "as original sin does in theology. Adam bit the apple, and thereupon sin fell on the human race. Its origin is supposed to be explained when it is told as an anecdote about the past. Long, long ago there were two sorts of people, one, the diligent, intelligent and above all frugal élite; the other, lazy rascals, spending their substance, and more, in riotous living" (873). What exactly is the original economic sin? It comes down to consuming an excess of value in a scarcity of time. In Genesis, the punishment for original sin is work: Adam is fated to earn his bread by the sweat of his brow. In political economy, the punishment is working for others: the riotous rascals sell their "skins" to the frugal elite:

> The legend of theological original sin tells us certainly how man came to be condemned to eat his bread in the sweat of his brow; but the history of economic original sin reveals to us that there are people to whom this is by no means essential. Never mind! Thus it came to pass that the former sort accumulated wealth, and the latter sort finally had nothing to sell except their own skins. And from this original sin dates the poverty of the great majority who, despite all their labor, have up to now nothing to sell but themselves, and the wealth of the few that increases constantly, although they have long ceased to work. (873/741)

Marx adds that although the tale of the two sorts is recited all the time, it seems to belong to no time at all. It is repeated day after day, and yet it remains current "every day." Nor can it be credited exclusively to the account of Adam Smith. For it is the property of everyone who owns productive capital. "Such insipid childishness is every day preached to us in the defence of property," Marx adds, for "as soon as the question of property is at stake, it becomes a sacred duty to proclaim the standpoint of the nursery tale as the one thing fit for all age-groups and all stages of development" (873–74). The tale of the two sorts "fits" any historical context and yet remains unique, irreducibly singular, "the one thing." Hence its moment is always now. No matter how many times it recurs, nor in how many contexts, it draws critical attention away from the role played by force in the production of events. "In actual history," Marx counters, "it is a notorious fact that conquest, enslavement, robbery, murder, in short, force, play the greatest part," notably in transforming the small property owners of the English countryside into the industrial working class of the English cities (874, 878–79). Smith recites the tale of the two sorts not to explain the emergence of the capital relation but to justify it, enlisting the interpretation of history in the enforcement of morality and the formation of ideology.

Savage Time

As "Adam bit the apple," so Marx takes a bite from Smith's *Inquiry into the Origins and Causes of the Wealth of Nations*, as if to suggest that the Adam of theology lends the means of persuasion to the Adam of political economy. When Eastman recites the tale of the two sorts, translating riot into wildness and frugality into civilization, he bites off the same morsel of discourse. He casts his passage between cultures in a literary form that exists only in passage between contexts. For the tale of the two sorts is the sort of "historical object" that overflows its historical frame, participating in history by subtracting itself from history, as if burdened with the very inertia that Eastman attributes to the improvident race: "contented with the old" and resistant to "new improvements."

Although the tale fails to explain how capitalist societies came to be divided into two opposing classes, it does supply political economists with an argument in defense of the capitalist relations of production. What it lacks in explanatory power it makes up in persuasive force. And its persuasiveness is directly proportionate to its potential for repetition. The political economists recite it because it can be made to fit one context after another: they "preach" it every day because it can be displaced from day to day.

According to Jacques Derrida, a force of rupture is part of the structure of every signifying "mark," whether spoken or written, linguistic or nonlinguistic.[4] A mark, such as a linguistic sign, comes to emergence by detaching itself from "the present" of its emergence. It is intelligible insofar as it is repeatable. It has always already broken with its current author and world and is therefore free to drift toward other authors and worlds: "a written sign carries with it a force of breaking with its context [*une force de rupture avec son contexte*], that is, the set of presences which organize the moment of its inscription. This force of breaking," Derrida adds, "is not an accidental predicate, but the very structure of the written" (317/377). The force of rupture introduces an element of spacing into the field of discourse. There is space between signs and space within signs. The space between them allows the interpreter to distinguish one unit of a sign chain from another, for example, "riotous rascals" from "the frugal elite." The space within them allows the interpreter to distinguish every sign from itself, for example, the Adam of Genesis from the Adam of *Wealth*. Only because spacing is always already at work in discourse is it possible to "lift a written syntagma from the interlocking chain in which it is caught or given" and graft it into other chains "without making it lose every possibility of functioning, if not every possibility of 'communicating,' precisely." Spacing makes repetition possible. "No context can enclose" the syntagma, Derrida stresses. "Nor can any code" (317). Nor can any referent. For spacing intervenes even between signs and things. Otherwise a signifying mark could not refer to its object when the thing itself is not present, which is what a sign is conventionally assumed to do.

The tale of the two sorts is a sign chain, or syntagma, repeated according to a fixed set of rules of formation. It is longer than a sentence but shorter than the various texts in which it recurs. Hence it is a part, or morsel, of discourse rather than a whole, and though it can set to work in any number of contexts, it does not belong to any context in particular.[5] It is a complex sign chain, yet it displays the three traits that, according to Derrida, define the individual mark. First, it persists beyond the present of its inscription. Thus it can be repeated in any empirically determined context without becoming the property of one empirically determinable author. Second, it harbors a force of breaking with its context, which displaces it toward other contexts, making it "the one thing fit" for all ages. Third, an effect of spacing divides it from itself, so that it can be repeated at different "stages" without losing its pertinence or its force. It is the same emerging in the form of the always new.

Significantly, two of the predicates that characterize the tale of the two sorts belong to one of the sorts it describes. The tale therefore behaves like the riotous rascals it opposes to the frugal elite. Its form is mirrored in its content. And vice versa. What results is a homology. The tale exceeds the limits of its context just as the rascals exceed the limits of thrift and foresight; the tale survives beyond the present of its inscription just as the rascals survive beyond the precapitalist present of their emergence. In short, the tale tends to do what it describes, going savage in the act of saying what savage economies are. The homology, moreover, is the necessary consequence of a failure of spacing. There is no distance between the tale and its referent. Rather, the one folds over the other as if there were no boundary between them. The tale breaks with the present of its inscription, but it cannot break with the characters it portrays. It can only transport them from one context to another. Consider what happens when they recur, as if for the first time, in Smith's *Wealth of Nations*.

Smith argues that two "circumstances" determine a nation's wealth. One is the productivity of its workers. The other is the proportion between the number of workers employed in productive labor and those employed in unproductive labor.[6] There can be no doubt which he considers the determining factor. It is the way he makes his case, though, that makes it a fitting case for the study of discursive inertia. Smith projects the difference between low and high productivity onto the opposition between savagery and civilization, transforming two sorts of labor into the characteristic traits of two competing races. A "savage nation" has low productivity. Hence it cannot feed and clothe its population no matter how many people it employs in "useful labor":

> Among the savage nations of hunters and fishers, every individual who is able to work, is more or less employed in useful labour, and endeavours to provide, as well as he can, the necessaries and conveniencies of life, for himself, or such of his family or tribe as are either too old, or too young, or too infirm to go a hunting and fishing. Such nations, however, are so miserably poor, that from mere want, they are frequently reduced, or, at least, think themselves reduced, to the necessity sometimes of directly destroying, and sometimes of abandoning their infants, their old people, and those afflicted with lingering diseases, to perish with hunger, or to be devoured by wild beasts. (lx)

Savage nations are characterized by "want," which Smith defines as a surplus of lack. They work all the time and yet accumulate nothing for the future. Their low productivity compels them to sacrifice the young, the old, and the sick, just to survive in the present. A nation with high productivity, in contrast, employs a comparatively small number of workers in productive labor, and yet it has enough wealth to support a lavishly unproductive class:

> Among civilized and thriving nations, on the contrary, though a great number of people do not labour at all, many of whom consume the produce of ten times, frequently of a hundred times more labour than the greater part of those who work; yet the produce of the whole labour of the society is so great, that all are often abundantly supplied, and a workman, even of the lowest and poorest order, if he is frugal and industrious, may enjoy a greater share of the necessaries and conveniencies of life than it is possible for any savage to acquire. (lx)

The "separation" of one "race" from another mirrors the division of one "employment" from another. A worker in a "rude" society is responsible for several tasks and performs none of them well, whereas a worker in an "improved" society is responsible for one task and performs it with ever-increasing dexterity in an ever-decreasing amount of time (5). Savage nations, though they accumulate without cease, are nonetheless guilty of the sin of waste, notably waste of life. They perform a surplus of work and earn a surplus of want. Civilized nations, though they waste vast amounts supporting those who do not work, are nonetheless blessed with the virtues of frugality and industry. They perform a scarcity of toil yet enjoy a surplus of stock.

The division of labor arises from a "propensity" that all human beings, in Smith's view, hold in common: "the propensity to truck, barter, and exchange one thing for another" (14). We truck; therefore we are human. "Nobody," he explains, "ever saw a dog make a fair and deliberate exchange of one bone for another with another dog" (14). We differ only in the way we truck. The "rude" sort do not conduct exchanges, enter into contracts, or accumulate surpluses. They lack foresight. Hence they have no time but the now:

> In that rude state of society in which there is no division of labour, in which exchanges are seldom made, and in which every man provides every thing for himself, it is not necessary that any stock should be accumulated or stored up beforehand, in order to carry on the business of the society. Every man endeavours to supply by his own industry his own occasional wants as they occur. When he is hungry, he goes to the forest to hunt; when his coat is worn out, he clothes himself with the skin of the first large animal he kills: and when his hut begins to go to ruin, he repairs it, as well as he can, with the trees and the turf that are nearest it. (299)

Rude man does not put food away now because he does not understand that he will be hungry later. He does not make a new coat before his old one frays because he does not foresee the long-term effects of wear and tear. He does not maintain his hut today because he does not predict that it will leak tomorrow. Rude man, in sum, fails to anticipate. Everything that Smith says about him indicates that he is poor in futurity. He is the very opposite of the kind of being that Martin Heidegger, in *Being and Time*, calls Dasein: the anticipatory, future-oriented being that we ourselves—that is, we "Europeans"—are.[7]

The "improved" man, in contrast, enters into production in the present because he had the foresight to accumulate his tools and materials in the past. He earns the privilege of mastering the future in return for his deferral of gratification. Smith styles him as a "thoroughly" anticipatory being:

> when the division of labour has once been thoroughly introduced, the produce of a man's own labour can supply but a very small part of his occasional wants. The far greater part of them are supplied by the produce of other men's labour, which he purchases with the produce, or what is the same thing, with the price of the produce of his own. But this purchase cannot be made till such time as the produce of his own labour has not only been completed, but sold. A stock of goods of different kinds, therefore, must be stored up somewhere sufficient to maintain him, and to supply him with the materials and tools of his work, till such time, at least, as both these events can be brought about. . . . This accumulation must, evidently, be previous to his applying his industry for so long a time to such a peculiar business. (299–300)

The division of labor puts space between the now-already-past, the now-just-passing, and the now-to-come, opening the horizon of future-oriented, anticipatory time. It is the horizon of the "till." The previous accumulation of stock lets the improved man stay in production "till such time" as the products of past labor have been sold and the proceeds reinvested in the means and materials of future production. Labor is productive if it produces something "which lasts for some time at least after that labour is past" (360). The product is not only a quantity of congealed labor power but a quantity of congealed time, and possesses not just a value but a future-oriented duration. "It is, as it were, a certain quantity of labour stocked and stored up to be employed," Smith explains, "upon some other occasion"—an occasion that always comes later (360). Value is labor that lasts.

Unproductive labor, "on the contrary," fixes itself nowhere and so disappears the "instant" it is performed. It is an event without duration. Since it has no future, it cannot be anticipated. It happens exclusively in now-time. Smith describes it as an instantaneous squander of the worker's life force. It assumes the same form in civilized nations as in savage ones. Among the civilized, however, the opposite of industry is not called savagery but poetry:

> The labour of some of the most respectable orders in the society is, like that of menial servants, unproductive of any value, and does not fix or realize itself in any permanent subject, or vendible commodity, which endures after that labour is past, and for which an equal quantity of labour could afterwards be procured. . . . Like the declamation of the actor, the

harangue of the orator, or the tune of the musician, the work of all of them perishes *in the very instant* of its production. (361, emphasis added)

The catalogue of unproductive workers includes not only "churchmen, law-yers, physicians," and "buffoons" but "men of letters of all kinds" (361). Now-time is the horizon both of savagery and of writing, and especially of inventive discourses like drama, rhetoric, and music. The savage is once again the poet's double.

A nation can do two things with the value that the productive worker fixes in durable, future-oriented products. It can reinvest it in production. Or it can consume it as revenue. The value reinvested in productive capital replaces the tools and raw materials consumed in the production process. If the amount reinvested is greater than the sum advanced, production ex-pands and the number of workers employed in productive labor increases. The nation works. "Wherever capital predominates," Smith maintains, "in-dustry prevails" (367). The value spent as revenue purchases either "nec-essaries," such as food, clothing, and shelter, or "conveniencies," such as puppet shows, buffoonery, and books. The value of necessaries is equal to the value of labor, which is paid in wages. The value of conveniencies has no limit. If the amount consumed in revenue exceeds the sum reinvested in production, then production contracts and the number of workers em-ployed in productive labor decreases. The nation stagnates: "wherever rev-enue" predominates, Smith warns, "idleness" prevails (367).

The "principle" that compels a nation to accumulate its capital in means and materials of production is "parsimony." The principle that com-pels it to squander its capital on means of consumption is "prodigality." Parsimony, because it drives us to improve our condition, is "the principle which prompts to save"; prodigality, because it seduces us into yielding to the passion for present enjoyment, is "the principle which prompts to expence" (371–72). Each principle rests on an underlying moral judgment. Parsimony lies on the high road to piety; prodigality, on the primrose path to sin: "every prodigal appears to be a public enemy, and every frugal man a public benefactor" (371). Parsimony is a sign of moral rectitude; prodigality, of moral "perversion." One is a consecration; the other a desecration. The parsimonious man helps others; the prodigal cannot even help himself:

By what a frugal man annually saves, he not only affords maintenance to an additional number of productive hands, for that or the ensuing year, but, like the founder of a public workhouse, he establishes as it were a perpetual fund for the maintenance of an equal number in all times to come. . . . No part of it can ever afterwards be employed to maintain any but productive hands, without an evident loss to the person who thus perverts it from its proper destination.

The prodigal perverts it in this manner. By not confining his expence within his income, he encroaches upon his capital. Like him who perverts the wages of some pious foundation to profane purposes, he pays the wages of idleness with those funds which the frugality of his forefathers had . . . consecrated to the maintenance of industry. (369)

The parsimony principle, a prototype of Freud's reality principle, directs today's labor toward a "destination" that can only be reached after a delay. It projects the worker onto the horizon of the future—"all times to come"—in a "uniform, constant, and uninterrupted" sequence of instants. It is to history what syntax is to discourse: it inserts space between instants of time. The prodigality principle, a prototype of the pleasure principle, brings time to a halt, seducing the worker into turning away from the future and squandering the fruits of labor in a now that neither advances nor recedes but recurs: "the passion for present enjoyment . . . , though sometimes violent and very difficult to be restrained, is in general only momentary and occasional" (371–72). The prodigality principle is to history what the force of rupture is to discourse: it lifts an event out of the present of its emergence and makes it available for grafting into other chains of events.

Smith's example confirms that the form of the tale of the two sorts is modeled on its content. It recurs in the very now-time that it attributes to poets and to savage nations, and it shares its force of breaking with its context with those unproductive laborers whose work "perishes in the instant of its production" (361). What the tale portrays is therefore what it is. It is in this sense that it overlaps its referent, projecting a rule for the formation of discourses onto the sequence of historical events. Yet it has remarkably few things, in all, to say. For the little that it does say is governed by the parsimony principle. Hence, as if in compensation, it repeats it in as many different contexts as possible.[8]

It falls to George Bataille, the anti-Smith, to make it explicit that parsimony and prodigality are principles of the tale's structure as well as its themes. Consider the following passage from Erotism, first published in 1957. "There are two extremes," Bataille writes. "At one end, existence is basically orderly and decent. Work, concern for the children, kindness and honesty rule men's dealings with their fellows. At the other, violence rages pitilessly. In certain circumstances the same men practise pillage and arson, murder, violence and torture. Excess contrasts with reason. These extremes are called civilisation and barbarism—or savagery."[9] Like Smith before him, Bataille mistakes two determinations of time for two sorts of race: the civilized and the savage. The parsimony principle compels the civilized "to save" for later; the prodigality principle compels the savage to demand "enjoyment" now. One aims at accumulation in a future-oriented horizon of duration; the other, at expenditure in an instant of dissipation. Accumulation is not an accidental predicate of civilization, nor is expenditure an accidental predicate of savagery. Parsimony, rather, is the becoming-civilized of civilization, and prodigality the becoming-savage of savagery.

Bataille, however, does not perceive an absolute opposition between the "two extremes." He folds them together instead. The zone where they meet is language: "But the use of these words [civilization and barbarism] is misleading, for they imply that there are barbarians on the one hand and civilised men on the other. The distinction is that civilised men speak and barbarians are silent, and the man who speaks is always the civilised man" (186). To say that civilization speaks indicates that it binds signs into sign chains and sign chains into discourses. Hence it opens the space of context. To say that savagery is silent indicates that it interrupts the procession of discourse and breaks sign chains into particles.[10] Hence it discharges a force of rupture. Yet discourse requires both continuity and interruption. There can be neither speech nor writing without the spacing that links signs into chains or the irruption that breaks them free from the present context and makes other combinations possible. "Not only does 'civilised' usually mean 'us,' and barbarous 'them,'" he explains, "but also civilisation and language grew as though violence was something outside, foreign not only to civilisation but also to man, man being the same thing as language. Yet observation shows that the same peoples are alternately barbarous and civilized in their attitudes" (186). When we speak of "man," we speak of "language" too, for "man" and "language" are effectively "the same." The two sorts of man correspond to two incompatible possibilities of language. To speak audibly of civilization and savagery is to speak silently, sometimes violently, of discourse itself.

Living Unhistorically

Only the sort who are exposed to the horizon of accumulation, Bataille argues, enjoy the privilege of living historically. The sort who squander their future now have no history. There is no record of the "interminable millennia" in which "man" shook off "his animal nature," he says, because "man" in the animal condition makes nothing that lasts, nothing that could be interpreted later, whereas "man" in the human condition makes "tools" and leaves them behind, as legible traces, after he is gone (30–31). The difference between animality and humanity comes down to a difference between two sorts of time: between the future-oriented time that Bataille attributes to "civilization" and the now-time he attributes to "savagery." Savages, then, are humans who have too much animal in them, whereas "civilized men" are those who have mastered their own animality.

There is, however, nothing original in Bataille's speculations about humankind's passage from prehistory to history. He is only repeating what it was already possible, in more than one context, for an author of his time to say about time. Yet Schopenhauer had drawn a similar distinction between "animals" and "man" a century earlier in *The World as Will and Representation:* "They live in the present alone; he lives at the same time in the future and the past. They satisfy the need of the moment; he provides by the most ingenious preparations for his future, nay, even for times that he cannot live to see."[11] Animals inhabit "the same time" all the time. They divide the present from itself in order to repeat it endlessly. Humans put space between one moment and the next in order to project themselves out of the past, across the present, and into the future.

Neither is there anything original about Schopenhauer's variation on the tale of two sorts of time. "Consider the cattle," Nietzsche urges the reader of his *Untimely Meditations* in 1873, "grazing as they pass you by: they do not know what is meant by yesterday or today, they leap about, eat, rest, digest, leap about again, and so from morn till night and from day to day, fettered to the moment and its pleasure or displeasure, and thus neither melancholy nor bored."[12] Nietzsche's cattle do not recollect a now-that-is-past, nor do they anticipate a now-still-to-come. They "leap" and "leap again" in the now-just-passing. For they cannot leap beyond it. No matter how often the present recurs, it is always the same moment for them. "Thus the animal lives *unhistorically*," he concludes, "for it is contained in the present, like a number without any awkward fraction left over" (61). Nietzsche says of animals what Smith says of savage nations. His cattle are not creatures of flesh, however, but creatures of discourse, and they share their time with the tale that describes them. It does not develop, nor does it regress. It "leaps" from one context to the next but cannot leap beyond the present of its emergence. It is the sort that breaks with every determinable context, taking history's place without taking a place of its own.[13]

The tale of the two sorts is a remarkably animated creature of discourse. It does not record an inert narrative of past events but is itself an event irrupting repeatedly in the present, as if it were one of those forces that, according to Marx, take part in historical change. Paradoxically, its capacity to provoke change is directly proportional to its capacity to persist as it passes from one author and one context to other, different authors and contexts. Nor can it be confined to the writings of eighteenth- and nineteenth-century economists and philosophers. The following series of examples discovers it at work in the colonization of the Canadian prairies during the early years of the twentieth century. The series conforms to a pattern that would continue to organize the public debate about land title in western Canada until early in the twenty-first century. The question therefore remains: How can the same statement be repeated, and remain repeatedly effective, in an open-ended series of linguistic, social, and historical contexts?

On November 23, 1903, Father J. Hugonard, the principal of the Industrial School at Fort Qu'Appelle in what were then the Northwest Territories of Canada, submitted an unsolicited progress report to the Indian commissioner in Winnipeg, Manitoba. In it he states that the mission of his school, a joint venture of church and state, is to isolate aboriginal children from their families and cultures in order to transform them "from savages to civilized individuals." The mission's success depends on the school's ability to lift students out of the present-bound, hence savage inertia of unproductive labor and graft them into the future-oriented, hence civilized horizon of productive labor. It costs money, however, to teach the young to renounce unrestricted expenditure and embrace the accumulation of stock. A regime of parsimony requires a dangerous outburst of prodigality on the part of both the Catholic Church and the federal government. Hugonard says he is willing to risk the expense if he can be persuaded that "the country" stands to profit from it later:

> The object of the Government in establishing and maintaining these institutions at great cost to the country is undoubtedly to enable the Indian youth educated in them to become civilized and self-supporting men and women.
>
> The usefulness of these schools is in proportion to the success attained in transforming these young people from savages to civilized individuals and it is no use denying the fact that this success depends far less on the mode of education received than upon the circumstance in which these ex-pupils are placed upon leaving school.[14]

Hugonard is concerned that when students graduate and return home to their reserves, they will renounce the parsimony principle and fall back under the sway of the prodigality principle. The danger is especially great if they are going home to dance, for one instant of dancing can undo the effects of years of residential education. He goes so far as to claim that "the dance" is "the source of all the trouble that missionaries and Government officials have to contend with." Dancing is the recourse of savagery. It cuts across the path to "improvement" and bars access to futurity:

> A person unacquainted with the Indian question might think it a harsh and arbitrary proceeding to stop these dances, but it would only take a very short time if he lived amongst the Indians to convince him that the dances must be stopped before any permanent results can be obtained from our schools.
>
> Let him attend some of these dances where graduates of these schools were present and see them nearly nude, painted and decked out in feathers and beads, dancing like demented individuals and indulging in all kinds of debauchery; and if he had the progress and welfare of the Indian at heart I am satisfied he would not hesitate a minute but declare that the total suppression of these dances and pagan practices is the first essential towards progress and advancement.[15]

A true agent of progress would not "hesitate a minute," he argues, to keep "the Indian" from hesitating *in* the minute, because dancing spontaneously transforms civilized subjects into creatures of "debauchery" and confines them to that "very short time" in which animals and savages live. "I am convinced," he adds, "that Christianity and advancement, and paganism and indolence cannot flourish side by side; one or the other has to give way; paganism, dancing, and indolence are most natural to the Indian, who has no thought for the morrow." Indolence is a definitively savage inertia. Its time is limited to the day just passing. Industry, in contrast, is a powerfully civilizing force of "advancement." It opens up a horizon for the accumulation of stock: "systematic work and uninterrupted labor ensure a better mode of living; more farming is being done, cows are being milked and butter made, and the Indians are accumulating individual property; they are better clad and healthier, their children are healthier." Productive labor fixes itself in "more" and "better" things. Unproductive labor squanders itself more. Savages, by Hugonard's definition, are creatures of excess. They waste not only time and property but a surplus of both. "I contend," he concludes, "that Indian dances promote agitation against missionaries, Christianity, and authority on the reserve, nullify to a great extent efforts towards education; cause great loss of time, neglect and abuse of stock and horses, and foster degradation, debauchery, idleness, and craving for liquor among the Indians." Dancers exhaust so much of their life force in unproductive labor that they have none left to fix in land, livestock, and crops. But there is a more serious danger. The dance promises a "loss" of futurity itself. It removes the space between moments of time and reduces the temporal horizon to a present that repeats itself without limit.

Hugonard claims to be speaking from firsthand, lived experience, as if he were presenting the findings that anyone would reach if confronted with the same facts. Yet he could have composed his letter without leaving a metropolitan library. His arguments had already been recited by Smith more than a century earlier. To compel the Indian commissioner to suppress "these dances," he repeats "the one thing" that "fits" any context, lifting the tale of the two sorts out of the discourse of political economy and grafting it into the discourse of colonial administration. Why not tell another tale? It is not that Hugonard lacks invention but that, in Foucault's words, "few things, in all, can be said." [16] The poverty of discourse induces a surplus of repetition. But few things, in fact, need to be said. The repetition of the tale releases a chain of events that ends in an attempt by one society to eliminate another, indeed several others.

In January 1904 W. R. Tucker, an Indian agent at the Moosewoods Sioux Reserve, writes to the Department of Indian Affairs in Ottawa to remind his superiors that the dances of the Dakota or "Sioux" people are causing a great waste of labor power. "I have known them to dance 7 days in the week," he explains. "The men were too lazy to work or hunt in fact they were not able to as they had danced all their energy away and would lay around and sleep until it was time to go to another dance." [17] Dancing not only squanders the labor power that fixes value in its products but lays waste to the future in which value endures and products are bought, sold, and consumed. Too exhausted for industry, those who dance remain suspended in a state of indolence and inertia. Who are these creatures of excess? Eastman's family was among the Dakota refugees who removed to the Canadian prairies after the Minnesota Massacre of 1862.

The homology between savagery and prodigality is valid a priori. Hence it is precertified for repetition in every context. No proof is "necessary" to confirm it because it is validated by the fact that it has already—indeed always already—been said. That, at least, is what Frank Pedley, the deputy superintendent general of Indian affairs, writes to T. Cory, the Indian agent at Carlyle, Saskatchewan, in a 1909 letter: "It does not seem necessary to explain at any length the grounds upon which the Department holds this view, but it may say that in its long and wide experience of Indians under their varying conditions it has invariably found that dancing tends to waste their substance, to produce a dissipated and frivolous habit of mind and condition of body which are inimical to work and habits of self-reliance."[18] The "long and wide experience" to which Pedley refers is the experience of a long series of texts in which the opposition between parsimony and prodigality finally brings forth the dancer as an object of administrative control.

In 1910 the department spent an excess of discourse to keep the aboriginal people of the prairies from dancing at agricultural fairs and exhibitions. Administrators never tire of repeating in their correspondence that dancing directs labor power away from future-oriented production and squanders it instead in present-oriented consumption. The time of the dancer, says the agent at Portage la Prairie, Manitoba, lasts no longer than a day: "The Indian has little idea of time and does not attach much value to it, but has a wonderful appreciation of a gala day, so will give up anything to celebrate."[19] Those who live for the day, adds the agent at Brocket, Alberta, do not think to defer present enjoyment for future gain. They lack thrift because they lack foresight: "tho' many had considerable earnings or proceeds from sale of horses I would venture to say not one has returned with enough cash to purchase food for one days sustenance for themselves or families, and not taking into consideration considerable loss of time, they were at a considerable financial loss."[20]

What these administrators say early in the twentieth century about dancing echoes the tale that Smith tells in the latter half of the eighteenth century about feasting. Smith conceives of the feast, or "festival," as a rare case of civilized excess. To feast is to consume a slowly gathered surplus in a fleeting instant of enjoyment. The aim, he laments, is not to feed the hungry but to make a public display of squander: "Of two or three hundred weight of provisions, which may sometimes be served up at a great festival, one-half, perhaps, is thrown to the dunghill, and there is always a great deal wasted and abused."[21] The host who eats up the products of labor past squanders a capital that might otherwise employ labor in the future. Indeed he treats both time and capital like shit—"dung"—something to be expelled rather than accumulated, wasting both past and future in the same instant. Dancing and feasting are two variants of one original economic sin: the divorce of capital from productive labor.

The tale of the two sorts, though, is itself a laborer, and it acquires an increment of persuasive force every time it breaks with its present context. The more it is repeated, the harder it sets to work. Duncan Campbell Scott succeeded Pedley as deputy superintendent general of Indian affairs in 1913. Haunted by tales of "excessive indulgence in the practice of dancing"—not to mention "the more or less characteristic disinclination of the Indian for steady work"—he lobbied the superintendent general of Indian affairs, an elected member of Parliament, to amend the Indian Act to ban aboriginal people from dancing off reserve without the permission of a government agent.[22] The Parliament of Canada passed an amendment to section 149 of the Indian Act on June 12, 1914.[23] The limited range of what it was possible to say about aboriginal people gave legislators the means to restrict what aboriginal people could legally do with their bodies.[24] Dancers would now have to add a new move to their repertoire: getting around the law.

"Discourse"

But surely the time of this tale has passed. Surely we have progressed beyond the era when scholars and administrators uncritically classified human beings into a race of the present and a race of the future. Who today would knowingly recycle the discursive strategies of colonialism? Austin Clarke's ironic answer is "colonials."[25] His 1997 novel *The Origin of Waves* entertains the possibility that even after the end of the colonial project, now-time remains the only time available to the "post"-colonial subject. The plot hinges on a chance meeting. Two men who grew up together in Barbados run into each other on a snow-covered Toronto street and spend the rest of the day catching up in a nearby bar. They have not seen each other since they were boys playing on the beach. Tim settled in Toronto. John lived in Europe for many years and then moved to North Carolina. As children they were taught to think of themselves as "colonials"; as adults they still live in the time reserved for them in colonial discourse. Tim is not always sure, for example, whether any time has elapsed between that day on the beach and this day in the bar. He says that their conversation occurs in "concentrated time": a sort of time that folds one present over another without advancing into the future (111).

Clearly Tim has an issue with time. He experiences the present not as a transition from past to future but as a horizon of iteration. Time for Tim is like a crab, which advances by walking backward, or like a wave, which goes forward by "falling back upon itself" (5). John asks Tim what he does with his time. Tim confesses that he wanders the streets all day but goes "nowhere." John does not believe him. The motion that Tim describes not only violates the laws of physics but offends against the standards of properly human conduct. Walking and going nowhere, he says, is not something "a man" does. Only Nietzsche's cattle can leap—and leap again—without moving from one place to another:

> "Where you was going when I bounced-into you?" John says.
> "Nowhere."
> "A man have to go *somewhere*. You can't just be walking and not going nowhere! You can't be just going from one place to the next, and not going *anywhere!* You must have some direction, even if only in your mind. A man just don't walk that way. You just can't walk from one spot to another spot, and still not be going anywhere!" (69)

Tim, whose name is just one silent vowel short of "time," suffers from a repetition compulsion. And the way he talks echoes the way he walks. He tells John a love story that leaps "from one spot" to another, and from one time to another, without coming to rest anywhere in particular. He insists the episode happened when he was in college but admits it makes no difference to him whether it happened "years ago" or "last night." An instant from the past can return to him anytime as if it were happening in the present. "I find that I live in the past as if it is the present," he confesses, "They mean the same to me. At my age I prefer the past. So, what I'm telling you . . . the story I am telling you about last night is really the same story as that Friday night, years and years ago." No delay intervenes between a tale told now and one told years ago. They are, for Tim, "mixed into one" (81).

What does Tim mean, though, when he says "the same"? John asks him what he saw the last time they spent a day together on the beach in Barbados. Tim answers,

> "Ships"
> > "Ships? Nothing else?"
> > "And clouds"
> > "Ships and clouds?" (195)

John's astonished response, which repeats what Tim has already said, launches Tim into a meditation on the problem of repetition, which he compares to an echo: "He says this as if it is the echo to my memory, as if it is an echo, time and place here in this bar going back to that time with no change in the time or in the place, as if there is no alteration, and the bar is the beach" (195). In Tim's time, there can be iteration without "alteration."

A sign chain can be lifted out of one context and grafted to another as if there were "no change" in the "time" and the "place" of its inscription, as if no spacing intervened between the event of its first enunciation and the event of its repetition. "I see him as he was then," Tim says to himself, "and as I was then, as we are, *then*" (195). He speaks as if "then" *is* now, as if both instants, in Nietzsche's words, were "contained in the present." He does not recall the past in the form of memories, nor does he project himself onto future possibilities. Every time is the same time for Tim. Yet he is well aware that something is "missing" from his experience of temporality. "And thinking about it now, years later," he muses, "this thing about time . . . I am always missing time, time is always passing me" (203). Tim's time does not divide one context from another. Every moment folds back over the moment that went before: "now" is simultaneously "years later." When he speaks of "the same," then, he draws attention to a failure of spacing. The sameness of Tim's time depends on the lack of difference between moments he nonetheless perceives as different.

That, moreover, is why Tim's tale does not belong to him. It is his own story—indeed his life story, his autobiography—but he insists it would be "the same story" no matter who told it. For it is constituted by a force that breaks it free of its author. Someone else could repeat it right now, in the context unfolding right here, as if reciting it for the first time. "'It wasn't *me* I was talking about,'" Tim warns John. "'This story is not my story'" (126). John may be right to maintain that "a man" cannot go from one place to another without going anywhere at all. But some statements can. They have "a propensity to truck" from context to context and from author to author without undergoing a change in time or place. They cannot be fixed in any present but instead fold back on themselves like waves.

Michel Foucault, however, insists that a statement is exactly what cannot be repeated. "The enunciation," he bluntly states, "is an unrepeatable event." It is a point he repeats more than once in his 1969 monograph *The Archaeology of Knowledge*, which mounts a systematic rebuttal of the arguments advanced in this chapter, not least Tim's conception of time.[26] Foucault writes in defense of "contextualism," a genre of history that aims to explain an event by studying its "specific relationships" to events going on around it in a "circumambient historical space."[27] No critique of contextualism can ignore Foucault's defense of the privileges of context. Every event of discourse, he argues, is unique. The iteration of a statement necessarily alters it. Hence a statement (*énoncé*) cannot *not* be transformed as it leaps from one spot to another—even if it is repeated word for word—because its mode of "occurrence" (*instance*) is "proper" to it alone.[28] So how might

Foucault explain the repetition compulsion that governs the tale of the two sorts?

Foucault conceives of discourse as a condition of finitude. The description of statements aims to discover its parsimony principle. The question is not "According to what rules could other similar statements be made?" but rather, "How is it that one particular statement appeared rather than another?" (27). The "rules" he alludes to would make it possible to repeat the "same" statements. They would proliferate discursive events. What he seeks instead is a principle that restricts events of discourse: "we must grasp the statement in the exact specificity of its occurrence," he says; "we must show why it could not be other than it was, in what respect it is exclusive of any other, how it assumes, in the midst of others and in relation to them, a place that no other could occupy" (28). A statement is not a thing but an event. It is so irreducibly singular, moreover, so strictly limited, so exclusive, that it breaks with the events happening around it. Such an event "emerges" only in an instant of "historical irruption." In order for there to be an "irruption," though, there must occur an instant of irruption that fractures the continuity of historical time. The event of irruption can happen only in now-time. Yet now-time is the time of repetition. Hence a uniquely unrepeatable event is tied to a singularly repeatable unit of time. "It is certainly a strange event," Foucault admits, in part "because, like every event, it is unique, yet subject to repetition, transformation, and reactivation" (28). There is no repetition, he repeatedly states, and yet there is *some*. How can the repetition compulsion take hold of an event without thereby making it repeatable?

Foucault argues that you can repeat a sentence any number of times by arranging the same words in the same order according to the same rules of formation. But a sentence is not a statement. Nor is a proposition. Nor is a speech act. "A statement exists outside any possibility of reappearing," he affirms, "and the relation that it possesses with what it states is not identical with a group of rules of use" (89). This "relation" is governed by four conditions. First, a statement establishes a rule for the existence of the objects it names, designates, or describes. It does not refer to things outside of discourse (91). Rather, it brings objects into emergence on the surface of a discourse. Second, a statement is not uttered by a subject but emerges instead from a subject position, a "vacant place" that can be "filled" by any number of "different individuals" (95). Nevertheless, third, a statement is not so singular that it exists in a vacuum. For it takes place in a preexisting "field" of discourse: "there is no statement that does not presuppose others" (99). Fourth, a statement has a "material existence" (100). It happens in a poem, an advertisement, or an act of legislation, and the surface of its emergence gives it "a substance, a support, a place, and a date" that are unique. When its material context changes, "it too changes identity" (101).

If two people "say the same thing at the same time," they produce two "distinct" statements. If the same person repeats "the same sentence several times," she produces a series of "distinct" statements (101). The "form" of a statement is "endlessly repeatable," but the "statement itself," Foucault never tires of repeating, "cannot be repeated" (102). True, a sentence like "Dreams fulfill desires" has recurred over the centuries, but it "is not the same statement" in the works of Plato and Freud, for the two authors subject it to different conditions of use and modes of verification (103).

What if you purchase two consecutive editions of *The Wealth of Nations*, or, "better still," two volumes from the same printing? Have you bought two different works? Do they contain different chapters? Different arguments? On the contrary, says Foucault, you have at last come into possession of two copies of "the same set of statements." They may differ in font, ink, and paper, but such differences are "not important enough" to distinguish them from one another. Here at last is a verifiable case of repetition. How is it possible? Foucault explains that in this case an institution, the publishing industry, establishes protocols for the "reinscription" and "transcription" of book-length statements, rendering them inert enough to happen more than once: "The schemata of use, the rules of application, the constellations in which they can play a part, their strategic potentialities constitute for statements a *field of stabilizations* that makes it possible, despite the differences of enunciation, to repeat them in their identity" (103). The field of stabilizations gives statements a "constancy" that makes them both unrepeatable and yet "too repeatable" to be fettered to "a particular time and place" (104). After insisting that the statement is an unrepeatable event, he concludes that "the statement may be *repeated*—but always under strict conditions" (105). But there is more than one exception to Foucault's ban on repetition.

He notes that a statement is a commodity routinely exchanged for other commodities in the marketplace of discourse: "the statement circulates" or, to use Smith's phrase, the statement trucks (105). As it trucks, moreover, it puts a supplement into circulation, a surplus value fixed in a surplus object. "A series of signs will become a statement on condition that it possesses 'something else' . . . a specific relation that concerns itself—and not its cause, or its elements" (89). A statement is not a correlation between a signifier and a signified, or between a sign and a thing, a sentence and its meaning, a proposition and its referent. It does not stand for something else or indicate something about something else. A statement, rather, is an event of emergence. The task of the analysis of discourses is to investigate not only how it happens but what it allows to happen: "The question proper to such an analysis might be formulated in this way: what is this specific existence that emerges from what is said and nowhere else?" (28)

An object, however, can remain in existence only if the event of its emergence is capable of being repeated. The durability of objects depends on the iterability of statements. Hence the field of discourse is divided into areas of "regularity" that favor the emergence of some objects and preclude the emergence of others (38). Foucault calls them "discursive formations," and he conceives of them as regions of poverty. Statements are values—"things that are transmitted and preserved, that have value"—and yet, paradoxically, "however numerous they may be," these values "are always in deficit" (en déficit) (119–20/156). The economy of discursive formations, it turns out, is remarkably similar to the economies of savage nations. They squander a surplus of values—such as statements—in a scarcity of time. In discursive formations, as in savage nations, moreover, stock is both "numerous" and rare. There is at once too much and not enough. They take wealth and make it into poverty. The little that can be said today is all that it will be possible to say tomorrow. Under such conditions, repetition, though otherwise forbidden, is permissible as a strategy for "the administration" of the "scarce resources" necessary for the maintenance of objects (120). The savage economy of discourse makes a certain quantity of repetition inevitable. "This rarity of statements," Foucault concedes, "the incomplete, fragmented form of the enunciative field, the fact that few things, in all, can be said, explain that statements are not, like the air we breath, an infinite transparency; but things that are transmitted and preserved, that have value, and which one tries to appropriate; *that are repeated, reproduced, and transformed*" (119–20, emphasis added). Thus the interpreter of discourses is required to ask not just "What emerges when a statement happens?" but "What persists when a statement happens *repeatedly*?"

The History of the Damned

To speak of "savagery" is to repeat today what was said the day before, which means speaking as savages are said to do. It is the sort of discourse that unfolds in the time it attributes to savage nations—another indication that it is a discourse about discourse itself and, especially, about the temporality of discourse. Savage time begins in the morning and lasts until evening, and begins all over again when the sun rises the next day. Every day of it is therefore "nowadays." Take, for example, Rousseau's portrait of "savage man," sketched in the "Discourse on Inequality" and published in Amsterdam in 1755. The portrait does not denote a state of affairs that an eighteenth-century reader could have experienced in the colonies but instead describes its own ekphrastic structure. "His soul, which nothing stirs," he says of savage man, "yields itself to the sole sentiment of its pres-. ent existence, with no idea of the future, however near it may be, and his projects, as limited as his views, hardly extend to the close of the day."[29] The portrait of savage inertia, a subset of the tale of the two sorts, partici- pates in history by excepting itself from history. But that is exactly why, in Rousseau's view, the reader should trust it. The "testimonies of History" are notoriously "uncertain," but the portrait of savage inertia, precisely be- cause it is unhistorical, seldom fails to exert a force of emergence. It can fit into any context because it breaks with every context. For it persists in now-time, like the "savage" it portrays:

> But without resorting to the uncertain testimonies of History, who fails
> to see that everything seems to remove from Savage man the tempta-
> tion as well as the means to cease being savage? His imagination depicts
> nothing to him; his heart asks nothing of him. His modest needs are so
> ready to hand, and he is so far from the degree of knowledge necessary to
> desire to acquire greater knowledge, that he can have neither foresight
> nor curiosity. . . . Forever the same order, forever the same revolutions;
> he lacks the wit to wonder at the greatest marvels; and it is not to him
> that one will turn for the Philosophy man needs in order to be able to
> observe once what he has seen every day. (142–43)

The portrait of "savage man" suffers from a characteristically savage iner- tia. Simply to utter it is to fold time. What Rousseau says in 1755 is what Smith will repeat in 1776 and what Clarke's Tim repeats again in 1997. No space intervenes between the now in which the savage remains "forever the same" and the now in which the portrait of savage inertia recycles its state- ments. For the "testimonies of History" are shot through with particles of savage time.[30] Rousseau's portrait does not prefigure the statements of Smith or Eastman or Clarke but repeats them in advance, in a time ahead of time. Some statement-events happen only in a present that endures with- out duration.

What, for example, is the time of this citation from the introduction to *The Native Tribes of Central Australia* by Baldwin Spencer and F. J. Gillen, published in 1897? The authors invite their readers to "imagine" they have been "transported" from their own cultural and historical context "to the side of some waterhole in the centre of Australia." What is happening there is going on right now, no matter whether you read about it in 1897 or in 2007:

> Early in the morning, if it be summer, and not until the sun be well up if it be winter, the occupants of the camp are astir. Time is no object to them, and, if there be no lack of food, the men and women all lounge about while the children laugh and play. If food be required, then the women will go out accompanied by the children and armed with digging sticks and *pitchis,* and the day will be spent out in the bush in search of small burrowing animals such as lizards and small marsupials. The men will perhaps set off armed with spears, spear-throwers, boomerangs and shields in search of larger game such as emus and kangaroos.[31]

The inhabitants of now-time rise first thing in the morning but do not go to work until the specter of scarcity—"lack of food"—propels them into motion. They know how to be "astir" without "setting off." They do not work for the future but confine themselves to the satisfaction of present wants, just as "Savage man," according to Rousseau, "has trouble giving thought in the morning to his needs in the evening."[32]

A few years earlier, but in the same particle of now-time, Bücher reiterates that there are "plenty of districts upon the earth" where "with a minimum of exertion" the "lowest" of races persist in the present by feeding on the fruits of uncultivated nature.[33] He insists that these "races" graze "like herds of animals" (one thinks of Nietzsche's cattle) because they do not think to accumulate what nature itself sets before them: "Stores of such fruits and roots they do not gather," but rather "each individual at once swallows what he finds" (9). This "at once" is the organizing principle of the portrait of savage inertia. The societies Bücher convokes, like the discourse that brings them repeatedly to emergence, lack the time of the till. "It is utterly impossible," he repeats, "to speak of foresight, in the sense of providing for the future, in connection with primitive peoples. Primitive man does not think of the future; he does not *think* at all" (12). Bücher, like Rousseau and Smith before him, treats time as a principle of racial classification, and now-time is the characteristic trait of the "uncivilized" races. Indeed it actively uncivilizes them. For it is their becoming-savage: "*the savage,*" Bücher iterates, "*thinks only of himself, and thinks only of the present.* What lies beyond that is as good as closed to his mental vision" (14). Not even the threat of starvation can persuade the inhabitants of the now to forgo present enjoyment and look ahead to future profit: "primitive man follows only the prompting of the moment . . . he thinks not of the future, nor of the past" (20).[34]

In the 1890s, Freud conceives of the cell as a savage in miniature, not a "savage man" but a kind of savage homunculus. Life on earth, he argues, borrows its principle of growth from the sun, but there is something in organic matter that resists the solar-powered, future-oriented time of evolutionary development and seeks to return to an earlier, simpler state, just as something compels certain discursive formations to repeat a repertoire of earlier and simpler statements. Indeed the homology is striking. The economics of multicellular organisms, as Freud understands it, mirrors the economics of the discourse about savage economics. Both are composed of "elementary particles" that recur in the present rather than endure from past to future. Each particle carries a discrete quantum of force and squanders it in now-time, though sometimes a particle briefly accumulates energy in order to squander it the more lavishly later. The following description of the elementary particle of life, from *Beyond the Pleasure Principle*, published in 1920, could double as an account of the repeatable particle of discourse:

> The elementary living entity would from its very beginning have had no wish to change; if conditions remained the same, it would do no more than constantly repeat the same course of life. . . . Every modification which is thus imposed upon the course of the organism's life is accepted by the conservative organic instincts and stored up for further repetition. Those instincts are therefore bound to give a deceptive appearance of being forces tending towards change and progress, whilst in fact they are merely seeking to reach an ancient goal by paths alike old and new.[35]

The inertia that Freud attributes to the elementary living entity, or cell, belongs equally to the statement he recites. The cell like "savage man," and like the discourse that brings savage man into emergence, is not disposed to change but tends instead "to repeat the same course." Just as the cell stores up every "modification" for "further repetition," so the discourse about savagery stocks up modes of utterance and repeats them without fixed limits. The event of recurrence, whether it occurs in life or discourse, irrupts in an instant that fractures the horizon of anticipation and duration. Even when life and discourse seem to be "tending towards change," they are really "seeking" to return to "an ancient goal" by every available "path." Freud calls the tendency of living things to return to an earlier state, a "drive" (36). Does a discourse have drives of its own?

Years earlier, in his unfinished 1895 manuscript "Project for a Scientific Psychology," Freud undertook, as he put it, "to represent psychical processes as quantitatively determinate states of specifiable material particles."[36] He means that mental activity has its material basis in the nervous system, which is composed of "particles" that today we call nerve cells or neurons. In James Strachey's translation, they are called "neurones." Each particle is invested with a discrete quantity of energy. The movement of quantities between particles generates the experiences of thought, will, and emotion. Freud's unsolved problem is to explain how differences in the quantity of energy translate into differences in the quality of experience.

A neurone exists either in motion or at rest. Motion ensues when a quantum of energy, which Freud names Q, enters the cell in an unbound flow. The cell, however, prefers to remain at rest. So it manages the incoming quantum either by discharging it in reflex action or by binding it up and storing it for future, specific action. Reflex action aims to rid the organism of excitations; it spends every quantum in the now. Specific action aims to prevent future excitations by making changes in the organism's environment; it opens up the horizon of anticipation. The discharge of energy is the nervous system's "primary function," but the binding of energy allows for a "secondary" and qualitative "development"—namely, consciousness—which takes three forms: thought, will, and feeling. The three modes of experience correspond to three ways of accumulating quantities of energy and are located in three systems of "neurones" (296). The system φ (phi) receives quanta from the outside world. It provides the organism with outer perception. The system ψ (psi) receives quanta from the body's internal organs, including the φ system (302–3). It provides inner perception. The system ω (omega) is the seat of consciousness, the "subjective side" of the nervous system's "physical processes" (311). An external "stimulus" does not reach any of these systems, though, until it passes through the skin. So Freud, revising as he goes, lets Q represent energy arriving from outside the body and proposes $Q\acute{\eta}$ to represent energy flowing inside the body (296). $Q\acute{\eta}$ (Q-eta) is his shorthand for the life force, a kind of bioenergetic soul.

The "basic principle" of Freud's mental economics, as of Smith's savage economics, is "neuronal inertia." It is responsible for the fact that "neurones tend to divest themselves of Q" (296). The primary function of the nervous system maintains a regime of strict prodigality: it spends all of its quantities now instead of stocking them up for later. The secondary function observes a policy of grudging parsimony: it accumulates "a store" of $Q\acute{\eta}$, the life force, in order to respond to the stimuli reaching the ψ system

from the internal organs. Our major needs—"hunger, respiration, sexuality"
(297)—arise inside the body. Hence we cannot flee them. But the objects that
satisfy them lie outside the body. Hence the only way to return to rest is to
act on the world, quelling hunger, for example, by finding nourishment. But
even the secondary nervous system tends toward inertia. Although circumstances compel it to amass a stock of energy, it keeps the accumulation of
$Q\acute{\eta}$ "as low as possible" (297–98).

How does the nervous system accumulate its stock? The spaces between
neurones oppose the "discharge" of $Q\acute{\eta}$ and thereby generate a "resistance"
that holds energy inside the cell (298). Freud calls these spaces "contact-
barriers." They link living particles together by holding them apart. When
$Q\acute{\eta}$ passes through the system ω for the first time, the contact barriers of
the ω neurones suffer permanent changes, forming pathways that he names
Bahnungen or, in Strachey's translation, "facilitations" (300, 309). A facilitation is a quantity of life force fixed in a product of past mental labor. It
reduces the resistance between neurones, making them "more capable of
[the] conduction" of excitations (300). Henceforth, when energy enters the ω
system, it is more likely to take already "facilitated" pathways rather than
less permeable routes. Facilitations therefore encourage the repetition of
"preferred" passages. Because they bear the traces of previous excitations,
they afford the nervous system the *"possibility of representing memory"*
(299). Together they comprise the ψ system, the material substrate of complex thought. In contrast, the neurones that discharge energy without a
trace "do not *think* at all," like Bücher's primitives, because they do not fix
energy in a durable product, like Rousseau's savages. They comprise the φ
system. The ψ system is the nervous system's civilized and frugal elite; the
φ system, its riotous and savage rascals. Freud's mechanical model of the
nervous system is another variation on the tale of the two sorts.

Just as the principle of neuronal inertia compels the elementary particles of life to return to an "earlier" and "simpler" state, so a principle of
rhetorical inertia compels certain elementary particles of discourse to persist in the now even as they leap between historical and cultural contexts.[37]
These particles display the kind of "organic elasticity" that Freud attributes
to the elementary living substance. They are by nature "conservative."
They facilitate the repetition of an existing order of discourse while resist-
ing the onset of a new one.[38] It is only fitting, then, that the temporality
of facilitation receives its canonical formulation in an essay with a highly
"facilitated" surface. The essay is Walter Benjamin's "On the Concept of
History." And it is "facilitated" in the sense of "geared for repetition." For
it recycles the portrait of savage inertia even as it elevates savage time into

the first principle of historical materialism. Benjamin's is another of those texts that do what they say and are what they are about.

He maintains that the fabric of history is "filled full" by repeatable "splinters" of now-time (*Jetztzeit*), not in the passive sense of cluttered but in the active sense of formed, shaped, filled out.[39] These splinters, or particles, are the contour rather than the container of events. Historians can mobilize them in one of two ways. The advocates of "historicism" insert spacing among the now-just-passed, the now-just-passing, and the now-to-come, as if to hold open the future-oriented horizon of civilization and accumulation. The advocates of "historical materialism" conceive of the present as an irruption that interrupts the series of causes and effects. They revive the possibility of savage time. "Historicism," explains Benjamin, "contents itself with establishing a causal nexus among various moments in history" (397). It tells one moment from the next like beads in a rosary. "The historical materialist," in contrast, "cannot do without the notion of a present which is not a transition, but in which time takes a stand and has come to a standstill" (396). Materialist historiography collects events that may be separated by thousands of years and makes them simultaneously present, like stars in a constellation (397). A particle of historical now-time happens again as if happening for the first time. Every day of *Jetztzeit* is therefore nowadays. For the materialist historian, "there can be no appearance of repetition in history," Benjamin adds in his *Arcades Project*, "since precisely those moments in the course of history which matter most to him, by virtue of their index as 'fore-history,' become moments of the present day."[40] Only for a "redeemed" humanity does "the past" become fully "citable"—and thus repeatable—in all its moments."[41] The damned, it seems, are condemned to recite bits of it, because each "splinter" can be repeated in any context while belonging exclusively to the context where it is happening now.

The history of the damned can only be written in a time gone savage. In "On the Concept of History," Benjamin calls such a time "messianic." He endows his messiah, however, with savagery's characteristic trait. Messianic events happen in a paradoxical "arrest of happening" that brings anticipatory time to a halt and interrupts the chain of causes and effects, fracturing "the course of history" into particles that the historical materialist recombines into more dialectical configurations (396). "It is not that what is past casts its light on what is present, or what is present its light on what is past; rather," he explains in *The Arcades Project*, "what has been comes together in a flash with the now to form a constellation."[42] Not only can there be no historical events, but there can be no interpretation of historical events, without recourse to savage time. Perhaps that is why the discourse that says what savages are repeatedly mimics what it says that savages do.

Later critics have perhaps cited no particle of Benjamin's discourse more often than his reading of Paul Klee's *Angelus Novus*. But has anyone noticed how he superimposes Klee's painting onto the portrait of savage inertia?

> There is a picture by Klee called *Angelus Novus*. It shows an angel who seems about to move away from something he stares at. His eyes are wide, his mouth is open, his wings are spread. This is how the angel of history must look. His face is turned toward the past. Where a chain of events appears before *us*, he sees one single catastrophe, which keeps piling wreckage upon wreckage and hurls it at his feet. The angel would like to stay, awaken the dead, and make whole what has been smashed. But a storm is blowing from Paradise and has got caught in his wings; it is so strong that the angel can no longer close them. This storm drives him irresistibly into the future, to which his back is turned, while the pile of debris before him grows toward the sky. What we call progress is *this* storm.[43]

The angel of history does not turn to face his future possibilities. Instead he flies backward into the horizon of improvement. Hence he lacks foresight. He takes what "we" perceive to be "a chain of events" and compresses them into the instant just passing. Hence he is fettered to the present. Though he is "caught" in the storm from paradise, the products of past labor pile up at his feet like "debris." Hence he oversees a scene of expenditure and waste. Benjamin's angel does not think of the future. What lies beyond the present is as good as closed to his mental vision. But still "progress" sweeps him along.

It is a picture already familiar to the historian of discursive formations. In 1897 Spencer and Gillen depict "progress" as a catastrophe that is "irresistibly" propelling the aboriginal people of central Australia out of a present in which they rest inert and into a future that has neither space nor time for them. The dilemma of these "Australian tribes" prefigures the plight of Benjamin's backward angel. For the "time" of the "native," like that of the angel, is always already up: "The time in which it will be possible to investigate the Australian native tribes is rapidly drawing to a close, and though we know more of them than we do of the lost Tasmanians, yet our knowledge is very incomplete, and unless some special effort be made, many tribes will practically die out without our gaining any knowledge of the details of their organisation, or of their sacred customs and beliefs."[44] Indigenous societies are the angels of *pre*history. They turn their back on the future and watch as the wreckage of the past piles up at their feet. Yet that wreckage, according to Spencer and Gillen, is them. Still the ethnographers do not ask for the storm of progress to abate. All they want is enough time to study the living portrait of prehistory before it fades for good. The horizon of anticipation is extending its borders, and there is little time left for now-time. The moment is coming—indeed it is always about to arrive—when the people of the present will have spent all of the time that remains to them, except, perhaps, for one last surplus particle. Again the question recurs. What inertia compels Spencer and Gillen to confine indigenous societies to a time that interrupts the storm of progress and is always about to end but never does?

CHAPTER TWO

The New Barbarism

That mountain there! That cloud there! What is "real" in that? Subtract the phantasm and every human *contribution* from it, my sober friends! If you *can!* If you can forget your descent, your past, your training—all of your humanity and animality. There is no "reality" for us—not for you either, my sober friends.—*Friedrich Nietzsche,* The Gay Science

Monsters of Energy

Sometime between the fall of 1887 and the winter of 1888, Nietzsche enriches his notebooks with a tale of two other sorts. First he offers a "view" of the Europeans of "the future." They possess a stock of riches that culminates, anticlimactically, in poverty: "the most intelligent slave animals, very industrious, fundamentally very modest, inquisitive to excess, multifarious, pampered, weak of will."[1] Nietzsche asks whether these weaklings can give rise to another, stronger sort (*Art*), one equipped with "*classical* taste": "this means will to simplification, strengthening, to visible happiness, to the terrible, the courage of psychological nakedness." The arrival of the classical sort—which will happen only after "tremendous socialist crises"—will invert rather than complete the causal sequence of historical events. Europe is going to enter a "classical" age only *after* modernity has been exhausted. There is a past, says Nietzsche, that has not happened yet: "Problem: where are the *barbarians* [*Barbaren*] of the twentieth century" (§868)? Consider the irony. In the 1880s, while Europe is endeavoring to bring civilization to the societies it considers barbaric, Nietzsche looks forward to a time when the barbarians will bring civilization to Europe. The coming barbarism will not be the recourse of an earlier age. Nor will it precipitate Europe's decline. It will be an improvement, though not in the Enlightenment's sense. Nor, moreover, will it be something entirely "new." The barbarism that is returning to Europe makes a fold in the future-oriented horizon of development.

What sort of barbarians will the new barbarians be? Does Nietzsche foresee the return of that "magnificent *blond beast*" who stalks the pages of *The Genealogy of Morality,* avidly "prowling round for spoil and victory"?[2] The blond beast is the sort of barbarian who holds an excess of force within a containing limit. He is a fragile vessel, though, because he tends to explode at the first opportunity: "this hidden center needs release from time to time, the beast [*das Tier*] must out again, must return to the wild [*die Wildnis*]:—Roman, Arabian, Germanic, Japanese nobility, Homeric heroes, Scandinavian Vikings—in this requirement they are all alike. It was the noble races which left the concept of 'barbarian' [*Barbar*] in their traces wherever they went" (25/786). Today this barbaric energy lies dormant among the "good men" of Europe, where it is "held in check" by "custom, respect, habit, [and] gratitude," as well as "spying on one another" and "peer-group jealousy" (24). But these constraints only serve to put the "hidden center" under pressure, as steam builds in a boiler. When the good Europeans leave home and arrive "where the strange, the foreign, begin"—a limit that Nietzsche generically names "the wilderness"—before long the energy compressed in them erupts and they suddenly rediscover the joy of torturing others. Enter Nietzsche's monster (*das Ungeheuer*): "in the wilderness [*in der Wildnis*] they compensate for the tension which is caused by being closed in and fenced in by the peace of the community for so long, they *return* to the innocent conscience of the wild beast [*Raubtier*], as exultant monsters [*Ungeheuer*], who perhaps go away having committed a hideous succession of murder, arson, rape and torture, in a mood of bravado and spiritual equilibrium as though they had simply played a student's prank" (25/786).

The monster's escape is a variation on the "heart of darkness" theme. Joseph Conrad's version is perhaps better known to English-speaking readers. With his aunt's help, Marlow, Conrad's narrator, fulfils his boyhood dream of sailing up the Congo River in West Africa, where he witnesses the depravity of Mr. Kurtz, an ivory trader who has installed himself as a petty tyrant at Kisangani. Everyone agrees that Kurtz is "an exceptional man."[3] Indeed the novel styles him as a paradigm of the good European. "All Europe," Marlow stresses, "contributed to the making of Kurtz" (50). The good European advocates an imperialism that balances economic exploitation with humanitarian compassion. He has gone to Africa not just to get rich but to serve "the cause of progress" (13), which entails, in the words of Marlow's aunt, "weaning those ignorant millions from their horrid ways" (16). Kurtz is both a promoter of trade and an "emissary" of pity (28). His methods, however, include cutting off people's heads and putting them on poles. Marlow, echoing Nietzsche, blames "the wilderness" for undo-ing Kurtz's humanitarian mission and releasing his "hidden center." Africa is an enchantress who has put him under a spell, freeing him from every "restraint" and inviting him to indulge the "instincts" that Europe held in check (43). Marlow is the dilapidated knight who undertakes a perilous journey to rescue him: "I tried to break the spell, the heavy mute spell of the wilderness that seemed to draw him to its pitiless breast by the awakening of forgotten and brutal instincts," for it is "this alone," he insists, that "be-guiled [Kurtz's] unlawful soul beyond the bounds of permitted aspirations" (65). Conrad projects the monster within onto the landscape without, as if to circumvent a prohibition by way of fantasy.

Are "the barbarians of the twentieth century" coming in answer to the call of *die Wildnis*? Or do they heed some other imperative? Nietzsche in fact distinguishes two sorts of barbarians: the beast and the titan. "I point to something new," he remarks in an 1885 fragment, "certainly for such a democratic type"—he does not specify which type [*Wesen*]—"there exists the danger of the barbarian [*des Barbaren*], but one has looked for it only in the depths [precisely where Conrad will look a decade later]. There exists also another type [*Art*] of barbarian [*Barbaren*], who comes from the heights: a species of conquering and ruling natures in search of material to mold. Prometheus was this kind of barbarian [*Barbar*]."[4] The blond beast rises up to the human world from "the depths" of an animal ("brutal") world: he is a monster of destruction. The titan whom the gods called "Forethought" comes down to the human world from "the heights" of the divine world: he is a monster of invention.

Nietzsche conceives of Prometheus, the barbarian of the heights, as a plastic artist, a molder of forms. His conception follows classical precedent. In the *Metamorphoses* Ovid recalls that Prometheus is said to have cre-ated humankind by mixing clay with water and molding it in the image of the gods.[5] Then he turned the eyes of the new species toward heaven. The Prometheus who rages against Zeus in Aeschylus's *Prometheus Bound* says that before he took pity on humans, whom the Olympians contemp-tuously called "creatures of a day," they lived in holes like ants. He adds that he raised them above the other animals by teaching them the arts—not only carpentry and agriculture but arithmetic, medicine, and writing.[6] Aeschylus's Prometheus brings civilization to ancient Europe and confers forethought on a species that formerly had no time but now-time. He is a prototype of the good European.

Nietzsche claimed to have uncovered the "kernel" of the Prometheus myth a decade earlier, in *The Birth of Tragedy*. What it teaches, he argues, is that sacrilege is a "necessity" imposed on every "titanically striving individual." The human titan is the artist.[7] To make art, moreover, is to transgress a prohibition. It means surpassing a forbidden limit. The Promethean artist does not steal fire from the gods and give it to humans but rather takes actualizing energy from nature (*phûsis*) and confers it on works of imitation (*mimêsis*). Whatever belongs to nature, as Aristotle explains in the *Physics*, is a principle of change, and change is the actuality of what exists potentially.[8] Natural things, in brief, have both *dynamis*, the capacity for change, and *energeia*, the power to actualize capacities. They are the source of their own production. They grow by themselves, move around, increase and decrease. Things made by human skill (*technê*), in contrast, such as a bed or a cloak, do not have an internal impulse toward self-production. They can neither move nor grow, increase nor decrease, without human help. The artist's particular skill lies in imitation, which makes likenesses of things, actions, and events.

Olympian law forbids the artist to confuse the self-producing products of nature with the manufactured products of human art. Only natural things are permitted to move by themselves from potentiality to actuality. The work of art is limited to copying them. The inventions of the new Prometheus, however, do both. He not only fashions plastic images but endows them with an internal, self-acting principle of change. His sacrilege lies in folding *phûsis* into *mimêsis*, which in the view of Nietzsche's contemporaries is the characteristic error—and moral lapse—of the savage philosopher. "In himself," Nietzsche argues, "the Titanic artist found the defiant faith that he had the ability to create men and at least destroy Olympian gods" (70). He copies his portrait of the "Titanic artist" from Goethe, rather than Aeschylus, on the grounds that Goethe's Prometheus allows us to understand what Aeschylus's *Prometheus Bound* "only allows us to sense": namely, that Promethean art infringes on nature's exclusive right to produce things that produce themselves. Goethe's Prometheus defends his crime before Zeus in a defiant stanza: "Here I sit, forming men / in my own image, / a race to be like me, / to suffer, to weep, / to delight and to rejoice, / and to defy you, / as I do" (69). Ovid says that Prometheus molded humans in the divine image. The Romantic Prometheus makes them in his own image. His art is self-mirroring. First he crafts a species "like" himself—"Ein

Geschlecht, das mir gleich sei"⁹—and then, taking the forbidden step from imitation to animation, he infuses them with a life like his own. His images contain the source of their own production. They are living likenesses that move and grow, increase and decrease. The Romantic Prometheus does not just imitate natural phenomena, then, but multiplies them. That, however, is the least of his crimes. After he finishes his formative labor, he gives the energeia that served him as a means of invention to the creatures he invented, endowing humans with a capacity for actualization that exceeds what Olympian law permits them. He mixes the human with the divine. The "tragic artist," says Nietzsche, "as he creates his figures," is "like a fecund divinity of individuation" (132). Artistic invention fixes an excess of self-actualizing energy within the limits of a self-contained mimetic form. The artwork opposes a force that exceeds a limit with a limit that holds back an excess of force. Art is therefore the strife between excess and limit. So too, as found in the previous chapter, is the savage economy of discourse.

Nietzsche names the two artistic powers (künsterliche Mächte) after "the two art deities of the Greeks," Dionysus and Apollo (33). Dionysus, or excess, personifies the prodigality principle; he ruptures boundaries and gathers individuals into "primordial unity" (37). Apollo, or limit, personifies the parsimony principle; he puts limits around things and gives them form. Dionysus incites acts of "excess" (Übermaß) and loss of self-awareness; Apollo promotes the search for "measure" and self-knowledge (46/34). Dionysian intoxication squanders its forces in now-time; Apollonian forms endure in future-oriented time. The Dionysian world resonates with "non-imagistic" sounds; the Apollonian world is populated with plastic "images" (64). The Dionysian, like Prometheus, is "'barbaric'" ("Barbarische"); the Apollonian is the zone of culture (46/34). Dionysus is the "suddenly swelling" tide that stirs up the surface of the waters; Apollo is the shore that holds them back. "For Apollo wants to grant repose to individual beings," Nietzsche explains, "precisely by drawing boundaries between them" (72). Yet Dionysus exceeds every boundary that Apollo draws: "that wonderful phenomenon which bears the name Dionysus," he repeats sixteen years later, in Twilight of the Idols, "is explicable only in terms of an excess of force."¹⁰

No matter what he names them—gods, titans, or barbarians—monsters of energy recur throughout Nietzsche's discourse. No context can contain them. Sometimes he projects them backward into a time already passed, such as the Athenian golden age; sometimes he projects them forward into a time to come, such as the "twentieth century." But he always comes back to them. Even when he leaves one phase of his thought behind, he brings his monsters with him to the next. The discourse named "Nietzsche" is home to statement-events that happen for the first time by happening again, as if shot through with particles of savage time:

> One always sees only those effects of the spirit that make men weak, delicate, and morbid; but now there are coming
>
> new barbarians [*neue Barbaren*] { cynics experimenters conquerors } union of spiritual superiority with well-being and an excess of energy [*Ueberschuss von Kräften*].[11]

The "new barbarians" make no expenditure without a corresponding accumulation. First they fill out the limits of Apollonian measure, and then they rupture them in acts of Dionysian excess. Their "task" (*Aufgabe*) is to stock up a "slowly acquired treasure" of actualizing energy and give it away (*aufgeben*) without getting anything in return. "How do men attain great energy [*Kraft*] and a great task [*Aufgabe*]?" (§995). They inherit a stock accumulated by earlier "generations" and spend it now on acts of invention. The instant of expenditure breaks with the future-oriented, anticipatory time of accumulation. Monsters of energy are thus two sorts at once, both a frugal, civilized elite and a riotous band of savage rascals:

> there are men who are the heirs and masters of this slowly-acquired manifold treasure of virtue and efficiency—because, through fortunate and reasonable marriages, and also through fortunate accidents, the acquired and stored-up energies [*Kräfte*] of many generations have not been squandered and dispersed but linked together by a firm ring and by will. In the end there appears a man, a monster of energy [*Ungeheuer von Kraft*], who demands a monster of a task [*Ungeheuer von Aufgabe*]. For it is our energy [*Kraft*] that disposes of us. (§995)

Modernity's good Europeans are too weak willed to organize the actualizing energy that slumbers in them. They irrupt into violence without bringing anything new to emergence. Hence they do not make history. Monsters of energy have the Apollonian capacity to bind "monstrous" Dionysian energies within the "ring" of an iron will. They are the plastic artists of history. They actualize the new by spending the accumulated resources of the past.

The monster comes out into the open in *Twilight of the Idols*, where Nietzsche entrusts the figure of "the genius" with Prometheus's stock of actualizing energy (*energeia*). Nietzsche's "great man," however, is less a person than an act, a quantum of energy under way between epochs. He does not fulfill an idea, defend a cause, or found a nation. He blows up without foresight and without aim. Yet the explosion is no accident. Nietzsche calls it a fatality: a necessary accident that overthrows existing social and political forms and molds new ones from the ruins.[12] Yet the new order turns out to be a recourse of the old:

> Great men, like great ages, are explosives [*Explosiv-Stoffe*] in which a monstrous energy [*ungeheuere Kraft*] is stored up: their precondition is always, historically and physiologically, that for a long time much has been gathered, stored up, saved up, and conserved for them—that there has been no explosion for a long time. Once the tension in the mass has become too great, then the most accidental stimulus suffices to summon into the world the "genius," the "deed," the great destiny. . . .
>
> Great men are necessary, the age in which they appear is accidental; that they almost always become masters over their age is only because they are stronger, because they are older, because for a longer time much was gathered for them. . . . The genius, in work and deed, is necessarily a squanderer: that he gives himself away [*daß es sich ausgibt*], that is his greatness. . . . He flows out [*Er strömt aus*], he overflows [*er strömt über*], he uses himself up, he does not spare himself—and this is a calamitous, involuntary fatality, no less than a river flooding the land.[13]

The "genius" is the titanic artist of history: a quantum of actualizing energy "monstrous" enough to blast open the causal series of events.[14] He conserves the conventionally savage art of expenditure and is consumed in a sacrifice that precludes the possibility of self-sacrifice, for a gift [*eine Gabe*] is annulled if the giver is repaid either with thanks or with a sense of deserving thanks. "I love him whose soul squanders itself," says Zarathustra, "who wants no thanks and returns none: for he always gives away and does not want to preserve himself."[15]

The artist and the genius are not Nietzsche's only monsters of energy. The world, as he pictures it in the mid-1880s, is one too. The world-monster consists of a finite quantity of force distributed among a diversity of forms. The artist of history can displace quantities of world energy from one form to another but cannot liberate new ones:

> This world: a monster of energy [*ein Ungeheuer von Kraft*], without beginning, without end, a firm, iron magnitude of force that does not grow

bigger or smaller . . . as a whole, of unalterable size, a household without expenses or losses, but likewise without increase or income . . . set in a definite space as a definite force . . . a play of forces and waves of forces, at the same time one and many, increasing here and at the same time decreasing there.[16]

The world is a monster—apparently a sea monster—of potential energy, a vast reservoir of capacities and possibilities. The new barbarian is monster enough to actualize them, releasing a quantum from its place within one set of limits, like Dionysus, and setting it in place among new limits, like Apollo. Hence the world exists in two times at once. It endures in future-oriented time of increase and decrease and yet persists all the while in a present without "beginning" or "end." It contains an internal principle of change yet remains "unalterable."

Jean-Luc Nancy says the monster theory comes down to Nietzsche as part of the legacy of German Romanticism. Romanticism, as Nancy observes in "Myth Interrupted," was the Promethean project to steal actualizing energy (energeia) from nature (phûsis) and grant it unlawfully to discourse (logos). The early Romantics—"Schelling, Hölderlin, Hegel, and the Schlegels"—held that a "freely creative power" had accumulated in one sort of discourse more than any other.[17] This discourse was "mythology." They did not limit their speculations to ancient mythology, though, but sought a new mythology capable of molding a new humanity. "The notion of a 'new mythology,' which appeared in Jena around 1798," says Nancy, "contains both the idea of a necessary innovation in order to create a new human world on the ground of the finished world of ancient mythology, and at the same time the idea that mythology is always the obligatory form—and perhaps the essence—of innovation. A new humanity must arise from [and] in its new myth" (51). How was myth to facilitate the emergence of another, newer humanity? The Romantics conceived of it as the sort of discourse that participates in the realization of reality, which is how Spencer will define savage philosophy a decade later. The language of myth does what it says. "Fundamentally, mythos is the act of language par excellence," but an act in which "being engenders itself by figuring itself" (54). Myth is Promethean because it molds figures in its own likeness and invests them with a capacity for self-production. It is the sort of fiction that founds a world—"the cosmos structuring itself in logos" (49). The world (cosmos) founded by the discourse (logos) of myth (mythos) does not exist prior to, or outside of, the act of utterance (53–54). Myth does not follow nature; nature, and that includes human nature, follows from myth. *Mythos* is *logos* that steals *energeia* from *phûsis*. Nancy classifies it as a genre of "autofictioning." "Myth," he explains, "is the transcendental autofiguration of nature and of humanity, or more exactly the autofiguration—or the autoimagination—of nature as humanity and of humanity as nature" (54). This is a roundabout way of saying that myth is animation and that its master trope is prosopopoeia, which confers human attributes, beginning with life, on what lacks them. Nancy adds that the "romantic desire" for autofictioning motivates Nietzsche's call for a new barbarism: "For Nietzsche, who is at least in part heir to this romantic desire for a 'new mythology,' the freely creative power he likes to credit to the Greeks more than to anyone else stems from the 'mythic feeling of lying freely': the desire for myth is expressly directed toward the mythic (fictive) nature of (creative) myth" (45–46). But is it true that Nietzsche credits a surplus of energeia to the Greeks "more than to anyone else"? His contemporaries, after all, credit it to the savage philosopher instead.

Nancy offers a more detailed account of the dangers of autofictioning in the 1990 essay "The Nazi Myth," cowritten with Philippe Lacoue-Labarthe. "Myth," they confirm, "is a fiction, in the strong, active sense of 'fashioning,'" [18] because it proposes, and even imposes, "models or types" for an individual, a city, or a nation to imitate (297). In short, myth is a means of group identification, which occurs in two stages. First the members of the group mold themselves in myth's likeness. Then they mistake its form for their own. In this way myth "assures" them of their shared identity (297). Nancy and Lacoue-Labarthe point out that the project of collective self-fashioning became a characteristically German obsession in the "two centuries" leading up to the National Socialist period: "what Germany wanted to create," they maintain, was "its own subject" (299). German nationalism was a struggle for control of the "means of identification" (299). To "create" a national subject, Germans required a "model" for group imitation (301). The Romantics had already found one in "the archaic Greece of group rituals, of bloody sacrifices and collective intoxications": the Greece that Nietzsche personifies in the figure of Dionysus (301). After the first world war, Nazism revived the Romantic premise that myth has the power to mold a new humanity in the artist's image: "the power," as Nancy and Lacoue-Labarthe put it, "to bring together the fundamental forces and directions of an individual or of a people" (305). The Aryan race was said to be the proper "locus" of this "productive or formative power"—this energeia. "The Aryan," Nancy and Lacoue-Labarthe explain, "is not only one type among others, he is the type in which the mythic power itself, the mother-nature of all types, presents itself" (309). To identify with the Aryan myth was to "participate" mystically (307) in the Aryan soul, for myth was Aryanism's intrinsic source of self-production. The Aryans were said to have inherited the capacity for autofictioning from the Greeks, "the great Aryans of antiquity" (309). The force that Nazism called myth, the authors suggest, was the same force that Nietzsche named Dionysus.

Nancy and Lacoue-Labarthe trace the source of Nazi ideology back to the characteristic error of savage philosophy. Nazism emerges, they conclude, at the limit where mimêsis folds over into phûsis, investing works of imitation with an energeia that properly belongs to natural things (309). Their portrait of Nazi ideology is modeled on Lucien Lévy-Bruhl's portrait of savagery, which was drawn in the early twentieth century: "the German tradition adds something to the classical, Greek theory of mythic imitation, of *mimêsis*," they argue, and this surplus, this extra "something," is a "theory of fusion or mystical participation" (302): the same theory that, according to Lévy-Bruhl, governs the procedures of savage thought. It is participation that makes savage thought savage.[19] And, Nancy and Lacoue-Labarthe argue, it is what makes Nazi ideology Nazi. Nazis reason as savage philosophers do. They assume that mimêsis takes part in phûsis, for they distinguish but confusedly between them. Thus Nancy and Lacoue-Labarthe "add something" of their own to Nazism. They inject it with the legacy of savage philosophy. Although they claim to have discovered its characteristic trait—the "specific difference" (295)—they have in fact classified Nazism as a species of the genus "savagery," adding another entry to the catalogue of forbidden forms of thought. In response to the crimes of National Socialism, they can only exclaim, impotently, "Those savages!" But that is what savages are for. They are the one thing fit for any context. They take history's place in cases where historical understanding is pressingly required but none is presently available.

In "Myth Interrupted," Nancy casts his net wider still. He claims that "a whole modernity," not just Romanticism or National Socialism, enlisted myth's actualizing energy in the monstrous task of fashioning a newer, better humanity. "This formulation in fact defines," he says, "beyond romanticism and even beyond romanticism in its Nietzschean form, a whole modernity: the whole of that very broad modernity embracing, in a strange, grimacing alliance, both the poetico-ethnological nostalgia for an initial *mything* humanity and the wish to regenerate the old European humanity by resurrecting its most ancient myths, including the relentless *staging* of these myths."[20] Nancy sketches a "very broad modernity" indeed. He neglects to mention that in "modernity" the nostalgia for autofictioning is balanced by an opposing project to separate the recitation of fiction from the act of foundation. This project is positivism. If, as Nancy maintains, a "whole" modernity "wishes" to found a new order of nature, especially human nature, on an order of discourse, then why do so many post-Romantic writers dismiss autofictioning as the error of culturally and racially inferior societies? Only a child or a savage philosopher, so the story goes, would fail to respect the limit between *logos* and *cosmos*. The civilized adult confuses them only in dreams and hallucinations. This *other* modernity, the one that Adorno and Horkheimer personify as "the Enlightenment," models the distinction between savagery and civilization on the opposition between fact and fiction. The Enlightenment, they argue, did not aspire to build a cosmos on the ground of a logos, but sought instead to put a boundary between them: "From now on being divides into the *logos* . . . and into the mass of all things and creatures without."[21] Savagery folds logos and cosmos together; civilization puts them apart. Nancy's critique of autofictioning only reinforces the division. He draws a limit around postwar European civilization in order to shield it from the recourse of Nazi barbarism, but he conceives of Nazism as a forbidden transfer of actualizing energy from nature to representation. He attacks one form of state-sponsored racism, Nazism, by rehearsing the logic of another, imperialism.

Is Nancy right to affirm that Nietzsche attributes the "freely creative power" of myth to those "Aryans of antiquity," the Greeks, more than "anyone else"? There is, after all, another power that Nietzsche attributes exclusively to "Americans." He describes it as a kind of kinetic energy. *Kinesis*, moreover, is Aristotle's term for change, which has three forms: coming to be, ceasing to be, and variation.[22] The energy that Nietzsche attributes to the Americans "more than to anyone else" is a pure potential for movement between forms. Americans are the sort who change too freely. They possess an excess of variation. He calls this characteristically American kinesis "restlessness" (*die Unruhe*). In the first, 1878 volume of *Human, All Too Human*, he warns that it exposes European-American "civilization" to the threat of a "new barbarism":

Modern restlessness [*Die moderne Unruhe*].—Modern agitatedness [*moderne Bewegtheit*] grows greater the farther west we go, so that to the Americans the inhabitants of Europe seem one and all ease-loving and epicurean creatures, though in fact they are swarming among one another like bees and wasps. This agitatedness is growing so great that higher culture can no longer allow its fruits to mature; it is as though the seasons were following upon one another too quickly. From lack of repose our civilization [*unsere Zivilisation*] is turning into a new barbarism [*in eine neue Barbarei*]. At no time have the active, that is to say the restless, counted for more.[23]

The new barbarism that he deplores in 1878 inverts the new barbarism that he sees coming in the 1880s. Here the "higher task" (*Aufgabe*) is to give up (*aufgeben*) as little energy as possible in the longest time possible (133). There it is to discharge a surplus of energy in a particle of now-time. Here the "free spirit" deplores expenditure as a uniquely "modern"—and uniquely "Western"—vice. Zarathustra, in contrast, extols it as a virtue.

The Nietzsche of *Human, All Too Human* exiles Dionysus to the colonies, which suggests that his notion of the actualizing energy that "too freely" exceeds its limits is more ambivalent than Nancy lets on. When he returns to the critique of restlessness three years later, in aphorism 329 of *The Gay Science*, Nietzsche reaffirms that to squander energeia is "the distinctive vice" of "the new world," but adds that Americans have acquired the prodigality principle through an infusion of "Indian blood."[24] It is now miscegenation that makes Americans work too much. An excess of savage "haste" has broken the bounds of civilized "reflection": "There is something of the American Indians [*Es ist eine indianerhafte*], something of the ferocity [or "savagery," *Wildheit*] peculiar to the Indian blood [*Indianer-Blute*], in the American lust for gold; and the breathless haste with which they work—the distinctive vice of the new world—is already beginning to infect old Europe with its ferocity [*das alte Europa wild zu machen*] and is spreading a lack of spirituality like a blanket" (§329). Nietzsche does indeed racialize the capacity to actualize what exists potentially, but does not, as Nancy claims, credit it to the Aryans of antiquity "more than to anyone else." He grants it just as freely to those he names "Indians" (*die Indianer*) and "savages" (*die Wilde*). The world is a monster of energy, and whether we spend it or save it determines what we are. Restlessness, since it obeys the prodigality principle, is a biological-genetic trait of savage peoples; contemplation and reflection, since they obey the parsimony principle, are biological-genetic characteristics of civilized peoples.

The Tale of the Two Zones

The Nietzsche of *Human, All Too Human* no longer personifies excess as Dionysus and limit as Apollo but likens them instead to two "ages" in the development of culture. The past age is barbarism. The coming age, still not fully arrived, is civilization. Modernity is the unfinished passage between them. In aphorism 236, he projects the two ages of history onto two zones of the globe, signifying succession in time by contiguity in space. Predictably, the two zones differ in how they spend a finite supply of energy. The coming age is temperate and cool: it follows the parsimony principle. The past is tropical and hot: it follows the prodigality principle. Nietzsche's globe is a monster of thermal energy:

> *The zones of culture.*—One can say metaphorically that the ages of culture correspond to the various climatic belts, except that they are ranged one after the other and not, as in the case of the geographic zones, side by side. In comparison with the temperate zone of culture into which it is our task [*Aufgabe*] to pass over, that of the past produces, taken as a whole, the impression of a *tropical* climate [*tropischen Klimas*]. Violent antitheses, the abrupt transition of day to night and night to day, heat and vivid color, reverence for everything sudden, mysterious, terrible, the swiftness with which a storm breaks, everywhere a prodigal overflowing [*Überströmen*] of the cornucopias of nature; and, on the other hand, in our culture a bright yet not radiant sky, a clear, more or less unchanging air, sharp, occasionally cold: thus are the two zones distinguished from one another.[25]

The thermodynamics of history presupposes a thermodynamics of race. In the tropical zone, time comes to a stop in the present: events happen by "abrupt transition" and with "reverence" for the "sudden." Things tend toward excess: of heat, of "antitheses," and of growth. In temperate regions, the air is cooler and calmer. The light is "bright" but not blinding. There is less of things. Nietzsche adds that "earlier," warmer "peoples" have not risen as high on the ladder of development as later, cooler "peoples" have. "To us," he says, "the very *existence* of the temperate zone of culture counts as progress." But even "we" do not live there yet; "our task" (*Aufgabe*), rather, is "to pass over" (§236).

In aphorism 251, he compresses the two zones of culture into the two "ventricles" of a "double brain" (*Doppelgehirn*). The geothermal division of the globe recurs as a biochemical division of the nervous system, the macrocosm serving as a model for the microcosm. The tropical ventricle generates an excess of heat in the form of "fantasy" and "illusion." The temperate ventricle fixes heat in the more durable form of "truth" and invests it in the production of "science." The ventricle that squanders energy

is what remains of Dionysus, who is now the prototype of barbarism. The
ventricle that binds energy within a containing limit is what remains of
Apollo, now the prototype of civilization. The two art energies, once racialized, are no longer exclusively Greek but expand to cover the entire
globe. The boundary-breaking force presides over tropical excesses, while
the individuating, form-giving force supervises the cooling of the temperate
zone. The possibility of science depends on whether the principle of excess
can be contained by the limiting principle. Nietzsche endorses the Socratic,
dialogical rationalism that he attacked in *The Birth of Tragedy:*

> a higher culture must give to man a double brain, as it were two brain
> ventricles [*zwei Hirnkammern*], one for the perceptions of science, the
> other for those of non-science: lying beside one another, not confused
> together, separable, capable of being shut off; this is a demand of health.
> In one domain lies the power-source [*die Kraftquelle*], in the other the
> regulator: it must be heated with illusions, onesidednesses, passions, the
> evil and perilous consequences of overheating must be obviated with
> the aid of the knowledge furnished by science.— If this demand of higher
> culture is not met, then the future course of human evolution can be
> foretold almost with certainty: interest in truth will cease the less plea-
> sure it gives; because they are associated with pleasure, illusion [*die Il-
> lusion*], error [*der Irrtum*] and fantasy [*die Phantastik*] will regain step
> by step the ground they formerly held: the ruination of science, a sinking
> back into barbarism [*das Zurücksinken in Barbarei*], will be the immedi-
> ate consequence. (§251)

The double brain installs a boundary between "error" and "knowledge,"
but nothing prevents the two sides from making an exchange. The tropical
ventricle, or "power source," produces energy in the form of pure potentiality. The temperate ventricle, or "regulator," acquires potential energy
and actualizes it. The labor of actualization can follow one of two paths:
it tends toward either illusion or knowledge. If the power source supplies
the regulator with too much heat, then the boundary between the ventricles fails and the double brain becomes single again. Fantasy assumes the
place of science. The temperate zone heats up and thought becomes tropical
once more. Civilization gives way to a new barbarism. The "freely creative
power" that *this* Nietzsche credits to the generic savage "more than to anyone else" is hardly an object of "desire," Romantic or otherwise. Rather it
is an object of caution. For whether it is bound or unbound determines the
"future course of evolution."

A decade later, in *Twilight of the Idols*, Nietzsche speaks cryptically of the "gray morning" when "reason" wakens with a "yawn" to "the cockcrow of positivism."[26] Heidegger maintains that an "extreme positivism" governs Nietzsche's discourse from 1879 to 1881.[27] Positivism, by Heidegger's definition, takes it for granted that "representation must respect, right from the start and constantly . . . what lies before us from the outset, what is constantly placed before us, the *positum*. The latter," he explains, "is what is given in sensation, the sensuous" (152). Positivism aims to establish correspondences between signs and things and accepts only those correspondences that can be verified directly, by perception, or indirectly, by experiment. Positivist representation adds nothing to its object and subtracts nothing from it. Nietzsche, in his positivist phase, renounces any claim to the actualizing energy of art and instead gives fire back to the gods. He ranks the "perceptions of science," which are the achievements of a temperate civilization, above those of "non-science," which are the errors of tropical barbarism.[28] Scientific perception respects the positum. Artistic perception enriches it. When culture passes from a tropical, artistic age to a temperate, scientific one, the range of perception contracts. Fewer objects are given to the senses. The positum is circumscribed within ever stricter limits. The scientist sees and feels less than the artist or savage philosopher does: "even in dreams," says Nietzsche, "we do not experience what other earlier peoples beheld while awake" (§236). Only "the artists" lament the closure of the senses, and Nietzsche stresses that he is no longer one of them: "But should we not be permitted to rejoice at this change, even allowing that the artists [*die Künstler*] have suffered badly through the disappearance of tropical culture [*tropischen Kultur*] and find us non-artists a little too sober" (§236)? The question situates artists in the very position where "earlier peoples" are conventionally located. Artists, like "savages" and "primeval" peoples, are guilty of wasting energeia. In consequence they neither "progress" into the future nor recede into the past, but can only repeat themselves in the now: "it is at least open to doubt," he therefore adds, "whether the past three millennia evidence a course of progress in the arts" (§236). The intoxication of art is a recourse of savage inertia.

One genre of savage art tends more than the others to confuse illusion with knowledge, smuggling an excess of tropical, barbaric heat into the cooler, more temperate atmosphere of civilization. It is mythology. Nietzsche says it is a product of "forgetfulness." The artists who composed the world's myths were not yet able to distinguish between what exists actually in "reality" and what exists potentially in "images." Hence they "confused one thing with another," enriching what was given to sensation with an excess given by imagination. Temperate peoples experience such forgetfulness only in dreams. Nietzsche's "savages" and "primeval" peoples experience it "by day and in waking." They conserve the tropical art of dreaming while awake. What fuels this art, furthermore, is an excess of metaphor, the capacity to discover "similarities" between things that are not manifestly "the same":

> *Dream and Culture.*—The function of the brain that sleep [*Schlaf*] encroaches upon most is the memory; not that it ceases altogether—but it is reduced to a condition of imperfection such as in the primeval ages of mankind [*in Urzeiten der Menschheit*] may have been normal by day and in waking. Confused and capricious as it is, it continually confuses one thing with another on the basis of the most fleeting similarities: but it was with the same confusion and capriciousness that the peoples composed their mythologies, and even today travelers observe how much the savage [*der Wilde*] is inclined to forgetfulness, how his mind begins to reel and stumble after a brief exertion of the memory and he utters lies and nonsense out of mere enervation [*Erschlaffung*]. But in dreams we all resemble this savage; failure to recognize correctly and erroneously supposing one thing to be the same as another is the ground of the false conclusions we are guilty of in dreams; so that, when we clearly recall a dream, we are appalled to discover so much folly in ourselves.—The perfect clarity of all the images we see in dreams which is the precondition of our unquestioning belief in their reality again reminds us of conditions pertaining to earlier mankind, in whom hallucination was extraordinarily common and sometimes seized hold on whole communities, whole peoples at the same time. Thus: in sleep and dreams we repeat once again the curriculum of earlier mankind. (§12)[29]

The positivist Nietzsche can hardly be said to voice a nostalgia, much less a desire, for an initial, mything humanity. Nor does he credit myth's freely creative power to the Greeks more than the societies he calls savage. Instead he claims to be "appalled" that metaphorical thought, "confusing one thing with another," continues to exercise its forbidden power to actualize what exists in fantasy. Mythology makes "reality" out of "images." Nancy's term for this error is "autofictioning." Nietzsche favors the term "hallucination." It is not only a "primeval" mode of thought, he maintains, but a racially inferior one.

Living Signs

Nietzsche shares his post-Romantic caution toward mythology with the so-called founder of modern ethnology, E. B. Tylor.[30] The positivist and the eth-nologist agree that mythological discourse is too prodigal with metaphor. Indeed metaphor is itself a kind of prodigal, for it discharges a surplus of living, discursive forces. Just as overexpenditure is a characteristic trait of savage economies, which belong simultaneously to modernity and to pre-history, so anyone who wastes a quantum of verbal energeia in a particle of now-time is a savage philosopher.[31] For Tylor as for Nietzsche, metaphor is a characteristically savage mode of expenditure.

Tylor argues that mythology endeavors to explain what causes change. Paradoxically, though, its fundamental theme is also the principle of its structure. Mythology does not just talk about change. It provokes it. And that is precisely the problem. The "ancient savage philosophers," says Tylor, traced changes in nature to the actions of a host of invisible and intangible beings called spirits. The philosophy of spirits is called animism. Mythology is the archive of its findings, a savage *Physics* that borrows its postulates from savage rhetoric. Tylor speculates that their research led the savage philosophers to venture two great hypotheses. They assumed, first, that a spirit commonly known as the soul oversees changes inside the body, and second, that a host of disembodied spirits, ranging from the lingering souls of the recent dead to distant and immortal gods, oversee changes in the outer world. Animism consists, accordingly, of "two great dogmas": a soul doctrine and a spirit doctrine.[32] The soul doctrine aims to explain how people die and why they dream:

> It seems as though thinking men, as yet at a low level of culture, were deeply impressed by two groups of biological problems. In the first place, what is it that makes the difference between a living body and a dead one; what causes waking, sleep, trance, disease, death? In the second place, what are those human shapes which appear in dreams and vi-sions? Looking at these two groups of phenomena, the ancient savage philosophers probably made their first step by the obvious inference that every man has two things belonging to him, namely, a life and a phan-tom. These two are evidently in close connexion with the body, the life as enabling it to feel and think and act, the phantom as being its image or second self; both, also, are perceived to be things separable from the body, the life as able to go away and leave it insensible or dead, the phan-tom as appearing to people at a distance from it. (428)

The soul dogma rests on the distinction between "a life" and "a phantom." A "life" is a quantum of energy that keeps a body in motion. What lives, moves. A "phantom" is a sign that stands for the body when the body cannot make itself present. What moves, signifies. A soul is the combination of a life and a phantom. It is a sign that imitates the body's form and acts with its physical force:

> It is a thin unsubstantial human image, in its nature a sort of vapour, film, or shadow; the cause of life and thought in the individual it animates; independently possessing the personal consciousness and volition of its corporeal owner, past or present; capable of leaving the body far behind, to flash swiftly from place to place; mostly impalpable and invisible, yet also manifesting physical power, and especially appearing to men waking or asleep as a phantasm separate from the body of which it bears the likeness; continuing to exist and appear to men after the death of that body; able to enter into, possess, and act in the bodies of other men, of animals, and even of things. (429)

At once an "unsubstantial image" and a "physical power," the soul is a sign that contains its own intrinsic principle of change. It effects a forbidden union of imitation and nature, mimêsis and phûsis. Considered as an image, it is mimetic: it "bears" the body's "likeness." Considered as a power, it is kinetic: it flashes restlessly "from place to place." It is something both material, since it acts on "other bodies," and immaterial, since it is "mostly impalpable and invisible." The soul-sign leaves the body as it sleeps, carrying its image across vast distances in a splinter of time. "The New Zealanders," Tylor explains, "considered the dreaming soul to leave the body and return [he calls this the "dream exit" of the soul] even traveling to the region of the dead to hold converse with its friends [this is the "dream visit" to the soul]" (441). If it does not return, the body dies. Hence the soul-sign has the power to kill its referent in the act of representing it.

In *Human, All Too Human*, Nietzsche speculates that mythology not only records the movements of living signs but puts them to work. Myths are tales about the spirit world that have the forbidden capacity to actualize the events they narrate. They mobilize discursive *energeia* by speaking of beings that live only in discourse. When the "primordial" philosophers encountered the spirit world in their dreams, they did not dismiss it as the false image of the waking world. Dreams were as real for them as the objects they experienced in daylight hours. They were titanic, plastic artists, and they endowed the products of fantasy with life and motion.

When they dreamed, therefore, they made contact with a "second" real
world:

> The man of the ages of barbarous primordial culture [*roher uranfängli-*
> *cher Kultur*] believed that in the dream he was getting to know a *second*
> *real world* [*eine zweite reale Welt*]: here is the origin of all metaphysics.
> Without the dream one would have had no occasion to divide the world
> in two. The dissection into soul and body is also connected with the old-
> est idea of the dream, likewise the postulation of a life of the soul, thus
> the origin of all belief in spirits, and probably also of the belief in gods.
> "The dead live on, *for* they appear to the living in dreams": that was the
> conclusion one formerly drew, throughout many millennia.[33]

Dreams supplied "barbarous" philosophers with a coherent system of binary
oppositions: human and divine, body and soul, sensuous and nonsensuous.
Nietzsche calls the system "metaphysics," even though it lacks one of the
central binarisms of western European thought: the opposition between imitation and nature. In an animist metaphysics, nothing is more alive than
the sign, which alone confers life on what lacks it, making the spirit world
"real." Life is not just what the discourse of mythology describes. It is what
it does. The living sign is both its form and its content. How else could it
enrich the first real world with a second one?

Tylor argues that the spirit dogma operates on the principle of personification, displacing human emotions and intentions onto inhuman, often
inanimate, objects and events. He finds the canonical statement of the
personification principle in Hume's *Natural History of Religion*, "perhaps
more than any other work the source of modern opinions as to the development of religion."[34] Hume, in turn, recycles the premises of poetic logic,
which Vico had already outlined in *The New Science:*

> There is an universal tendency among mankind to conceive all beings
> like themselves, and to transfer to every object, those qualities, with
> which they are familiarly acquainted, and of which they are intimately
> conscious. We find human faces in the moon, armies in the clouds; and
> by a natural propensity, if not corrected by experience and reflection, as-
> cribe malice or good-will to every thing, that hurts or pleases us. Hence
> the frequency and beauty of the *prosopopoeia* in poetry; where trees,
> mountains and streams are personified, and the inanimate parts of na-
> ture acquire sentiment and passion. And though these poetical figures
> and expressions gain not on the belief, they may serve, at least, to prove

a certain tendency in the imagination, without which they could neither be beautiful nor natural.[35]

The living sign, because it reproduces the body's force and likeness, is subject both to the laws of motion and to the laws of discourse. The study of motion is physics, which expresses its laws in mathematical formulas. The study of mimetic discourse is poetics, which expresses its laws in rhetorical "figures" or tropes. Tylor, however, perceives no clear difference between them. Savage poetics is an earlier, "ruder" physics, just as physics is the modern inheritor of poetics. Animism, for Tylor, is an expression of what Nietzsche, in *The Birth of Tragedy*, calls "theoretical optimism," the belief that thought, by following the thread of causality, can illuminate "the deepest abysses of being."[36] The first philosophers were right to search for the origins and causes of change—they put humanity on the path to science—but wrong to assume that natural events are self-evidently "analogous" to discursive ones. Says Tylor,

> It was no spontaneous fancy, but the reasonable inference that effects are due to causes, which led the rude men of old days to people with such ethereal phantoms their own homes and haunts, and the vast earth and sky beyond. Spirits are simply personified causes. As men's ordinary life and actions were held to be caused by souls, so the happy or disastrous events which affect mankind, as well as the manifold physical operations of the outer world, were accounted for as caused by soul-like beings, spirits whose essential similarity of origin is evident through all their wondrous variety of power and function.[37]

Nietzsche lists some of the ways in which "present-day savages" (*die jetzigen Wilden*) attribute changes in sensory things—such as the motions of objects and the diseases of the body—to the actions of supersensory spirits. His examples are borrowed from John Lubbock, who published *The Origin of Civilisation* in 1870, one year before *Primitive Culture* and two years before *The Birth of Tragedy*. Because the ancient savage philosophers modeled the causes of events in their own unpredictable human image, they concluded that nature is lawless and therefore arbitrary:

> In those ages one as yet knows nothing of natural laws; neither earth nor sky are constrained by any compulsion; a season, sunshine, rain can come or they can fail to come. Any conception of *natural* causality is altogether lacking. When one rows it is not the rowing which moves the

ship: rowing is only a magical ceremony by means of which one compels
a demon to move the ship. All illness, death itself is the result of magical influences. Becoming ill and dying never occur naturally; the whole
conception of a "natural occurrence" is altogether lacking . . . When
someone shoots with the bow, there is still an irrational hand and force
[*Kraft*] at work in it; if the wells suddenly dry up, one thinks first of all
of subterranean demons and their knavery; it must be the arrow of a god
through whose invisible action a man suddenly sinks down. In India (according to Lubbock) a carpenter is accustomed to make sacrifices to his
hammer, his axe and his other tools; a Brahman treats the crayon with
which he writes, a soldier the weapon he employs in the field, a mason
his trowel, a labourer his plough in the same way. The whole of nature
is in the conception of religious men a sum of actions by conscious and
volitional beings, a tremendous complex of *arbitrariness*.[38]

Lubbock denies that the ancient savage philosophers invented the spirit
doctrine to explain how we die and why we dream. They wanted instead to
explain why things move. "The savage, indeed, accounts for all movement
by life," he argues. "Hence the wind is a living being. Nay, even motionless
objects are regarded in a particular stage of mental progress as possessing
spirits."[39] If it moves, it lives, and if it lives, it is because it harbors a living
sign. Lubbock cites the testimony of John and Richard Lander, who claim
that the people living on the Niger River thought a watch was alive because
they saw its hands move.

Tylor reserves the name "fetishism" for the doctrine that living but
immaterial forces are embodied in, or attached to, or convey influence
through, material objects. "Any object whatsoever," he points out, "may be
a fetish."[40] And that includes the living sign. No wonder, then, that there
is a fetishism of discourse. Lubbock, though he disagrees with Tylor's definition, includes writing in the class of sensory things deemed capable of
conducting nonsensory energies.[41] There are places in Africa, he says, where
discourse itself is used as a cure for certain diseases: "the priests or wizards
write a prayer on a piece of board, wash it off and make the patient drink
it. Caillié met with a man who had a great reputation for sanctity, and who
made his living by writing prayers on a board, washing them off, and then
selling the water, which was sprinkled over various objects, and supposed to
improve or protect them" (16). The peddler of texts assumes that the impalpable forces of discourse can produce palpable changes in the body's organs.
There is a discursive *energeia* that yields nondiscursive consequences: this

is the first principle of magical criticism. But you do not have to go to Africa to find people who say so.

Metaphorical Animation

Tylor classes fetishism as one of a "great class of facts" that participate in history by subtracting themselves from history. The storm of progress carries them along but does not move them forward. They are "survivals": "These are processes, customs, and opinions, and so forth, which have been carried on by force of habit into a new state of society different from that in which they had their original home, and they thus remain as proofs and examples of an older condition of culture out of which a newer has been evolved."[42] Survivals "remain." They "last." They are governed by the law of savage inertia, which manifests itself as a "force of habit." They have meaning only when taken out of context, for they cannot be limited to any of the "states" in which they continually recur:

> When in the process of time there has come general change in the condi-
> tion of a people, it is usual, notwithstanding, to find much that mani-
> festly had not its origin in the new state of things, but has simply lasted
> on into it. On the strength of these survivals, it becomes possible to
> declare that the civilization of the people they are observed among must
> have been derived from an earlier state, in which the proper home and
> meaning of these things are to be found; and thus collections of such
> facts are to be worked as mines of historic knowledge. (71)

The Nietzsche of *Human, All Too Human* more than once observes that "the dream" is what survives today of an "earlier" mode of human consciousness: "the dream takes us back again to remote stages of human culture [*in ferne Zustände der menschlichen Kultur*] and provides us with a means of understanding them better."[43] It is a "piece" (*ein Stück*) of primeval thought carried on into the present from an earlier, *pre*historical human condition. The "conclusions" that "man still draws in dreams," he argues, the first philosophers drew "*when awake.*" What "we" perceive as representations "they" experienced as reality. "According to travelers' tales," he notes in parentheses, "savages [*die Wilden*] still do this today [*heute noch*]." Nietzsche's savage philosophers perceive no difference between dreaming and waking, signs and things. Nor do the artists and poets of any age, tropical or temperate. Art and especially poetry are survivals of ancient savage philosophy. Nietzsche suggests that if we know how to "mine" them, we can experience a state that we might have thought was lost forever: "The poet and the artist, too, *foists upon* his moods and states of mind causes which are not the true ones; to this extent he recalls an earlier humanity and can aid us to an understanding of it" (§13). The poet is an artist who mistakes the copy for the original and the effect for the cause, enriching the positum in the act of representing it—just like the savage philosopher.

Nietzsche resumes the interpretation of dreams in the first, 1882 edition of *The Gay Science*—"Oh, these men of former times knew how to *dream* and did not find it necessary to go to sleep first"—but gives it a turn that might surprise the reader of *Human, All Too Human*—"And we men of today [*von heute*] still master this art all too well, despite all of our goodwill toward the day and staying awake."[44] The Nietzsche of 1882 puts himself in the position that another, earlier Nietzsche reserved for "savages." Not only does he say of "men of today" what he formerly said of "men of former times"—that they sleepwalk in daylight—but, more importantly, he identifies himself with them. No longer does he speak of "the artist" from the vantage of the "nonartist." Instead he declares, "We artists!" He renounces positivism by going stereotypically savage. And he takes his philosophy with him. "It is quite enough to love, to hate, to desire, simply to feel," he affirms, "and right away the spirit [*der Geist*] and power [*die Kraft*] of the dream [*des Traumes*] overcome us, and with our eyes open, coldly contemptuous of all danger, we climb up on the most hazardous paths to scale the roofs and spires of fantasy [*der Phantasterei*]—without any sense of dizziness, as if we had been born to climb, we somnambulists of the day! We artists! [*Wir Künstler!*]" (§59). The earlier Nietzsche warned that the overproduction of "fantasy" threatened to enervate scientific enquiry and sink Europe into a new barbarism. This Nietzsche ranks himself among those who ascend toward fantasy as toward the "heights." By embracing an art that he previously declared "savage"—the art of sleepwalking in daylight—he makes himself into a survival of "primeval humanity." What accounts for the change in his moral valuation of the artwork?

Nietzsche detours through positivism in order to purge his thought of the possibility that mimêsis endows its products with an intrinsic source of change. First he displaces Prometheus onto the figure of the savage poet, and then, like old Zeus, he persecutes him. The savage poet, however, is a substitute for Nietzsche himself. He embraces positivism in order to attack his own Romanticism. At least that is how he interprets *Human, All Too Human* a decade later in *Ecce Homo:* "I was overcome with *impatience* at myself," he confesses, but adds that, nevertheless, "I realized it was high time for me to think back to *myself*."[45] The effort of thinking back to himself brings him back to the hypotheses of savage philosophy, which is no longer Greek but belongs now to a new, generic barbarism in which there survive elements of Greek mythology. At the same time he constructs the new barbarism on one of the twin pillars of animism—the spirit doctrine—which explains why the animist hypotheses that he debunked in the late 1870s recur in the texts from the late 1880s. Still, as he suggests in *Daybreak*, he cannot endorse the hypotheses he once ridiculed without first dispelling a lingering sense of shame:

> During the great prehistoric age of mankind, spirit [*Geist*] was presumed to exist everywhere and was not held in honor as a privilege of man. Because, on the contrary, the spiritual (together with all drives, wickedness, inclinations) had been rendered common property, and thus common, one was not ashamed to have descended from animals and trees (the *noble* races thought themselves honoured by such fables), and saw in the spirit that which unites us with nature, not that which sunders us from it.[46]

When the ex-positivist embraces "the spiritual," he is guilty of a certain "wickedness," as if, like Prometheus, he had committed sacrilege. But he says there is no shame in renouncing truth in favor of error or, in the lexicon of positivism, "knowledge" in favor of "illusion." Rather it is "noble" to do so. Only "prejudice" keeps good Europeans from acknowledging what the people of "prehistoric ages" already knew: that everything in nature participates in a single, uniform life force. Nietzsche calls it "spirit" in 1881. He adopts the phrase "will to power" in the following apostrophe, dated 1885: *"This world is the will to power—and nothing besides!* And you yourselves are also this will to power—and nothing besides!"[47] Nietzsche thinks his way back to the spirit doctrine after a long detour. But what he proposes when he arrives is a curiously acephalous animism, for he renounces the personification principle. The "spiritual," he argues, includes "everything that exists." It is neither the "privilege" nor the exclusive property of human beings.

The ancient philosophers did not err when they endowed inanimate objects with a principle of change. Their mistake was to personify it. They were right to conclude that the world is a sea of living forces, wrong to mold those forces in the human image:

> On the *Origin of Religion.*—In the same way as today [in 1888] the uneducated man believes that anger is the cause of his being angry, spirit

the cause of his thinking, soul the cause of his feeling—in short, just as
there is still thoughtlessly posited a mass of psychological entities that
are supposed to be causes—so, at a yet more naive stage, man explained
precisely the same phenomena with the aid of psychological personal
entities. Those conditions that seemed to him strange, thrilling, over-
whelming, he interpreted as obsession and enchantment by the power
of a person. (§135)

The positive sciences repeat this mistake today. They endeavor to uncover
the causes of change but forget that the notion of causality is a survival of
the personification principle—what Hume calls "the prosopopoeia." Natural scientists, like savage philosophers, model the concept of cause on the
pattern of the self-conscious, self-producing, human "ego," for they assume
that change happens because someone—or some*thing* acting like some-
one—provokes it. But there is no doer behind the deed, no agent behind
the act. Positivism, because it projects a subject onto a series of subjectless
events, proceeds by the logic of fetishism. But it does not have exclusive
rights to the error of projection. In *Twilight of the Idols* Nietzsche argues
that fetishism survives, more than anywhere else, in the elementary unit of
discourse: the sentence. It is generative grammar itself that puts a subject
behind every action. We go savage every time we speak because we treat
rules for the combination of signs as if they were laws for the emergence of
events:

> We enter a realm of crude fetishism when we summon before conscious-
> ness the basic presuppositions of the metaphysics of language, in plain
> talk, the presuppositions of reason. Everywhere it sees a doer and doing;
> it believes in will as *the* cause; it believes in the ego, the ego as being,
> in the ego as substance, and it projects this faith in the ego-substance
> upon all things—only thereby does it first *create* the concept of "thing."
> Everywhere "being" is projected by thought, pushed underneath, as the
> cause; the concept of being follows, and is a derivative of, the concept
> of ego.[48]

Although he renounces the personification principle, Nietzsche cannot do
without the animist premise that people and things participate in a "play of
forces." The forces of discourse, like those of nature, actualize what exists
potentially. Discourse is an impersonal yet "titanic" artist that fashions
the concepts of "being" and "substance" in the ego's image. Indeed it "creates" them, endowing signs with the capacity to move and change by them-

selves. Discourse itself is the new barbarian: a post-Romantic, posthuman Prometheus.

Tylor agrees that discourse is what survives today of a prehistoric and savage "method" of reasoning: a "simple" mechanism "carried on" into a more "complex" age. "Comparing the grammars and dictionaries of races at various grades of civilization," he complains, "it appears that, in the great art of speech, the educated man at this day substantially uses the method of the savage, only expanded and improved in the working out of the details."[49] He likens the savage "art" of discourse to the fire that Prometheus reputedly gave to humanity at the threshold of history. For a long time it fueled the development of culture, but now it is beginning to outlive its usefulness: "Language is one of those intellectual departments in which we have gone too little beyond the savage stage, but are still as it were hacking with stone celts and twirling labourious friction-fire" (2:446). Like all things "savage," the language machine generates an excess of heat but performs a scarcity of work. Tropes are especially hot, and the two that burn with the most intensity are metaphor and metonymy: "The two great methods of naming thoughts and stating their relation to one another, viz., metaphor and syntax, belong to the infancy of human expression, and are as thoroughly at home in the language of savages as of philosophers" (1:238). These hottest of tropes, however, are fundamental laws for the formation of discourses, and not even the most civilized natural scientist can reason without them. Metaphor is the law for selecting signs from a code. Syntax, or metonymy, is the law that organizes them into sign chains. Metaphor works by substitution, associating one sign, a "thought," with another, a "name," on the basis of similarity. Metonymy works by contiguity, placing signs side by side according to the rules of generative grammar.[50]

The two master tropes lie at the foundation not just of positive science but of magical thought as well. Contagious magic, Tylor explains, consists of "the practices whereby a distant person is to be affected by acting on something close to him" (116). It obeys the law of metonymy. Things that were once side by side are assumed to continue to act on each other from a distance. Imitative magic exploits the similarities between means and ends. It obeys the law of metaphor. Whatever is done to a copy is assumed to happen to the original, for example, when you chew on a piece of wood to soften someone's heart (118). Metonymy and metaphor are survivals of magic in the house of discourse. They do not point to correspondences between thought and its object, but rather open paths for the transmission of forbidden forces. They haunt positivism with the specter of an irreducible potentiality for error. Not only is there something discursive in the casting of spells, but there is something magical in the formation of knowledge.

Tylor indicates he is appalled that even today the most "highly developed" scientific knowledge can only be communicated by a "machine" that operates on the laws of animism, and yet civilization, which has invented so many technologies, has discovered no other "engine" for "expressing modern thought." Science can speak only if it draws on magic's power source:

> The language by which a nation with highly developed art and knowledge and sentiment must express its thoughts on these subjects, is no apt machine devised for such special work, but an old barbaric engine added to and altered, patched and tinkered into some sort of capability. Ethnography reasonably accounts at once for the immense power and the manifest weakness of language as a means of expressing modern educated thought, by treating it as an original product of low culture, gradually adapted by ages of evolution and selection, to answer more or less sufficiently the requirements of modern civilization. (239)

The hottest of tropes is metaphor, for it conserves the actualizing energy of mythology, that tropical art of dreaming while awake. Metaphor fits the signified ("meaning") to the signifier ("sound"), thereby producing the sign: "one great means of giving new meaning to old sound is metaphor, which transfers ideas from hearing to seeing, from touching to thinking, from the concrete of one kind to the abstract of another, and can thus make almost anything in the world help to describe or suggest anything else" (234). Metaphor does not create new signs ex nihilo. It recycles old signs by a process that rhetoricians call catachresis. It can graft a "new" signified onto an "old" signifier by mapping cognition onto sensation ("thinking" onto "touching"), or by folding one sense onto another ("hearing" onto "seeing"), or by treating ideas as if they were things ("the abstract" as "the concrete"). Metaphor is therefore a force of invention. It brings newness into the world by the oldest of means. Sooner or later, though, the "old barbaric engine" overheats. Not only does it give new meaning to old sound, but it gives it to excess, endowing the inventions of discourse with a principle of change. But Tylor was certainly not the first to conceive of metaphor as a force of actualization.

Aristotle says in the *Poetics* that metaphor is a part of diction that gives something the name of something else.[51] There are fours ways of conducting the exchange. If you say "here stands my ship," you give to a species (lying at anchor) the name of a genus (standing). If you say "truly has Odysseus done ten thousand deeds of worth," you give to a genus (many) the name of a species (ten thousand). If instead of drawing wine from a vase, you "cut" it with the "long-edged bronze" of a bowl, you give to one species (drawing) the name of another species (cutting) of the same genus (taking away). If you call your wine bowl the "shield of Dionysus" or your shield the "wine-bowl of Ares," you are drawing a four-point analogy: the wine bowl is to Dionysus what the shield is to Ares (57b). Each substitution discovers and exploits a resemblance between one sign and another. Jacques Derrida confirms that "metaphor has always been defined as the trope of resemblance," namely, "the resemblance between two signs, one of which designates the other"; Paul de Man agrees that the "classical definition" of metaphor, which reaches "from Aristotle to Roman Jakobson," conceives of it as "an exchange or substitution of properties on the basis of resemblance"[52] Tylor's concern, though, is not that metaphor discovers too many resemblances but that it too freely creates them. Not only can it make anything suggest anything else, but, worse, it can summon objects of discourse into emergence in the extradiscursive world. However, the anxiety about metaphor cannot be explained in terms of the resemblance theory of the *Poetics* but must instead be gauged with reference to the actualization theory of Aristotle's *Rhetoric*.

Aristotle takes up the question of metaphorical actualization during the discussion of wit in the section on style. Rhetoric enlists wit in the service of understanding. To learn "easily," Aristotle explains, is "naturally pleasant to all," and so the words that we find most pleasant are those that "produce knowledge for us."[53] He adds that "it is metaphor that particularly has this effect" (235/1410b). Metaphor is thus a productive trope. It has the capacity to bring something new before the understanding. Still newness only emerges if the event of understanding interrupts everything that came before it (the already familiar) and everything that follows it (the still strange). Hence metaphor carries a force of breaking with the continuum of received ideas. The break occurs when metaphor suddenly compels its "hearer" to acknowledge a similarity between dissimilar things: "when the poet calls old age a reed," for example, "he produces understanding and recognition through the generic similarity: for both have lost their flower" (235/1410b). Metaphor surprises its hearer with the truth of what ought to be considered untruth: "what the hearer hears becomes clearer to him through its being the opposite to what he thought, and the mind seems to say, 'How true, and I was wrong'" (239/1412a). The production of new understanding collapses differences in what Benjamin calls the now of recognizability.

Whether new understanding emerges depends on how fast metaphor posits a resemblance between "related but not obvious things" (239/1412a). Wit is a function of speed. And it does its best work in now-time. "Both style [saying things properly] and enthymemes [reasoning deductively from probabilities] must be witty," Aristotle maintains, "that produce swift understanding for us" (235/1410b). Two factors thwart the event of recognition: obviousness and obscurity. A familiar metaphor cannot reveal an unexpected similarity between dissimilar things; an unfamiliar metaphor shows no similarity at all and so fails to produce anything new. The sorts of metaphors that discover truth in untruth are "either those of which recognition occurs as soon as they are spoken, especially if it had not pre-existed, or those in which the intellect of the hearer is but a little behind" (235/1410b). Although metaphors by analogy are the "most celebrated," those that have "vividness" are the most likely to make understanding "swift" (236–37/1411a–b). What gives a sense of "vividness"? Aristotle argues that "vividness is produced by things that indicate actuality" (238/1411a), and he includes among them the animation of inanimate objects. Metaphor is most likely to produce swift, and therefore new, understanding when it confers life on what lacks it: "as Homer's usage often is, making the inanimate animate through metaphor" (238/1411b–12a). The force of recognition emerges from the act of animation. But what distinguishes the "animate" from the "inanimate"? In the *Physics* Aristotle says it is change, which he defines as the actualization (*energeia*) of what exists potentially (*dynamis*).[54] What lives, changes, by coming to be or by ceasing to be or by varying its size or its position. The evocation of one sort of change, though, makes metaphor especially vivid: the change from rest to motion. Homer, above all other poets, makes things actual by making them move: "he makes all things moving and alive" because, as Aristotle puts it in the *Rhetoric*, "actuality is a movement" (238/1412a).

Natural things contain an intrinsic principle of change. They are the agents of their own production. Artificial things have an extrinsic principle of change. They depend on the artist's skill to make them actually what they are potentially. A block of wood has the potential to become a statue of Hermes, but though a tree can grow by itself, a statue cannot sculpt itself.[55] Nature and art do come together, however, in poetry. The limit at which they meet is metaphor, which effects an unnatural passage from potentiality to actuality. Aristotle cites an example from Euripides—"With shooting feet the Greeks"—who, like Homer, makes description lively by making what he describes move. "In all these cases," Aristotle concludes, "through the 'things' being made animate they appear to be actual [*energounta*]" (238/1412a).[56] Metaphor harbors a stock of actualizing energy. The event of actualization, however, depends on a simultaneous act of animation, which is a change from rest to motion.

At the threshold of modern ethnology, the art of metaphorical animation recurs as the animist theory of causality. Aristotle's commentary on epic and tragic rhetoric supplies a model for Tylor's portrait of savage philosophy. Savages do what Homer and Euripides did: they assume that "actuality is a movement" and make movement a characteristic trait of living things. If something moves, it is because it is alive; if it is alive, it is because it has a soul, for the soul, as Aristotle defines it in *On the Soul*, is the actuality of a body that has life potentially within it.[57] Tylor's savages believe that discourse is a body that has life potentially within it. They are, anachronistically, unconverted Aristotelians. Aristotle did not fully distinguish physics from rhetoric. Neither do savage philosophers. They sustain their discourse about animism at the limit where nature folds into discourse. Hence they personify the species of metaphor that steals the principle of change from phûsis and confers it on mimêsis. But that is how savages are made.

When Paul Ricoeur resumes, or rather "reactivates," the theory of discursive energeia in *The Rule of Metaphor*, he plays down the tradition that metaphor substitutes one name for another on the basis of resemblance and proposes instead that metaphor is a "calculated error" that introduces something new into the nondiscursive world. In metaphor, an "aberrant" word not only interrupts a sign chain but disrupts its logic, attributing predicates to a subject not usually thought to possess them, as in the verse, "La terre est bleue comme un orange."[58] Metaphor, for Ricoeur, as for Aristotle, brings truth to emergence in the form of untruth, signifying both "is like" and "is not." Blue, it says, both is and is not orange. Metaphor is therefore a case of "categorial transgression."[59] When Homer "makes all things moving and alive," he lifts objects from the category of the inanimate and grafts them into the category of the animate, where they do not properly belong. Yet a transgression of this kind is a highly productive error. It breaks up existing schemes of classification and thereby prepares for the "invention" of new ones. Metaphor, Ricoeur concludes, has a "heuristic function" (22). It is an inventive, indeed Promethean, event because it assembles and disassembles categories of thought by endowing familiar objects with unfamiliar qualities, for example, by reclassifying seemingly lifeless things in the class of living ones. He says it is a "complement" to the "logic of discovery": a technique of imitation that has the capacity to shift nature's limits (22). Ricoeur dares to conceive of metaphor as a principle of change in the physical sense. But that is how savage philosophers are traditionally said to think.

In "Creativity in Language," Ricoeur argues that words—he means, strictly speaking, naming words—have "sense" and "reference" (express meanings and make truth claims) only in the context of a sentence.[60] They take on different meanings, moreover, in different sentences. The fact that words have several senses is called "polysemy" (124, 126). Conventionally, polysemy is assumed to pose a "threat" to the process of communication (127). Communication aims "to convey information from speaker to hearer," but because words are polysemous, the hearer has to distinguish the meanings the speaker intends from those the speaker connotes as an unintended surplus. If the hearer cannot distinguish denotation from connotation, then the act of communication is prey to "ambiguity": it is open to several interpretations at once. Ambiguity can lead in turn to equivocation: the hearer is left hesitating between competing interpretations. If left unresolved, equivocation ends in misunderstanding: there is no transfer of information from speaker to hearer. The act of communication falls short of its aim (126).

Conventionally, the speaker and the hearer rely on the action of context to reduce the equivocity of utterances to "univocity" (127). To find the meaning that best suits the matter at hand, the hearer tests the speaker's words for "semantic pertinence," for "when we speak, only a part of the semantic field of a word is used," and the rest is set aside for use in other contexts (127). Metaphor, however, is a semantic *im*pertinence that interrupts the corrective action of context: "a clear case where polysemy is preserved instead of being screened" (132). An utterance rich in metaphor confronts the hearer with a surplus of meaning and deflects communication into equivocation. Yet metaphorical excess does not always lead to misunderstanding. Sometimes, in Aristotle's words, it produces new understanding instead. It is both a form-breaking and a form-giving, Dionysian and Apollonian, energy. It destroys "old" schemes of classification by finding "new" similarities between objects from mutually exclusive categories. The destruction of old forms makes it possible to gather otherwise incompatible species into a freshly minted genus. In this way metaphor dismantles existing forms of knowledge and builds new ones from the ruins.[61]

> Could we not say that the dynamics of metaphor [its potential energy, or dynamis] consists in confusing the established logical boundaries for the sake of detecting new similarities which previous categorization prevented our noticing? In other words, the power of metaphor [its actualizing energy, or energeia] would be to break through previous categorization and to establish new logical boundaries on the ruins of the preceding ones. If we take this remark seriously, we may wish to draw the ultimate consequence and say that the dynamics of thought which breaks through previous categorization is the same as the one which gen-

erated all classifications. In other words, the figure of speech which we classify as metaphor would be at the origin of all semantic fields. (131)

Existing classifications are too obvious to yield new understanding. So the order of knowledge rests inert until living metaphor comes to reanimate it, shattering ossified categories and generating fresh ones (132). Ricoeur exemplifies the process: he revives the dormant potentiality of Aristotle's notion of metaphorical actualization by carrying it forward into a new context and reactivating it. "Aristotle once more observes"—"once more," that is, in Ricoeur's reanimation of Aristotelianism—"that it is from metaphor that we can best get hold of something fresh, for 'when Homer calls old age stubble, he teaches and informs us through the genus, for both have lost their bloom'" (131). The "metaphorical twist" supplements rather than respects the positum, actualizing in the world what exists potentially in discourse: "a discourse which makes use of metaphor has the extraordinary power"— the extraordinary energeia—"of redescribing reality" (132). Metaphorical energeia completes what nature leaves incomplete. It exceeds the limits of restricted mimesis and extends the field of general mimesis: "the strategy of discourse implied in metaphorical language is neither to improve communication nor to insure univocity in argumentation, but to shatter and to increase our sense of reality by shattering and increasing our language" (132–33). Ricoeur revives a premise that Tylor and Nietzsche attribute to savage philosophers: metaphor, like Prometheus, takes the principle of change from nature ("reality") and gives it to discourse ("language"). It is Apollonian insofar as it draws boundaries, Dionysian insofar as it breaks them.

Tylor, however, warns that metaphor not only undermines the communication of "modern educated thought" by letting "almost anything . . . suggest anything else" but stifles the production of positive knowledge by substituting fiction for fact. The office of our thought is to respect the positum. Metaphor enriches it, making description so vivid that it takes the place of lived experience. The sort of discourse that spends energeia too freely is "myth." Tylor accuses it of the Promethean sacrilege of making the ideal real. "First and foremost among the causes which transfigure into myths the facts of daily experience," he remarks, "is the belief in the animation of all nature, rising at its highest pitch to personification. This, no occasional or hypothetical action of the mind, is inextricably bound in with that primitive mental state where man recognizes in every detail of his world the operation of personal life and will."[62] What Tylor calls "transfiguration" is a hierarchically racialized version of metaphorical actualization. Paradoxically, he claims that savage philosophers conduct the labor of actualization so effectively that there is no metaphor in myth. They purge myth of metaphor by an excess of metaphor:

> To the lower tribes of man, sun and stars, trees and rivers, winds and clouds, become personal animate creatures, leading lives conformed to human or animal analogies, and performing their special functions in the universe with the aid of limbs like beasts or of artificial instruments like men; or what men's eyes behold is but the instrument to be used or material to be shaped, while behind it there stands some prodigious but half-human creature, who grasps it with his hands or blows it with his breath. The basis on which such ideas as these are built is not to be narrowed down to poetic fancy and transformed metaphor. They rest upon a broad philosophy of nature, early and crude indeed, but thoughtful, consistent, and quite really and seriously meant. (285)

Myth makes events actual by making them lively and makes them lively by making them move. The ancient savage philosophers, though, took the further, more "serious" step of inquiring into the causes of movement and concluded that whatever moves has a soul. Without metaphor there would have been no "philosophy of nature," for "philosophy" borrows its heuristic resources from rhetoric and poetics and redirects them to physics, the study of change.

Aristotle attributes skill in vivid description to Homer above all poets. Tylor says it typifies "the lower tribes" more than any other kind of society, including "the Greeks." Whereas Homer *compares* old age to stubble, however, savage philosophers affirm that the "sun and stars" *are* living beings. The "less educated races" do not just make description lively. They bring what they describe to life. They are so capable of metaphor that they are incapable of metaphor. Where the subject of positivism perceives a figure of discourse, the subject of myth experiences a living event. Tylor cites the example of the waterspout:

> Poetry has so far kept alive in our minds the old animative theory of nature, that it is no great effort to us to fancy the waterspout a huge giant or sea-monster, and to depict in what we call appropriate metaphor its march across the fields of ocean. But where such forms of speech are current among less educated races, they are underlaid by a distinct prosaic meaning of fact. Thus the waterspouts which the Japanese see so often off their coasts are to them long-tailed dragons, "flying up into the air

with a swift and violent motion," wherefore they call them "tatsmaki," "spouting dragons." Waterspouts are believed by the Chinese to be occasioned by the ascent and descent of the dragon; although the monster is never seen head and tail at once for clouds, fishermen and sea-side folk catch occasional glimpses of him ascending from the water and descending to it. (292)

An *in*appropriate metaphor takes part in change instead of describing it. The result is an event of *in*appropriation that lets possibilities framed in discourse blossom forth in the extradiscursive world. The upsurging waterspout is not like a dragon. It is a dragon.

According to Ricoeur, poetry, since it is rich in metaphor, has the "power to make contact with being."[63] Tylor concedes that metaphor bears a charge of actualizing energy but displaces it onto "the old bards and orators" of "past ages" in order to distance it from the positivist horizon of the present. Ironically, though, the figures who personify the force of discursive invention are the inventions of Tylor's own actualizing utterance. His discourse performs the very conjuring trick that he attributes to poetic logic, classing creatures of "fancy" in the category of "reality." He "shatters and increases" the limits of the world by shattering and increasing the limits of discourse. Yet that is what the "bards and orators" supposedly do:

> Analogies which are but fancy to us were to men of past ages reality. They could see the flame licking its yet undevoured prey with tongues of fire, or the serpent gliding along the waving sword from hilt to point; they could feel a live creature gnawing within their bodies in the pangs of hunger; they heard the voices of the hill-dwarfs answering in the echo, and the chariot of the Heaven-god rattling in thunder over the solid firmament. Men to whom these were living thoughts had no need of the schoolmaster and his rules of composition, his injunctions to use metaphor cautiously, and to take continual care to make all similes consistent. The similes of the old bards and orators were consistent, because they seemed to see and hear and feel them: what we call poetry was to them real life. (297)

Savage philosophers group representation and reality, mimêsis and phûsis, in the same genus: the genus of things that make themselves actually what they are potentially. "The difficulty in interpreting language like this," Tylor warns, "is to know how far it is seriously and how far fancifully meant"

(293). Conventionally, the interpreter reduces the polysemy of metaphor by replacing a semantically impertinent, or "fanciful," term ("I hear the chariot of the heaven-god") with a semantically pertinent, or "serious," one ("I hear thunder").[64] What today's "schoolmaster" considers impertinent, though, the "men of the past" heard and felt, for they observed no categorial difference between animate and inanimate being. Their "living thoughts" found expression in living signs. Tylor fashions his savage poets in the image of Aristotle's Homer and then sets them in motion to personify the hypothesis of "past ages."

Why does the event of actualization happen in "the East" more than the West or the North? The Nietzsche of *Human, All Too Human* suggests it is because the difference between positive observation and vivid description is a marker of racial difference. "Europe," he claims, "has attended the school of consistent and critical thinking," whereas "Asia still does not know how to distinguish between truth and fiction [or "truth and poetry," *Wahrheit und Dichtung*]." Reasoning from cause to effect makes Europe actually what it is potentially: "Reason in school has made Europe Europe." Classing poetry alongside reality makes Asia "Asiatic."[65] There is no doubt which mode of thought the positivist considers "superior."

Tylor endorses the racialization of metaphor. What China, Japan, and Islam have in common, he suggests, is the characteristically "Asiatic" vice of overindulging in acts of discursive actualization. Predictably, their vice compels them to confuse fact and fiction:

> The merest shadowy fancy or broken-down metaphor, when once it gains a sense of reality, may begin to be spoken of as an actual event. The Moslems have heard the very stones praise Allah, not in simile only but in fact, and among them the saying that a man's fate is written on his forehead has been materialized into a belief that it can be deciphered from the letter-like markings of the sutures of his skull. One of the miraculous passages in the life of Mohammed himself is traced plausibly by Sprenger to such a pragmatized metaphor.[66]

In Tylor's Asia, metaphor, if sufficiently vivid, precipitates an event of "materialization." It does not just allow the hearer to grasp something new. It gives being to something new. The "stiffening of metaphor" proceeds from the "mistaken realization [that is, the metaphorical actualization] of words" (415). Metaphor fuels the "crystallization" of sense ("story") into reference ("history") or, to use another metaphor, "transfigures" objects of discourse into products of nature (415, 285). Its Promethean energy even hardens signs into bone. For Tylor this is the greatest sacrilege of all. Yet it is how he invents his "Moslems."

Tylor, like the positivist Nietzsche, foresees that culture will one day pass from a tropical to a temperate age. Indeed the course of development is already having a cooling influence on metaphor's "friction-fire." The event of actualization still recurs today—"our own day"—in the poet's "conscious fictions," but the "transition" from myth to science put limits on metaphor's tropical excesses. Though poets continue to believe in "the reality of ideas," they have grudgingly learned to distinguish metaphorical "realization" from "real life." Though they continue to make fictions, they now know how to distinguish them from facts:

> A poet of our own day has still much in common with the minds of uncultured tribes in the mythologic stage of thought. The rude man's imaginations may be narrow, crude, and repulsive, while the poet's more conscious fictions may be highly wrought into shapes of fresh artistic beauty, but both share in that sense of the reality of ideas, which fortunately or unfortunately modern education has proved so powerful to destroy. The change of meaning of a single word will tell the history of this transition, ranging from primaeval to modern thought. From first to last, the processes of *phantasy* have been at work; but where the savage could see *phantasms*, the civilized man has come to amuse himself with *fancies*. (315)

The savage sign is a "phantasm": a combination of phantom and life. The poetic sign is a "fancy": a phantom whose life is confined to the limits of discourse. The two sorts differ only in the amount of energy they discharge. A phantasm possesses an intrinsic principle of change. It makes itself actually what it is potentially. A fancy does not. Metaphor continues to make description vivid but no longer makes it move. Reality has made itself master of ideality.[67]

Tragic Magic

The Nietzsche of *The Birth of Tragedy* echoes Tylor's premise that poetry is a forbidden technique of crystallization. The force that drives it, naturally, is metaphor. What the positivist later calls poetry is for the tragic poet real life. For tragedy is a survival of animist thought. The tragic poet inhabits a

world of images that "live" because they "act" or, more precisely, because
they move: "nothing could be more certain," he affirms, "than the fact that
a poet is a poet only insofar as he sees himself surrounded by figures who
live and act before him and into whose inmost nature he can see." [68] There
is an uncanny likeness between Nietzsche's portrait of the tragic poet and
Tylor's portrait of "the old bards and orators." The tragic consciousness
endows dramatic characters with souls and speaks of dramatic action as if
it were an actual event. "For a genuine poet," this Nietzsche argues, "metaphor [Metapher] is not a rhetorical figure but a vicarious image [Bild] that
he actually beholds in place of a concept [eines Begriffes]. A character is for
him not a whole he has composed out of particular traits, picked up here
and there, but an obtrusively alive person [lebendige Person] before his very
eyes, distinguished from the otherwise identical vision of a painter only
by the fact that it continually goes on living and acting" (63/51). An "image," like a soul, is a living sign. It possesses its own principle of change.
After the poet invents it, it continues to move by itself. And it is metaphor
that gives it the spark of life. Indeed the force of metaphor is capable of
fashioning "a host of spirits" that hover in between animate and inanimate
being (64/51). The poet who wields this most tropical of tropes practices
the "primeval"—and magical—art of actualizing ideas by animating them:
"let anyone have the ability to behold continually a vivid play and to live
constantly surrounded by hosts of spirits," Nietzsche promises, "and he
will be a poet" (64). In the tradition of Aristotle, he cites the example of
Homer, whose poetry remains the locus classicus for the discussion of vivid
description: "How is it that Homer's descriptions are so much more vivid
[anschaulicher] than those of any other poet? Because he visualizes so much
more vividly" (63–64/51). Metaphor, which sets all things in motion, makes
the image actually what it is potentially, enriching tragic mimêsis with
the principle of phûsis. Nietzsche's formula for Promethean art replicates
Tylor's formula for savage philosophy almost point for point. Or rather the
savage is Prometheus racialized according to the requirements of the era of
imperialism. The same rule governs the formation of both.

    When the tragic actors enter the stage, they pass on the power of
actualization—what Nietzsche calls the "artistic gift"—to the audience.
"The Dionysian excitement is capable of communicating this artistic gift to
a multitude," Nietzsche explains, "so they can see themselves surrounded
by such a host of spirits [Geisterscharen] while knowing themselves to be
essentially one with them" (64/51). The chorus provides a focal point for
the event of dramatic actualization. The actors of the chorus stand on the

border between animate and inanimate being. They live and move by themselves; the characters they play do not. As soon as the action begins, though, the actors confer their life force onto their characters. They give them soul, a principle of change, making them live by letting them move. Tragedy, for this earlier Nietzsche, is a genre of soul migration. The souls of the actors pass into the body of the chorus, and the chorus passes on the force of self-production to the audience, which is in turn invited to mold itself in the chorus's image. What ensues is a "magical transformation." The chorus and the audience are "one" during the performance because they share the same life force until the action ends: "This process of the tragic chorus is the dramatic proto-phenomenon: to see oneself transformed before one's own eyes and to begin to act as if one had actually entered into another body, another character" (64). Tragic magic aims at group identification: "a whole throng," Nietzsche adds, "experiences the magic of this transformation" (or, "feel themselves magically transformed [*verzaubert*]") (64/52). The actors give life to the dramatist's characters and to the audience that identifies with them, gathering the unorganized masses into one living, collective body. Tragedy is therefore a change first from lifelessness to life and then from individual to collective life. "Such magic transformation [*Verzauberung*]," he stresses, "is the presupposition of all dramatic art" (64). Tragic drama steals the principle of change back from nature. Years later he argues that the passage of energeia to art from nature produces a state of "frenzy." Predictably, he styles the artist as a man who seeks sexual mastery and the thing as a woman who resists him:

> What is essential in such frenzy [*Rausch*] is the feeling of increased strength and fullness [*das Gefühl der Kraftsteigerung und Fülle*]. Out of this feeling one lends to things, one *forces* them to accept from us, one violates them—this process is called *idealizing* [*idealisieren*]. . . . In this state one enriches everything out of one's own fullness: whatever one sees, whatever one wills, is seen swelled, taut, strong, overloaded with strength. A man in this state transforms things until they mirror [*widerspielgeln*] his power—until they are reflections [*Reflexe*] of his perfection. This *having* to transform into perfection is—art.[69]

Art is a "mirror," he says. The mirror, however, does not reflect nature; nature, rather, reflects the mirror, molding itself in art's image. There is no distinction between the art that imitates nature and the art that completes what nature leaves incomplete, restricted and general mimesis. In an inversion of the natural order, art supplies nature with a principle of change. Phûsis is mimêsis in action. Nature comes from art no otherwise than living.

Traditionally, Platonism accuses imitation of being unfaithful to things in themselves. In an unfinished preface for a new edition of *The Birth of Tragedy*, written between 1886 and 1888, Nietzsche counters that things are unfaithful to themselves. "The antithesis of a real and an apparent world," he insists, "is lacking here [that is, in *The Birth of Tragedy*]: there is only *one* world, and this is false, cruel, contradictory, seductive, without meaning— A world thus constituted is the real world. *We have need of lies* in order to conquer this reality, this 'truth,' that is, in order to *live*."[70] Only an imitation that masters the art of deception is capable of being true to nature, for "reality" is itself frenzy, pure transformative energy: "This ability itself, thanks to which he violates reality by means of lies, this artistic ability of man *par excellence*—he has it in common with everything that is. He himself is after all a piece [*ein Stück*] of reality, truth, nature: how should he not also be a piece of *genius in lying!*" (§853).[71] The "ability" that Nietzsche alludes to is metaphor, the art of representing what is in terms of what it is not. Metaphor is a "piece," or survival, of nature's logic because it mimics the natural art of lying.

Imitation and nature are not two opposing modes of being, then, but two ways of spending the forces of life. When we say that one thing belongs to representation and another to reality, we are not "respecting" them, as positivism demands, but gauging how much was spent enriching them, as economic morality demands. A greater expenditure produces an impression of fact; a lesser expenditure, an impression of fiction. That is all that the opposition between them entails:

> Critique of "reality": where does the "more or less real," the gradation of being in which we believe, lead to?—
>
> The degree to which we feel life and power (logic and coherence of experience) gives us our measure of "being," "reality," not-appearance. (§485)

What we call reality is more vivid than what we call representation. Nothing, moreover, is more vivid than our own consciousness: the certainty that "I think, I feel, I will." We fashion the actual in the image of the animate, and the most animated of things is our own subjectivity. The force of metaphor therefore makes reality in our image. The positum that Tylor and the positivist Nietzsche would defend from the projections of savage philosophers is itself, for the artistic Nietzsche, a projection of the self-conscious human "ego." The real world is what survives today of the spirit doctrine:

> we *created* the world on this basis as a world of causes, a world of will, a world of spirits. The most ancient and enduring psychology was at work here and did not do anything else: all that happened was considered a doing, all doing the effect of a will; the world became to it a multiplicity of doers; a doer (a "subject") was slipped under all that happened. It was out of himself that man projected his three "inner facts"—that in which he believed most firmly, the will, the spirit, the ego. He even took the concept of being from the concept of the ego; he posited "things" as "being," in his image, in accordance with his concept of the ego as cause.[72]

Reality is a mirror of the animating metaphor. What is most actual, because most vivid, is what most resembles human consciousness. The very concept of a thing in itself—of a reality independent of ideality—is the survival of a prehistoric personification. Hence even the staunchest positivist is unwittingly an animist:

> The subject: this is the term for our belief in a unity underlying all the different impulses of the highest feeling of reality . . . we believe so firmly in our belief that for its sake we imagine "truth," "reality," "substantiality" in general.— "The subject" is the fiction that many similar states in us are the effect of one substratum: but it is we who first created the "similarity" of these states; our adjusting them and making them similar is the fact, not their similarity (—which ought rather to be denied—).[73]

The categories of thought arise from the recognition that different experiences both are and are not alike. The agency that discovers the resemblances between them is metaphor. It created the category of "the subject" by demonstrating the similarity between "different impulses," just as it created the category of "reality" by demonstrating the similarity between changes in the subject and changes in the subject's environment. Thus the subject, including the subject of art, is a lie that the artist, overfull with actualizing energy, imposes on things. So too is reality or nature. Nietzsche no longer invites his audience to identify with the image projected by art energy but to recognize it as a lie the artist tells in order to live.

Subtract the subject and there survives only the deed, the act itself: a pure, headless doing. "The question," Nietzsche remarks in 1887, is "whether that which 'posits things' [*was 'Dinge setzt'*] is not the sole reality [*allein real ist*]" (§569). There is no being but being-invented. He calls it "becoming," and although he conceives of it as a fiction that founds, still it cannot, as Nancy warns, provide a model for mass identification, for it is a headless, and therefore subjectless, event: an animism without spirits. Becoming dispenses with "that which posits" and provokes an "action" of positing instead: "no subject but an action, a positing [*Setzen*], creative, no 'causes and effects'" (§617). Being *is* not. Rather, becoming happens—but only insofar as it happens *again.* Reality, for Nietzsche, is a lie that recurs: "That *everything recurs* is the closest *approximation of a world of becoming to a world of being*" (§617). What matters—and what matter is—is what can be repeated. The living depend on it: "Life is founded upon the premise of a belief in enduring and regularly recurring things" (§552). One region of experience is more reliable than others if resemblances are said to recur more often there than anywhere else.

Repetition "crystallizes" semantic impertinence, always wrong and arbitrary, into semantic pertinence, always right and necessary, solidifying what was fresh into what is merely commonplace: "The reputation [*Ruf*], name [*Name*], and appearance [*Anschein*], the usual measure and weight of a thing, what it counts for—originally almost always wrong and arbitrary, thrown over things like a dress and altogether foreign to their nature and even to their skin—all this grows from generation unto generation, merely because people believe it, until it gradually grows to be part of the thing and turns into its very body [*Leibe*]."[74] Metaphor shatters and increases the limits of reality only as long as it is lively. Sooner or later it dies and is buried in the background of language, where it becomes just a name like any other. It is then that the savage inertia of discourse, according to Nietzsche, knits words into "skin" and even, according to Tylor, hardens them into bone.

CHAPTER THREE

The Mana Type

To live in intimacy with a stranger, not in order to draw him closer, or to make him known, but rather to keep him strange, remote: unapparent— so unapparent that his name contains him entirely. And, even in discomfort, to be nothing else, day after day, than the ever open place, the unwaning light in which that one being, that thing, remains forever exposed and sealed off.—*Giorgio Agamben, "The Idea of Love"*

Entelechy

The school of "savage psychology" holds that the souls of the living and the dead come to talk to us when we sleep. We experience their visits as dreams. Tylor cites an example from J. Leighton Wilson's *Western Africa: Its History, Condition, and Prospects*, published in 1856. In "Southern Guinea," says Wilson, a retired Presbyterian missionary, the dead bring "cautions, hints, and warnings" to the living, and on waking the living share the wisdom of the dead with family, friends, and neighbors. The more they talk about their dreams, the more dreams they have to talk about:

> The habit of relating their dreams, which is universal, greatly promotes the habit of dreaming itself, and hence their sleeping hours are characterized by almost as much intercourse with the dead as their waking are with the living. This is, no doubt, one of the reasons of their excessive superstitiousness. Their imaginations become so *lively* that they can scarcely distinguish between their dreams and their waking thoughts, between the real and the ideal, and they consequently utter falsehood without intending, and profess to see things which never existed.[1]

Tylor ranks the dreams of the "modern savage" on par with Homer's dream of Achilles. They stand as paradigms of "lively" description: "To the Greek of old, the dream-soul was what to the modern savage it still is. Sleep, loosing cares of mind, fell on Achilles as he lay by the sounding sea, and there stood over him the soul of Patroklos, like to him altogether in stature" (444). Savage dreams are living imitations, a genre of pictorial discourse so vivid that they add a supplement of "things that never existed" to the things that exist already. Tylor takes it as further proof that dreaming is a survival of the ancient and savage art of crystallization.

In *Comparative Mythology*, published the same year as *Western Africa*, Max Müller confirms that what today's dreamer perceives while asleep, "the ancient poets" perceived while awake. Syntax was for them "living expression." It conferred a soul on everything that changes. When the "Aryan" poets said "the day dawns," they assumed that the subject of the sentence was as alive as the person who uttered it. They were linguistic fetishists in Nietzsche's sense. "As long as people thought in language," Müller explains, "it was simply impossible to speak of morning or evening, of spring and winter, without giving to these conceptions something of an individual, active, sexual [because every noun had a gender], and at last personal character."[2] Poetry was the exercise rather than the imitation of life. The prosopopoetic act recurs today in the "more conscious fictions" of modern poets. Wordsworth's skill at vivid description vies with Homer's: "We are wont to call this poetical diction, and to make allowance for what seems to us exaggerated language. But to the poet it is no exaggeration, nor was it to the ancient poets of language" (75). "Even in our time," syntax continues to put a doer behind every deed, for "though we have the conception of nature as a power, what do we mean by power, except something powerful" (73)? The poets of "mythopoeic ages," however, did more than exaggerate. They assumed that imitation shares nature's "power" to produce change. Living expression was nature in act, and it acted to excess. "Every word, whether noun or verb," says Müller, "had still its full original power during the mythopoeic ages. Words were heavy and unwieldy. They said more than they ought to say" (82). The sign did not represent ideas but multiplied them. It did not describe objects but enriched them with qualities they would not otherwise have possessed. "Where we speak of the sun following the dawn, the ancient poets could only speak and think of the sun loving and embracing the dawn. What is with us a sunset, was to them the Sun growing old, decaying, or dying. Our sunrise was to them the Night giving birth to a brilliant child; and in the Spring they *really saw* the Sun or Sky embracing the earth with a warm embrace" (82–83, emphasis added).

Only later was actualizing energy denied to the language of myth and made the exclusive property of natural things.

Nothing is more commonplace in the late nineteenth-century discourse about culture than to affirm that the mythopoeic phase of development recurs daily in the games of the civilized child. Children, like savages, personify discursive energeia. Indeed they personify personification itself. There survives in them a "rudimentary" capacity to makes thing actual by making them lively. "Yet," Tylor maintains,

> the more we compare the mythic fancies of different nations, in order to discern the common thoughts that underlie their resemblances, the more ready we shall be to admit that in our childhood we dwelt at the very gates of the realm of myth. In mythology, the child is, in a deeper sense than we are apt to use the phrase in, the father of the man. Thus, when in surveying the quaint fancies and wild legends of the lower tribes, we find the mythology of the world at once in its most distinct and most rudimentary form, we may here again claim the savage as a representative of the childhood of the human race.[3]

Each stage in the development of the "civilized" individual corresponds to a stage in the development of the species. Childhood is the age of animism, and mythology is the archive of animist thought. The language of children revives the art of mythopoeic expression. They do not speak about things. They bring them to life by setting them in motion. "Even in civilized countries," Tylor continues, the animist doctrine of universal vitality reappears

> as the child's early theory of the outer world, nor can we fail to see how this comes to pass. The first beings that children learn to understand something of are human beings, and especially their own selves; and the first explanation of all events will be the human explanation, as though chairs and sticks and wooden horses were actuated by the same sort of personal will as nurses and children and kittens. Thus infants take their first step in mythology by contriving, like Cossette with her doll [in Hugo's *Les misérables*], "se figurer que quelque chose est quelqu'un" [pretending some*thing* is some*one*]; and the way in which this childlike theory has to be unlearnt in the course of education shows how primitive it is. (285–86)

Children are somnambulists of the day. They know how to dream while awake. Childhood is an age of reverie that elapses in between sleeping and waking. The task of "education," therefore, is to civilize the child-savage. The individual takes her first irrevocable step from child-savagery to adult-civilization when she learns to respect a distinction that the residents of West Africa, according to Wilson, do not: the distinction between "the real" and "the ideal." Education is Enlightenment, and Enlightenment, in the words of Adorno and Horkheimer, demands "the extirpation of animism."[4]

It is an extirpation that the narrator of Marcel Proust's *In Search of Lost Time* repeatedly fails to perform. He lingers instead on the threshold between the child-savage and adult-civilized stages of development, and we, his readers, enter the novel by adopting his point of view. When we read him, we take part in the mythopoeic art that he shares with another, older animist: his parents' country neighbor, Swann. Proust sets the stakes in the first three sentences of the first paragraph of *Swann's Way*, the first installment in the seven-volume series. The narrator recalls that he used to go to bed early. Sometimes he would fall asleep as soon as he put out his candle, only to be awoken by the thought that it was time to stop reading the book that he still seemed to be holding and extinguish the light. At the threshold of the novel, he locates reading on both sides of the threshold between waking and dreaming: a position that the disciplines of ethnology and comparative mythology reserve for savages and children.

Proust's narrator does not "stop reading" when he falls asleep. He just reads differently. Sometimes, he remembers, he would drift off so abruptly that he would "turn," without perceiving any transition, from reading a book to being a book: "I had gone on thinking, while I was asleep, about what I had just been reading, but these thoughts had taken a rather peculiar turn; it seemed to me that I myself was the immediate subject of my book: a church, a quartet, the rivalry between François I and Charles V. This impression would persist [literally, "would survive," *cette croyance survivait*] for some moments after I awoke."[5] He says of himself what Wilson says of the residents of West Africa: "[he] can scarcely distinguish between [his] dreams and [his] waking thoughts." Reading makes a fold "between the real and the ideal" until there is no difference between the reader and the text ("I myself was the subject of my book"), or between the text and its referent (between his reading about "a church" and him being a church). The narrator is the sort of reader who partakes of what he reads. He does not claim, as Nietzsche does, to sleepwalk in daylight. But he does sleep*read* at night.

So what are we doing when we read his narration? Where does the novel position us, his readers? Do we become like this narrator who becomes what he reads? Do we partake of the things we glimpse only through his eyes? Can we trust the point of view of a narrator who cannot tell dreams from waking thoughts? Ironically, the conclusions he draws while asleep are more credible than those he draws while awake. He says he used to dream that he was the subject of a book. His dreams are in fact correct. He "really" is the subject of Proust's novel. Only when he wakes does he make the mistake of thinking he exists outside of the book that *we* are reading, perhaps before we go to sleep at night. His dreams tell it like it is. They give us instructions about reading. What else do they say? When the narrator is awake, he reads about "a church." When asleep, he becomes one, conferring his face and voice on something that lacks them. What his dreams *also* say, then, is that reading "turns" inanimate objects into living, self-conscious ones. Reading, in short, occurs in the mode of prosopopoeia. When we read the narrator's account of reading, we do exactly what he says he does when he reads. We confer a life like our own on an otherwise lifeless character who pauses on the threshold of a novel to remind us that reading brings the inventions of fiction to life. We animate him, endowing him with face, voice and the capacity to speak, and the first thing he says after coming to life is that reading is an event of animation, the sort of event that, in Tylor words, takes animism to its "highest pitch." Proust's novel confirms from the outset that prosopopoeia is the fundamental, generative act of reading novels.[6] Yet Tylor insists that prosopopoeia is the characteristic trait of savage philosophy. Taking prosopopoeia literally is what makes savage philosophers savage. So it seems we all go a little savage when we read. Convention requires us to confer a life like our own on the characters in fiction. We, Proust's readers, take part in the books we read just as Proust's narrator takes part in the books he reads.

Yet Gérard Genette argues that the action of the novel aims precisely to guide the narrator away from the threshold that he shares with his readers. The novel, according to Genette, records the narrator's "painful apprenticeship" in the "value and function of language."[7] He conceives of this apprenticeship (*apprentissage*), moreover, as a development, indeed an evolution, from child-savagery, which is the recourse of mythopoetics, to adult-civilization, which is a state of ironic self-observation. At first, Genette explains, the child-narrator confuses signs with things, but over time experience teaches him to respect the difference between them. Apprenticeship is the extirpation of animism. A novel that begins by putting the reader in the savage position ends by lifting the narrator out of it. Genette burdens Proust with a civilizing mission. But is his moral posturing justified? Is the novel an allegory of improvement?

The narrator's recollections of childhood are inextricably bound up with his experience of linguistic signs, especially place-names. Genette claims that as a child the narrator succumbs to "the realist illusion," which is the error of assuming that "what one names is *as one names it.*" The child-narrator reads too much into things. Or, more precisely, he reads things into names. His realism has two premises. First, he believes there is an "active relation" between the signifier, or expression-form, and the signified, or content-form. Genette calls this "the semantic illusion" (237). Second, the narrator assumes there is an "identity" between the signified and the referent. Genette calls this "the referential illusion" and says it consists of mistaking an ideal for a real connection (249). His definition of the "realist illusion" echoes the definition of magic discussed in the introduction. The child-narrator, he claims, treats names as if they were things. He falls prey not just to any realism, then, but to a conventionally savage realism. This is the error that the novel is supposed to correct.

The narrator's semiotics carefully distinguishes words from names. Words, he says, reproduce the images of things. Names, in contrast, remake things in their own image. Words respect what is given in sensation. Names enrich it. Words typify things. Names personify them, making them actual by making them more "like" those who utter them:

> Words present to us a little picture [*image*] of things, clear and familiar, like the pictures hung on the walls of schoolrooms to give children an illustration of what is meant by a carpenter's bench, a bird, an anthill, things chosen as typical of everything else of the same sort. But names present to us—of persons, and of towns which they accustom us to regard as individual, as unique, like persons [*comme des personnes*]—a confused picture [*une image confuse*], which draws from them, from the brightness or darkness of their tone, the color in which it is uniformly painted, like one of those posters, entirely blue or entirely red, in which, on account of the limitations imposed by the process used in their reproduction or by a whim on the designer's part, not only the sky and the sea are blue or red, but the ships and the church and the people in the streets. (421/387–88)

A word is a sign, and the child-narrator agrees with Genette (and Saussure and Hjelmslev) that a sign is a correlation of two elements. A sound pattern—"bench" or "bird"— evokes an image pattern, and the image pattern in turn stands for a thing: not an individual thing but a genus or "type" of things, a bench or a bird in general. The relation between the signifier and the signified is arbitrary: the one does not partake of the other. The relation between the signified and the referent, however, is verisimilar: the one

pictures forth the other. The name too is a correlation of two elements: a
signifier, or "tone," and a signified, or "image." The form of the signifier,
moreover, determines the form of the signified: the sound pattern lends its
"tone" to the image pattern. The relation between them is not arbitrary.
Nor is it verisimilar. Although the signified is made in the signifier's image, it reproduces only one of its traits and excludes the rest. The narrator
explains that as a child he assumed that the city of Florence was something
"flower-like" because the "Flor-" in the signifier "Florence" evokes a "flo-
ral" signified. "As for Balbec," he adds,

> it was one of those names in which, as on an old piece of Norman pot-
> tery that still keeps the colour of the earth from which it was fashioned,
> one sees depicted still the representation of some long-abolished cus-
> tom, of some feudal right, of the former status of some locality, of an
> obsolete way of pronouncing the language which had shaped and wedded
> its incongruous syllables and which I never doubted that I should find
> spoken there even by the inn-keeper who would serve me coffee on my
> arrival. (421/388)

"Balbec" is a prosopopoeia, or animating metaphor: its "syllables" endow
the town with a face and with a voice that "pronounces" them in a distinctive way. The narrator perceives a real, physical connection not only
between the tone and the image (signifier and signified) but between the
tone and the town it personifies (signifier and referent), as if the name had
arisen directly from the place itself. Only years later does Doctor Brichot
inform him that "Balbec" is "probably a corruption of Dalbec," a combination of *dal*, meaning "valley," and, *bec*, meaning "stream," and a name
that once seemed uniquely tied to a place turns out to be a commonplace:
"valleystream."[8]

Genette stresses "how wrong it would be" if, after mistaking the signifier for the signified, the narrator were to confuse "the signified with the
referent, that is to say, the real object," but "this error," he immediately
adds, "is precisely the one committed by Marcel."[9] The narrator substitutes
a "dream" Balbec for the "real" Balbec, adding a place that does not exist to
the places that exist already:

> And yet nothing could have differed more utterly, either, from the real
> Balbec than that other Balbec of which I had often dreamed [*souvent
> rêvé*] when the wind was so strong that Françoise, as she took me to the
> Champs-Elysées, would advise me not to walk too close to the walls or I

might have my head knocked off by a falling slate, and would recount to
me, with many a groan, the terrible disasters and shipwrecks that were
reported in the newspaper.[10]

The child-narrator treats daydreams—reveries—as if they were realities,
and it is the act of reading—in this case the reading of a newspaper—that
folds waking and dreaming together. The name is the threshold where they
meet. What exists potentially in a name is as lively for him as anything he
encounters in the actual world:

> Doubtless whatever it was that my imagination aspired to, that my
> senses took in only incompletely and without any immediate pleasure,
> I had committed to the safe custody of names; doubtless, because I had
> accumulated there a store of dreams [parce que j'y avais accumulé du
> rêve], those names now magnetised my desires; but names themselves
> are not very comprehensive; the most that I could do was to include in
> each of them two or three of the principal "curiosities" of the town,
> which would lie there side by side, without intermediary. (422–23/389)

Genette concludes that the narrator invests names with the power to "crys-
tallize" fantasy into fact: "les noms propres . . . cristallisent la rêverie du
Narrateur."[11] He regards daydreams as survivals of mythopoeic consciousness, which makes things actual by making them lively. Ironically, Tylor
confesses that when he was a child he too mistook the "vividness" of signs
for an indication of "reality": "In the poetic stage of thought we may see
that ideal conceptions once shaped in the mind must have assumed some
such reality to grown-up men and women as they still do to children. I
have never forgotten the *vividness* with which, as a child, I fancied I might
look through a great telescope, and see the constellations stand round the
sky, red, green, and yellow, as I had just been shown them on the celestial
globe."[12] Genette says that an excess of vivid description characterizes "the
poetic stage of language" (l'état poétique du langage).[13] Tylor says it typifies "the poetic stage of thought." Both treat poetry as an earlier, and lower,
phase of intellectual development. Both agree that the child-savage disposes
of a surplus of actualizing energy and learns, by a process of disenchantment, to spend it in moderation. But does the novel bear out the development theory?

   When the narrator asks Swann whether Balbec is the best place to view
"the most violent storms," Swann's reply does more than make description lively. It brings the object of description to life. "The church there,"

he answers, "built in the twelfth and thirteenth centuries, and still half Romanesque, is perhaps the most curious example to be found of our Norman Gothic" (417–18/384–85). Either Swann does not hear the narrator's question or he ignores it, because he tells him nothing about storms. Yet a lapse on the level of sense facilitates an emergence on the level of reference. "Gothic art seemed to me a more living [*plus vivant*] thing," the narrator recalls, "now that, detached from the towns in which until then I had always imagined it, I could see how, in a particular instance, upon a reef of savage rocks, it had taken root and grown until it flowered [*germé et fleuri*] in a tapering spire" (418/385). Swann's failure to answer the narrator's question makes his dream Balbec actual by making it live. The Gothic "takes root" in Swann's words and grows there, producing blossoms as flowers do. Swann's words are like flowers in Hölderlin's sense: the "spire" that blooms from them possesses its own principle of change.

The child-narrator thinks of names as an "atmosphere" in which "the life" he has "not yet lived" promises to become "real." They bring to actuality what has the potential to be. Only on this assumption can the force of discourse (*logos*) be said to rival the forces of nature (*phûsis*): "since I thought of names not as an inaccessible ideal but as a real and enveloping atmosphere into which I was about to plunge, the life not yet lived [*la vie non vécue encore*], the life, intact and pure, which I enclosed in them gave to the most material pleasures, to the simplest scenes, the same attractions which they have in the works of Primitives [*dans les oeuvres des primitifs*]" (423/390). When he maintains that the body of the name brings to life whatever has the potential for life, the narrator comes close to reproducing Aristotle's definition of the soul. According to Aristotle, the soul is the actuality of whatever has the potential to be "besouled."[14] Does the child-narrator mean to suggest that names are the souls of things? Does the name realize whatever has the capacity to become real? Not everything that has the potential to be actually comes to be. The life into which the narrator finally plunges does not unfold as he dreams it. He invests possibilities in the name that often prove impossible when he visits the place. What his "apprenticeship" teaches him, then, is that the name is the actuality of what has the potential both to be and to not-be. It is the potentiality (*dynamis*) of an impotentiality (*adynamia*). When he "plunges" into the life not yet lived, he launches simultaneously into a life never to be lived. He cannot choose one without accepting the other. Between them lies the "root" of his freedom and his responsibility.

It is no accident that the narrator likens names to "the works of Primitives." In a commentary on Aristotle's *On the Soul*, Giorgio Agamben remarks that "there is truly potentiality only where the potentiality to not-be does not lag behind actuality but passes fully into it as such."[15] Aristotle's affirmation of the potentiality of impotentiality recurs, in the early twentieth century, as the fundamental premise of savage philosophy. Agamben explains that for Aristotle "potentiality is not simply non-Being, simple privation, but rather *the existence of non-Being,* the presence of an absence" (179). The two potentialities do not oppose one another. Together *dynamis* and *adynamia* facilitate the labor of actualization. When Proust's narrator gathers them together in the name, he joins a tradition of thought that values potentiality on par with impotentiality. Freud calls those who affirm the potentiality of impotentiality "primitive people." They insist that the potentiality to not-be participates in the actualization of the potentiality to be. The unreal is for them a necessary moment in the realization of the real. When Aristotle affirms the potentiality of impotentiality, Agamben takes it as another indication of his "genius" (183).[16] When the same hypothesis is attributed to "savage philosophers," it is held up as proof of the inferiority of their thought. A savage philosopher, or more recently a postmodernist or magical realist, is anyone who dares to affirm the being of nonbeing.

Genette observes that the child-narrator endows names with the capacity to transform daydreams into essences, but warns that these essences are "not an abstraction" but "a profound material," indeed "a substance." Naming effects the "transubstantiation" of *im*potentiality into actuality, folding the ideal into the real, daydreams into conscious perception.[17] "That," the narrator confirms, "(for all that I was still in Paris) was what I saw, and not what was actually round about me."[18] Genette evaluates the narrator's theory of names as a forbidden recourse of magical thought, but adds that as the action of the novel advances, the narrator's "contact with reality" gradually teaches him to draw a limit between what has the potential to be and what has the potential to not-be, between the life "not yet lived" and the life never to be lived.[19] The narrator's apprenticeship, in short, "depoeticizes" the name. The fetishist of discourse submits to the discipline of things, passing from a child-savage to an adult-civilized phase of intellectual development: "belief in the truth of names is an ambiguous privilege of childhood," Genette argues, "one of those 'illusions to be destroyed' of which the hero must divest himself one after another in order to accede to the state of absolute disenchantment [*désenchantement absolu*] that precedes and lays the way for the [novel's] final revelation."[20] Although the adult narrator continues to encounter "essences" in his dreams, he learns to confine them to the borders of sleep. His slow "disenchantment" saps the name of its actualizing energy and liberates potentiality from the threat of impotentiality. Only because he struggles against the illusions of "magic," Genette suggests, does he qualify as a "hero." The antirealist critic cannot abide the suggestion that potentiality, as Agamben puts it, entails "the existence of non-Being." All potentiality, for Genette, is potentiality to be.

Yet the narrator insists that the images he stores in names grow "more real" the *less* they correspond to any place he could possibly visit. His interpretation of names is not a phase he grows out of but the principle of the world's growth. For there is no life outside of names. Change, says Aristotle, is the actuality of what has the potential both to be and to not-be: "Every potentiality is simultaneously the potentiality of the negation of what it is the potentiality of."[21] Names, says the narrator, have the potential to negate what they nevertheless have the potential to be. They realize the unreal even as they realize the real. What he "accumulates" in them is not just "a store of dreams" but a reality that surpasses reality's limits:

> But if these names thus permanently absorbed the image I had formed of these towns, it was only by transforming that image, by subordinating its reappearance in me to their own special laws; and in consequence of this they made it more beautiful, but at the same time more different from anything that the towns of Normandy or Tuscany could in reality be, and, by increasing the arbitrary delights of my imagination, aggravated the disenchantment [*la déception*] that was in store for me when I set out upon my travels. They magnified the idea that I had formed of certain places on the surface of the globe, making them more special and in consequence more real [*plus réels*].[22]

The "image" the name connotes is "different" but not separate from the "reality" it denotes. Only the potential for unreality can bring reality to emergence. The Balbec the narrator finally visits is unlike the Balbec that he invests in the name. Hence the actualization of what "Balbec" is potentially is "simultaneously" the negation of a potentiality that "Balbec" is the potentiality of. One Balbec actualizes itself by de-actualizing another. Dynamis passes into being by taking the risk of adynamia. "Every human power is *adynamia*, impotentiality," Agamben explains, which means that "every human potential" exists only "in relation to its own privation."[23] Without the potentiality for impotentiality, there would be no life to plunge into.

One reason why Genette projects a theory of development onto the theory of names is that he overinvests in Saussure's definition of the linguistic sign, which assumes that the world to which discourse refers is already fully actualized. For Saussure, the sign is an arbitrary—or better, immotivated—

correlation between a sound pattern, or signifier, and a thought pattern, or signified. There is no internal connection between the two—between, for example, the sound pattern "arbor" and the thought pattern "tree"—because the same concept can be evoked by other sound patterns in other languages.[24] In a 1939 essay, however, Émile Benveniste argues that Saussure bases the principle of arbitrariness on an unacknowledged "third term."[25] This term, according to Benveniste, is "reality" (46). What is arbitrary is not the correlation between signifier and signified—the sound pattern is "identical" with the thought pattern—but the correlation between the sign and its referent. "The sign overlies and commands reality," he insists, "even better, it *is* that reality (*nomen/omen*, speech taboos, the magic power of the word, etc.)" (46). Benveniste revives the fundamental premise of savage philosophy: "For the speaker there is a complete equivalence between language and reality" (46). How does the sign take "command" of its object? Benveniste leaves the question open. The answer, however, hinges on the unacknowledged third term.

In the text of Saussure's lectures, the thought pattern, or signified, is itself a signifier, though not a linguistic one. He represents it in the form of a stylized image. A written signifier, "arbor," appears underneath a black-and-white sketch of a deciduous tree:

It is as if Saussure were saying of signs what Proust's narrator says of names: that they evoke a confused image of things. The sketch, neither a sound pattern nor a thought pattern, does not depict a correlation between a signifier and a signified. It depicts a correlation between a signifier and a signifier.[26] A sound pattern evokes an image pattern, "arbor." Both signifiers evoke the thought pattern "tree." The thought pattern, however, is itself a signifier and comes no closer to the referent—the tree itself—than any other signifier does. Indeed there is no "tree" in reality. If you were to look out my window and ask "What tree is that?" I would ask you whether you meant the maple, the cherry, or the apple. You give me the name of a genus; I offer you the popular name of a species. The signified is itself a signifier and does not gesture toward an object. The sign's referent remains a deferred presence.

In contrast Peirce foregrounds the very problem that Saussure forecloses: the problem of thirdness. A sign, according to Peirce, determines an interpretant toward an object. The sign and the interpretant refer to the object "in the same way." The interpretant, however, is itself a sign that determines an interpretant toward the object, "and so on" to infinity.[27] Yet neither the sign nor the interpretant points to an object that already exists. Rather the object lies at the end of an infinite series of signs. "Reality," for Peirce, "can only be regarded as the limit of the endless series of symbols."[28] Symbols are the kind of signs that determine interpretants. They possess the attribute of thirdness. It is the passage from sign to interpretant, moreover, that opens a horizon for the object's emergence. Interpretation is the realization of the real. "And what do we mean by the real? It is a conception," Peirce maintains, "which we must first have had when we discovered that there was an unreal, an illusion, that is, when we first corrected ourselves."[29] The sign realizes the "real" only insofar as it realizes the "unreal" too. The actualization of what exists potentially is simultaneously the actualization of what exists impotentially. Because we approach the real by the detour of the unreal, which makes constant correction necessary, the realization of the real is "such that its being" can never be perfected. Reason, which is the capacity to use symbols in a self-controlled way, "must always be in a state of incipiency," says Peirce, "of growth."[30] The sign grows—becoming actually what it is impotentially—by determining an interpretant toward an object that neither of them reaches. Its capacity to "command" reality rests on its incapacity to command reality. What matters is not whether a thought corresponds to a thing, nor whether the image evoked by the name adequately portrays the place, but what the sign contributes to the actualization of what has the potential to not-be.

The name "Balbec" supplies Proust's narrator with the image of waves "expiring" at the base of a Gothic church. The name is a sign; the image, an interpretant. When he arrives in his dream place for the first time, however, he finds that there is not one "Balbec" but two. The church is located near the train station in "Balbec-en-Terre." The seashore lies twelve miles away at "Balbec-Plage."[31] He doubles the real Balbec with a dream Balbec only to find that the real Balbec was already double. This is one of those moments when, according to Genette, the narrator's "contact with reality" contradicts his reveries and give him a lesson in the interpretation of sensory experience. Yet Peirce insists there can be no "contact" between the sign and its object until interpretation has run its infinite course. "Hardly any symbol directly signifies the characters it signifies," he explains, "for whatever it signifies it signifies by its power of determining another sign signifying the same character."[32] The sign attributes predicates to the object, and each of these predicates—Peirce calls them "characters"; the narrator, "curiosities"—serves as an interpretant (307). Before the narrator arrives there, the name "Balbec" determines the "image" of a church on a storm-wracked shore to represent the place named Balbec; after he arrives, the name determines the image of a church in a land-bound square to represent Balbec-en-Terre. The second image is more fully realized than the first. Peirce resorts to metaphor to explain the actualizing relation between the sign and the interpretant: "We must suppose there is something like a sheet of paper, blank or with a blank space upon it upon which an interpretant sign may be written. What is the nature of this blank? In affording room for the writing of a symbol, it is *ipso facto* itself a symbol, although only a wholly vague one" (322). The sign is the blank. The interpretant is the sign inscribed on the blank. The inscription of the interpretant, moreover, completes what the sign leaves incomplete: "partial" (322). The interpretant "*is* the original symbol," Peirce maintains, but "in a more developed state" (322). When a sign determines an interpretant, it does not miss its object but crystallizes it more fully. Interpretation replaces a less definite sign with a more definite one, bringing the object farther down the path from potentiality to actuality, which is why "interpretation involves a power of the symbol to cause a real fact" (322). Yet every event of actualization is constantly haunted by its potentiality for impotentiality, because, according to Aristotle, "something with a potentiality for being admits both of being and of not being, so that the same thing has a potentiality both for being and for not being."[33]

The purpose of interpretation is to actualize a potentiality in which there would no longer be anything impotential. Yet interpretation was originally an impotentiality of unlimited potential. In the beginning, Peirce speculates (since an infinite series has no beginning), "there was an indeterminate nothing of the nature of a symbol," and this mythical first symbol determined an "infinite series of interpretants" that were at first "absolutely vague like itself" (323). In Peirce's myth of the origin, the original sign is a pure potentiality for impotentiality. But in its impotentiality lies all of its potential. It is "absolutely vague" because absolutely undetermined, indefinite, "a blank." Considered in logical terms, it is a subject without predicates; considered in semiotic terms, it is the sign of nothing in particular. Its potentiality to be is still fully immersed in its potentiality to not-be. Yet a sign, by definition, is something that "seeks to make itself definite" (323). Peirce conceives of it as a "purpose" in Aristotle's sense. It is animated by an intrinsic principle of change. Hence it makes itself actually what it is impotentially. The sign actualizes itself, moreover, by producing "an interpretant more definite than itself" (323). Reality emerges out of the endless determination of one sign by another.

Peirce's term for the actualizing event of interpretation, in which a potentiality struggles against its own impotentiality, is "entelechy." "The very entelechy of being," he adds, "lies in being representable" (324). Reality, for Peirce, is not something already given, a positum, that waits passively for signs to come and represent it. Signs, rather, take part in the realization of the real, actualizing a potentiality that remains burdened by its potential to not-be. Reality is therefore an unfinished project. Peirce insists it is still growing. All growth, moreover, is in signs: "A symbol is an embryonic reality endowed with power of growth into the very truth, the very entelechy of reality" (324). Entelechy—*entelekheia* in Greek—is Aristotle's *other* word for the actualization of what exists both potentially and impotentially, yet, according to Peirce, Aristotle's account of entelechy collapsed under the weight of its potential to not-be: "Aristotle gropes for a conception of perfection, or *entelechy*, which he never succeeds in making clear" (304). Peirce is probably alluding to the following passage from the *Metaphysics*, where Aristotle concedes that the difficulty with the "conception of entelechy" is that it requires us to ascribe actuality to things that are "normally" thought to lack it, such as objects of thought and desire. Entelechy seduces us into mistaking an ideal for a real connection, a possibility that the nineteenth century projects onto its portrait of savage philosophy. To conceive of entelechy, it is necessary to speak of thoughts as if they were things. Entelechy makes a forbidden fold between actuality and inactuality, being and nonbeing:

> Important note on terminology: the name *actuality*. In our discussion it is assimilated to entelechy. This constitutes a shift away from processes towards other things as well. For an actuality is thought most normally to be a process, and it is normal to hesitate before ascribing being in a process to things that do not have being, for all that certain other predicates are ascribed, such as that these non-entities are the objects of thought and desire. It is just being in a process that is not ascribed to them and this is because actual being is a precondition of being in a process, whereas such actual being is just what these things lack.[34]

For Peirce, "entelechy" is the completion of what nature leaves incomplete: the coming-to-being of what is not yet in being but nevertheless capable of being. Entelechy aims to make the sign "identical" with its object, effecting a "perfect," in the sense of complete, union of matter and form. "We may adopt the word," he remarks, "to mean the very fact, that is, ideal sign which should be quite perfect, and so identical,—in such identity as a sign may have,—with the very matter denoted united with the very form signified by it. The entelechy of the Universe of being, then, the Universe *qua* fact, will be that Universe in its aspect as a sign" (304). Until the process of interpretation completes the identification of the sign with its object, which happens only at the end of an endless series, actuality will continue to be haunted by its potential for impotentiality. Entelechy lets being persist in being able to not-be.

It is tempting to reserve the word *energeia* for the actualizing energy of metaphor and to adopt *entelekheia* to denote the actualizing energy of names. The narrator's interpretation of the place-name would then be not a misrepresentation but "the very entelechy" of the place. Only when he tries to pass directly from the sign to its object—which assumes that discourse is directly in "command" of reality—do names deceive him. The images he stores in a name like "Balbec" constitute a finite series of interpretants, and none is immediately in "contact" with the place itself, which is not fully actual until fully interpreted. Places, like "people," grow into themselves because they are animated by names "such as people have," and a name is an "embryonic reality" in the process of being completed. "I did not then," the narrator says of his childhood reveries,

> represent to myself cities, landscapes, historical monuments, as more or less attractive pictures [*tableaux*], cut out here and there of a substance that was common to them all, but looked on each of them as on an unknown thing, different in essence from all the rest, a thing for which my soul thirsted and which it would profit from knowing. How much more individual still was the character they assumed from being designated by names, names that were for themselves alone, proper names such as people have![35]

Proust's novel gathers entelechy under the law of prosopopoeia, endowing inanimate objects with a characteristically human attribute.

When he finally allows his readers a glimpse of the "seascape" at Balbec-Plage, the narrator naturally does not describe it directly. Instead he describes how it is reflected in the bookcases that line his hotel room, where every night he returns to the border between waking and dreaming: "that [room] which I found myself occupying had set against the walls, on three sides of it, a series of low book-cases with glass fronts, in which, according to where they stood, by a law of nature that [the room's upholsterer] had not perhaps foreseen, was reflected this or that section of the ever-changing view of the sea, so that the walls were lined with a frieze of seascapes, interrupted only by the polished mahogany of the actual shelves" (416). The sea comes before the narrator's gaze only after passing across a self-contained universe of living, moving signs: a universe that by a natural "law" mimics the "ever-changing" rhythm of natural things. The waves do not wash onto the shore but play across the shelves of a library. Where the seascape should be, a book-scape emerges. The universe of signs actualizes what nature is potentially, and what it is potentially is an image: "A question again of *phûsis* as *mimesis*."[36]

Meaning or Force?

When the narrator's father tells him to pack his bags for Venice, his excitement at the thought of visiting one of his dream places quickly turns to fever, and the doctor forbids him to travel for a year. Instead, every day his parents send him to the Champs-Élysées with the housekeeper, Françoise. But he finds the park "unendurable" because he experiences it directly rather than by way of discourse: "If only Bergotte had described the place in one of his books, I should no doubt have longed to get to know it, like so many things else of which a simulacrum [*le "double"*] had found its way into my imagination. This breathed life into them [*les faisait vivre*], gave them a personality [*une personnalité*], and I sought then to rediscover them in reality [*dans la réalité*]; but in this public garden there was nothing that attached itself to my dreams."[37] He desires to know only those places that possess human qualities, places that have "personality." What makes them live is that he can replace each of them with a replica (*un double*). Things acquire life, the power to become actually what they are potentially, from a genre of signs encountered in "books." Interpretation is animation, and animation proceeds by prosopopoeia, the master trope of mythopoesis: "the interpretant," Peirce confirms, "is *animated* by the original replica, or by the sign it contains, with the power of representing the true character of the object," though its "true character" is only the last, or "ultimate," interpretant in the series.[38] The simulacrum does not stand for a thing. Rather it is the potentiality of a thing, its soul. It alone has entelechy. Hence it alone determines a series of interpretants—"dreams"—that actualizes what has the potential to be and to not-be. If the Champs-Élysées gives the narrator nothing to desire, it is because it falls outside the "blank space" in which acts of inscription "breathe life" into objects of perception.

The doctor's ban on travel puts the narrator in a position where no action is possible but inaction is unthinkable. So he resorts to magic instead. Since he cannot visit other places, he takes comfort in reciting their names. He invents a genre of spells and incantations:

> the countries for which we long occupy, at any given moment, a far larger place in our actual life [*notre vie véritable*] than the country in which we happen to be. Doubtless, if, at that time, I had paid more attention to what was in my mind when I pronounced the words [*quand je pronon-çais les mots*] "going to Florence, to Parma, to Pisa, to Venice," I should have realized that what I saw was in no sense a town, but something as different from anything that I knew, something as delicious, as might be, for a human race whose whole existence had passed in a series of late winter afternoons, that inconceivable marvel, a morning in spring.[39]

The names he recites have the force of a charm. Uttering a charm, more-over, is an act of impotentiality, the coming to being of nonbeing. It does not refer to an actual town. It conjures up "something different," namely, an unreality that has more reality than the city he lives in. The charm is a blank in which a "morning" that will never happen nevertheless finds the means to occur.

How can an act of discourse—the pronunciation of a string of words—yield a nondiscursive consequence, even if it is only the actualization of an impotentiality? This is the problem that the theory of magical utterances aims to resolve. Magic is conventionally said to be a technique of "bridging" the "gap" between a potential to be and a potential to not-be: the art of ac-tivating what cannot—or cannot yet—be actualized. "The integral cultural function of magic," argues Proust's contemporary Bronislaw Malinowski, "consists in the bridging-over of gaps and inadequacies in highly important activities not yet completely mastered by man."[40] Magic takes action where no action is possible but inaction is unthinkable. If, as Aristotle argues, ev-ery potentiality is simultaneously the potentiality for the negation of what it is the potentiality of, then magic is the art of negating that negation. We resort to charms when "chance and accident" thwart the effort to actualize what exists potentially, undermining an otherwise rational pursuit of a de-sired end (139). The potential for impotentiality haunts every human design. Magic, though, promises to make the unreliable reliable, balancing fear of failure with hope for success.

Malinowski maintains that every magical performance has three parts: the rite, the performer, and the spell. The rite is a set of "ceremonial actions" fixed by convention (140); the performer is the "officiating minister" who ensures that convention is observed (140); the spell, "the most important constituent of magic," is a chain of force-bearing words (141). The rules for the formation of spells are recorded in "traditional lore" and, "more especially," in the archives of mythology, that great reservoir of actualizing energy. Malinowski stresses that "knowledge of magic means the knowledge of the spell; and in any act of witchcraft the ritual centers round the utterance of the spell" (141). The discourse on magic inevitably reduces magic to an "act" of discourse. The rite and the performer have no other role than to launch the spell, an utterance that completes what nature leaves incomplete. The spell, however, never fully exhausts its impotentiality. Thus a gap opens between the act of discourse and its physical consequences. The spell is an actualizing act that falls just short of actualization, and yet inactuality, as Aristotle argues and Agamben repeats, is a necessary moment in any process tending toward actuality.

The spell shares its potentiality for impotentiality with a larger class of utterances that endeavor to do rather than describe things. J. L. Austin calls them "illocutions" and defines them in opposition to two other genres of speech act.[41] Every utterance is necessarily a locutionary act, namely, the "performance of an act *of* saying something" (100). An utterance that achieves something by saying something, as when a speaker wins an audience's favor by discovering the available means of persuasion, is a perlocutionary act (101). An illocution, in contrast, is the "performance of an act *in* saying something" (99). When you utter a promise, for example, you commit yourself to a future course of action. But there is a problem with Austin's classification of speech acts. It leaves "the notion of an act" undefined (107). So what is an act exactly? He approaches the question, in classic Aristotelian fashion, by asking what we "normally" think an act is. "We have the idea of an 'act' as a fixed physical thing we do," he observes, but only a child, a savage, or a neurotic would believe that making a statement is enough to produce a physical change in things (107). We posit an intrinsic difference between verbal acts and physical ones. The potential to act verbally is the impotential to act physically. I can accomplish "physical things" by performing a perlocutionary act, for example, when I persuade someone to do something, but there is no internal connection between the verbal cause and its physical effect. The same result can be achieved by nonverbal means (107–8). Yet illocution is a case in which the saying is the doing. In uttering a promise, I commit myself. The event of discourse is coterminous with its nondiscursive consequence. The cause and its effect, however, are not *"in pari materia"* (in like case or position). Rather, something verbal makes a change in something physical. Austin notes that this sort of causation strikes us as unnatural.[42] Verbal acts, we think, do not "normally" have "bodily" consequences, although

> we seem to derive some assistance from the special *nature* of acts of saying something by contrast with ordinary physical actions: for with these latter even the minimum physical action, which we are seeking to detach from its consequences, is, being a bodily movement, *in pari materia* with at least many of its immediate and *natural* consequences, whereas, whatever the immediate and *natural* consequences of an act of saying something may be, they are at least not normally other further acts of saying something, whether more particularly on the speaker's own part or even on the part of others. So that we have here a sort of regular *natural* break in the chain, which is wanting in the case of physical actions, and which is associated with the special class of names for illocutions. (113, emphasis added)

The "nature of acts of saying something" runs counter to the "nature" of "physical actions." Illocutions nevertheless set the two sorts of "nature" into relation. Though they are events of discourse, they have the power to confer actuality on what exists potentially. In sum, they possess entelechy as natural things do, making something physically what it is verbally. What is slipping away here is the classical notion of physical causality; what is emerging in its place is a fundamentally discursive sense of causation. The emergence of this causality beyond causality remains today an unfinished project for the philosophy of language.

Austin's account of illocution comes close to endorsing Peirce's hypothesis that "a symbol could not be without that power of producing a real effect."[43] What is at stake, though, is not whether illocutionary acts produce physical effects but whether they produce them in physical ways. Is illocutionary causality molded in the image of physical causality? Or is another sort of causation at work? Austin concedes that "the divorce between 'physical' actions and acts of saying something is not in all ways complete," but still he declares that "it does not seem to prevent the drawing of a line for our present purposes were we want one, that is, between the completion of the illocutionary act and all consequences thereafter."[44] What he calls a "line" is in fact a hinge. Illocution folds together discursive acts with physical consequences to produce a "fundamentally different" category of causality altogether: "Or we could put the matter in a most important other way by saying that the sense in which saying something produces effects on other persons, or *causes* things, is a fundamentally different sense of cause from that used in physical causation by pressure, &c." (113n1). In the case of illocution, verbal causes produce consequences that are not quite physical and yet not quite nonphysical either.

Philosophy, however, does not fold. "There is a constant tendency in philosophy," Austin warns, "to elide" illocution "in favor" either of locution or perlocution. "Yet it is distinct from both" (103). A locutionary act has a meaning. A perlocutionary act enlists discourse in the performance of nondiscursive acts. An illocutionary act wields "a certain *force* in saying something" (121). But what kind of "force"—or rather what kind of entelechy—is it? Austin distinguishes the force of illocution from the force of truth: "Admittedly we can use 'meaning' also with reference to illocutionary force—'He meant it as an order', &c. But I want to distinguish *force* and meaning in the sense in which meaning is equivalent to sense and reference, just as it has become essential to distinguish sense and reference" (100). Sense, according to Frege, is the thought connected with a sign. Reference is the sign's truth value: it is true if it corresponds to its object, false if it does not.[45] An illocutionary force is neither meaningful nor true. But it has three sorts of consequences. If performed "happily," it secures uptake (I succeed in warning you if you grasp my utterance as a warning), puts other acts out of order (a ship christened the *Queen Elizabeth* can be called the *Generalissimo Stalin* only in jest), and invites a response without commanding one (my promise commits me to act, but promises are often broken) (116–17).

Illocutions actualize both what exists potentially, as when I make a commitment and keep it, and what exists impotentially, as when I make a commitment and break it. Aristotle says that things that become actually what they are potentially belong to nature. Austin speculates that illocutionary forces are what survives today of language in the state of nature. He classifies them as "primitive forms" of utterance. Couching a bias against "savagery" in evolutionary terms, he proposes that "primitive languages" did not yet distinguish utterances that state something (constatives) from those that do something (performatives), nor did they distinguish primary performatives, such as "I will," from explicit ones, such as "I promise I will"

(71–72). "Primitive languages" possess more force than meaning and are more physical than verbal, although Austin concedes he cannot prove it:

> The plausible view (I do not know exactly how it would be established) would be that in primitive languages it would not yet be clear, it would not yet be possible to distinguish, which of various things that (using later distinctions) we might be doing we were in fact doing. For example "Bull" or "Thunder" in a primitive language of one-word utterances could be a warning, information, a prediction, &c. It is also a plausible view that explicitly distinguishing the different *forces* that this utterance might have is a later achievement of language, and a considerable one; primitive or primary forms of utterance will preserve the "ambiguity" or "equivocation" or "vagueness" of primitive language in this respect; they will not make explicit the precise force of the utterance. (71–72)

It is a convention of the discourse about savage philosophy to affirm, repeatedly, that "primitive" peoples believe that names partake of the forces of things. In *The Secret of the Totem*, Andrew Lang remarks that "the savage belief in the intimate and wonder-working connection of names and things is a well-ascertained fact."[46] What forces do names and things share? He says only that the "early mind" discovers "a mystic and transcendental" connection between them (121). In *Totem and Taboo*, Freud remarks that "primitive races" believe that everything that is, including names, is endowed with a life force: "Primitive races (as well as modern savages and even our own children) do not, like us, regard names as something indifferent and conventional, but as significant and essential. A man's name, is a principal component of his personality, perhaps even a portion of his soul."[47] What Freud says of primitive languages echoes what Proust's narrator says of place-names. To utter the name of a dead man, Freud argues, "is equivalent to invoking him and will be quickly followed by his presence" (57). The savage sign and its object are not just *in pari materia* but of one substance. Place-names not only have a "personality," the narrator argues, but they communicate one. Indeed they "breathe life" into things. Hence a language of one-word utterances is a compendium of spells.

As a child, the narrator hears such a language murmuring all around him. A proper name, if uttered according to the proper conventions, exercises a power over him that rivals the force of a person's living presence. One day, as he stops to contemplate a hawthorn bush on the path by Swann's estate, he notices that a girl with "fair, reddish hair" is staring at him.[48] She has just enough time to sketch "an indelicate gesture" with one hand before her mother calls her "in a piercing tone of authority"(154/141).[49] The mother's call not only commands the girl's obedience—"securing uptake, taking effect and inviting a response"[50]—but supplies the narrator with an interpretant, endowing the otherwise anonymous girl with "an identity" that sets her apart from others and allows him to find her again later: "Thus was wafted to my ears the name of Gilberte, bestowed on me like a talisman [un talisman] which might, perhaps, enable me some day to rediscover her whom its syllables had just endowed with an identity, whereas the moment before she had been merely an uncertain image [une image incertaine]" (154–55/142). He conceives of the name as "a talisman," part of a magical charm. His name for the verbal act that lends certainty to the girl's "uncertain image," conferring actuality on one who has the potential not to be *for him*, is not magic, however, but love. There can be no love, moreover, without names. Even place-names inspire him with a "desire" that excites "something as profoundly personal as if it had been love, love for a person" (424/391). "Love" is the sign's relation to a reality that it never reaches.

The love-struck child-savage ranks the force of Gilberte's name on par with the forces of nature. A name is just one entelechy among others. Perhaps that is why he perceives no difference between verbal acts and physical ones:

> So it came to me, uttered across the heads of the stocks and jasmines, pungent and cool as the drops which fell from the green watering pipe; impregnating and irradiating the zone of pure air through which it had passed—and which it set apart and isolated—with the mystery of the life of her whom its syllables designated to the happy beings who lived and walked and traveled in her company; unfolding beneath the arch of the pink hawthorn, at the height of my shoulder, the quintessence of their familiarity—so exquisitely painful to myself—with her and the unknown world of her existence into which I should never penetrate. (155/142)

"Gilberte" joins "Bull" and "Thunder" in a mythopoeic language of one-word utterances. The narrator is the "primitive" who speaks it. Her name partakes of her "life" force and transmits it to her surroundings, acquiring the density of water and leaving palpable traces in the air: a question now of phûsis as logos. Later, in Paris, when he hears "Gilberte" ring out on the Champs-Elysées, he claims that he can feel the name brushing past his body, as if an "act of saying something" had joined the "the natural chain" of physical events (428/394). The utterance of her name now produces consequences "normally" reserved for bodies having mass and velocity, as if "Gilberte" had the "force" of a running fountain and as if its "trajectory" were governed not just by the rules of grammar and rhetoric but by the laws of momentum and gravity:

> "Goodbye, Gilberte, I'm going home now; don't forget we're coming to you this evening, after dinner." The name Gilberte passed close by me, evoking all the more forcefully the girl whom it labelled in that it did not merely refer to her, as one speaks of someone in his absence, but was directly addressed to her; it passed thus close by me, in action [*en action*] so to speak, with a force [*une puissance*] that increased with the curve of its trajectory [*son jet*] and the proximity of its target;—carrying in its wake, I could feel, the knowledge, the impressions concerning her to whom it was addressed that belonged not to me but to the friend who called it out, everything that, as she uttered the words, she recalled, or at least possessed in her memory, of their daily intimacy, of the visits that they paid to each other, of that unknown existence which was all the more inaccessible, all the more painful to me from being, conversely, so familiar, so tractable to this happy girl who let it brush past me without my being able to penetrate it. (428/394)

The friend performs an illocutionary act according to the conventions of polite society. She makes her friend a promise— "we're coming to you this evening"—and yet in uttering the friend's name, she liberates its entelechy. Without intending it, she promises the narrator access to an "existence" that has the potential to remain "unknown" to him, for the name she utters contains "everything" the narrator would like to know about Gilberte but cannot find out. The friend's promise sets in motion the potentiality of an impotentiality.

Naturally, when Gilberte comes into possession of the narrator's name, he is convinced that she has acquired a power over him, as if to name him sufficed to convoke his presence and control his movements. Indeed the act of naming transforms her, predictably, into a child-cannibal. It is not just his name that she holds between her lips but his body, stripped "naked." To be named is to be eaten alive. Could this be why the narrator never divulges his name to the reader in any definitive way?[51]

> I distinguished the impression of having been held for a moment in her mouth, myself, naked, without any of the social attributes which be-longed equally to her other playmates and, when she used my surname, to my parents, accessories of which her lips—by the effort she made,

a little after her father's manner, to articulate the words to which she wished to give a special emphasis—had the air of stripping, of divesting me, like the skin from a fruit of which one can swallow only the pulp. (437–38/403–4)

Is this another example of vivid description in the Homeric tradition? The metaphor that puts the narrator's "skin" into Gilberte's mouth at once gauges the force of his desire and satisfies it by displacement. His name partakes of his person, as if they were *in pari materia*. To manipulate one produces a change in the other, as required by the law of contiguous magic, which holds that things that were once in contact still act on each other from a distance.[52] But surely only a child or a savage would fail to tell verbal causes from physical effects, or those neurotics who, says Freud, "react just as seriously to thoughts as normal persons do to realities."[53]

Mana

Austin cautions that "philosophers" have traditionally "neglected" the study of illocutionary acts, preferring instead to treat "all problems" of discourse as "problems of 'locutionary usage,'" as if the many things that utterances do can be explained exclusively "in terms of 'the meanings of words.'"[54] This is the descriptive fallacy (100). "It was for too long the assumption of philosophers," he notes from the outset, "that the business of a 'statement' can only be to describe some state of affairs, or to 'state some fact,' which it must do either truly or falsely" (1). He proposes to supplement the study of locutions with a "doctrine of 'illocutionary forces.'" Austin's criticism of the philosophy of language, however, is not entirely accurate. Scholars had not in fact neglected the forces of discourse. Indeed by the time he lectured at Harvard in 1955, they had been discussing them for more than half a century. The debate did not take place in philosophy, though, but in anthropology, where "illocutionary forces" were assimilated to "the magic power of words."

Austin assumes "that the occasion of an utterance matters seriously, and that the words used are to some extent to be 'explained' by the 'context' in which they are designed to be or have actually been spoken in a linguistic interchange" (100). By 1955 this was hardly an original assumption. In their *General Theory of Magic*, published a decade before *Swann's Way*, Marcel Mauss and Henri Hubert argue that the sort of utterance in which "the occasion matters" most is the magical spell. For the "force" it deploys can only be "'explained'" by the "milieu" in which it is performed. Indeed

Mauss and Hubert perceive no limit between them: "The ideas of force and milieu are inseparable, coinciding in an absolute sense. They are expressed at the same time and through the same means. In fact ritual forms, those dispositions aimed at creating magical forces, are also the same as those which create the milieu and circumscribe it before, during or after the ceremony."[55] The "milieu" of a spell, like the "context" of an illocution, is not a physical location but a set of discursive conventions. The spell, like the illocution, is bound by rules. It is a formula uttered by someone who is authorized to utter it, who believes in its effectiveness, and who says it completely, correctly, and in the proper circumstances.[56] A spell performed with the wrong words or by the wrong person or in the wrong circumstances has no force. But what kind of force does a happily performed spell have?

Mauss and Hubert describe it as a "magical potential." The spell possesses dynamis, but not necessarily entelechy, for sometimes it is the negation of what it is the potentiality of. Although it is a nonmechanical force, Mauss and Hubert nevertheless define it in mechanical terms, as if to suggest that magical dynamis is not quite mechanical and yet not quite nonmechanical either: "The idea of magical force is moreover, from this point of view, quite comparable to our notion of mechanical force. In the same way as we call force the cause of apparent movements so magical force is properly the cause of magical effects: illness and death, happiness and health, etc" (107). Yet there is a link missing in the chain of magical causation. The cause and its effect are perceptible to the senses. The connection between them, though, is not. All the observer knows for sure is that when a spell is uttered, certain consequences usually follow. To say that one produces the other rests on a generalization from experience. The spell occurs in between the perceptible and the imperceptible. Its effectiveness depends on the perception of an imperception:[57]

> In this mysterious milieu, things no longer happen in the way they do in our world of the senses. Distance does not prevent contact. Desires and images can be immediately realized. It is the spiritual world and the world of spirits at the same time. Since everything is spiritual, anything may become a spirit. Yet although this power is illimitable and the world transcendental, things happen according to laws, those inevitable relations existing between things, relations between signs and words and the represented objects, laws of sympathy in general, laws of properties which are susceptible to being codified into a system of classifications. (107)

There is one region of the globe where, more than any other place, "force" and "milieu" come together to produce the sort of "one-word utterance" that, according to Austin, is typical of "primitive languages." "The idea," argue Mauss and Hubert, "is that found in Melanesia under the name of *mana*" (108). They credit its discovery to R. H. Codrington, who "admirably observed and described" it in his 1891 monograph, *The Melanesians: Studies in Their Anthropology and Folk-Lore* (108). Codrington's account encourages them to conclude that mana is both a physical action and a linguistic sign: "*Mana* is not simply a force, a being, it is also an action, a quality, a state. In other terms the word is a noun, an adjective and a verb" (108). The word "*mana*," they continue, variously means "a sorcerer's power, the magical quality of an object, a magical object, to be magical, to possess magical powers, to be under a spell, to act magically" (108). Sometimes a thing possesses "the thing called *mana*" without being mana; sometimes mana is a thing that "can be handled" and transmitted "through contact"; sometimes it is a force that brings inanimate things to life, "more especially the force of spirit beings, that is to say, the souls of ancestors and nature spirits" (109). Remarkably, "mana" is both the word for force and force itself. It is sign and object at once. "We could extend still further the meaning of this word," they speculate, "and maintain that *mana* is power *par excellence*, the genuine effectiveness of things" (111). Hence "mana" is the sort of sign that does what it describes. The word for the effectiveness of things is itself effective among things. It not only signifies the action of a power but sets a power into action, another case in which a discursive cause achieves physical effects: "This is what causes the net to bring in a good catch, makes the house solid and keeps the canoe sailing smoothly. In the farms it is fertility; in medicine it is either health or death" (111).

The utterance of such a word does not just act on the world but establishes a "world." This other world is a middle place (mi-lieu) in between discourse and nature, where there is no viable difference between the real and the ideal nor between discursive and mechanical forces. The word "mana" is for Mauss and Hubert what the name "Balbec" is for Proust's narrator:

> *Mana* is also a milieu, or more exactly functions as a milieu, which in itself is *mana*. It is a kind of internal, special world where everything happens as if *mana* alone were involved. It is the *mana* of the magician which works through the *mana* of the rite on the *mana* of the *tindalo* [Codrington says that a *tindalo* is the ghost of someone who had mana when alive], and which sets other *manas* in motion and so forth and so

on. In its actions and reactions there are no other forces involved apart
from *mana*. It is produced in a closed circuit, in which everything is
mana and which is itself *mana*. (112)

The "special world" is like the blank page, where, according to Peirce, the
reinscription of the sign lends definition to its object, actualizing what exists potentially by unfolding a series of replicas. In a mana milieu, a mana-
symbol determines a mana-interpretant toward a mana-object. The series is
ultimately circular, however, because its origin is immediately its end.

Codrington's interpretation is more cautious. He claims that mana is
"distinct from physical power" yet resides in physical things and produces
real, physical effects.[58] He conceives of it as a potentiality that exceeds the
limits of human potentiality. Mana makes it possible to act where action is
necessary but no action would otherwise be possible:

> The Melanesian mind is entirely possessed by the belief in a supernatural
> power or influence, called almost universally *mana*. This is what works
> to effect everything beyond the ordinary power of men, outside the com-
> mon processes of nature; it is present in the atmosphere of life, attaches
> itself to persons and to things, and is manifested by results which can
> only be ascribed to its operation. When one has got it he can use it and
> direct it, but its force may break forth at some new point; the presence
> of it is ascertained by proof. (118–19)

Although it is "impersonal," this more-than-natural "power" remains intimately "connected with some person who directs it." Codrington explains
that "all spirits have it, ghosts generally, some men" (119). He compares
it to heat, as if it were not just a magical but a characteristically tropical
potential: "all persons and things in which this supernatural power resides
are said to be *saka*, that is, hot. Ghosts that are powerful are *saka*; a man
who has knowledge of the things which have spiritual power is himself
saka; one who knows a charm which is *saka* mutters it over water, *saru'e*,
and makes the water 'hot,' *ha'asaka*" (191–92). Codrington makes the word
"mana" a general term for the living sign. He finds it personified in spirits
and claims that a spirit is both an image and an energy. It imitates the form
and exercises the life force of one who has died. When the living want mana,
therefore, they have to borrow it from ghosts: "If a stone is found to have a
supernatural power, it is because a spirit has associated itself with it; a dead
man's bone has with it *mana*, because the ghost is with the bone; a man

may have so close a connexion with a spirit or ghost that he has *mana* in himself also, and can so direct it as to effect what he desires" (119–20). The most effective way to establish a "connexion" with a spirit is to call it by name, for the name partakes of the soul no matter whether the body is living or dead. The illocutionary act of invocation is a "charm." Yet the Melanesians, he notes, call it a "mana": "certain forms of words, generally in the form of a song, have power for certain purposes; a charm of words is called a *mana*" (119). He explains that "a charm is powerful because the name of a spirit or ghost expressed in the form of words brings into it the power which the ghost or spirit exercises through it" (120).[59] To name a ghost is to set a ghostly power to work. This power, however, is the potentiality of an impotentiality. You acquire it by losing your life. Codrington's version of mana is a synonym for "entelechy," an exoticized variant of an idea that Peirce finds in Aristotle's *Metaphysics* and Proust's narrator, in place-names.

Nowhere is the mana of discourse more active than in the discourse in which mana itself is the object of inquiry. It discharges an excess of force in its own force-milieu. Lévi-Strauss argues that it is one of a class of signifiers that intervene where a word is pressingly required but none is presently available. Rhetoricians call them catachreses. The structural anthropologist calls them signifiers of the "mana type." His argument proceeds from Saussure's hypothesis that language is a system of differences without positive terms. The value of each linguistic unit is based on its contrast with the other units.[60] All of the units have to be simultaneously available in order for the system to function. Hence language could only have come into being "all at once." There was no evolution from a "primitive" language of one-word, multifunction utterances to a "civilized" language of multiword, single-function utterances. Rather, "a shift occurred from a stage when nothing had a meaning to another stage when everything had meaning," though "at the moment when the entire universe all at once became *significant*," he adds, "it was none the better *known* for being so."[61] Systems of thought grow out of the strife—or "fundamental opposition"— between "symbolism" and "knowledge." Symbolism comes about suddenly in now-time; knowledge "develops slowly and progressively" in future-oriented time (60). Symbolism, because it is based on relations of contrast, is generated out of the discontinuity between the signifier and the signified; knowledge, because it is based on relations of agreement, establishes areas of continuity between signifier and signified. The emergence of language gave humankind a detailed map of a vast territory, Lévi-Strauss explains, but people "spent millennia" determining which parts of the map, or signifier, correspond to "the different aspects" of the territory, or signified. What we call "progress" is a ceaseless cutting and matching of patterns from two incompatible levels (61).

The "mana type" enters into play in cases in which no match has been established between signifier and signified (63). We encounter a thing but have no name for it. So we resort to a stand-in. To explain the procedure, Lévi-Strauss cites "a most profound remark" made by Father Thavenet in the Jesuit Relations and cited by Mauss and Hubert. Thavenet's remark bears on "the Algonquin notion of *manitou*." He is concerned not with what it means but with what it does: "It more particularly designates any being which does not yet have a common name, which is unfamiliar; of a salamander, a woman said she was afraid: it was a *manitou*; people laughed at her, telling her the name salamander" (54).[62] Lévi-Strauss observes that "*manitou*" does not refer to a thing but "floats" over it instead, making it possible to discuss what is not yet named. Signifiers of this type do not mean; they act. Though they possess "a *zero symbolic value*," still they "enable symbolic thinking" to leap the gap between symbolism and knowledge, letting interpretation proceed where no discourse is possible but the failure of discourse is unthinkable (63). "That," according to Lévi-Strauss, "explains the apparently insoluble antinomies attaching to the notion of *mana*, which struck ethnographers so forcibly, and on which Mauss [and Hubert] shed light: force and action; quality and state; substantive, adjective and verb all at once; abstract and concrete; omnipresent and localised" (63–64). The zero signifier is a "pure" potential for meaning but is simultaneously the negation of whatever it is the potentiality of. It can take on any value at all because it has no value of its own.

Lévi-Strauss's discussion makes it possible to understand how the "mana type" draws its force from its milieu. The zero signifier sets to work in cases in which what can be said falls short of what can be known. Anthropology, according to Lévi-Strauss, is precisely such a case. Like every discursive formation, it suffers a rarity of statements, and the brute fact that few things, in all, can be said means that its language is too impoverished to cover the range of "indigenous thought." Empirical observation is constrained to draw on the resources of "aesthetic invention" but borrows so heavily that the discourse about magic can no longer be distinguished from the magic of discourse: "in one case," he concludes,

> the notion of *mana* does present those characteristics of a secret power,
> a mysterious force, which Durkheim and Mauss [and Hubert] attributed

to it: for such is the role it plays in their own system. *Mana* really is *mana* there. But at the same time, one wonders whether their theory of *mana* is anything other than a device for imputing properties to indigenous thought which are implied by the very peculiar place that the idea of *mana* is called on to occupy in their own thinking. (57)

Lévi-Strauss cannot do without the notion of a discursive force that Mauss and Hubert call mana, but he limits its operations to a narrowly defined milieu: mana "really is *mana*" in the discourse that describes it. To say "mana" there—and only there—is to perform a discursive act that has more-than-discursive consequences. The "power" that Mauss and Hubert call "mana" is the entelechy of their own discourse.[63] Lévi-Strauss adds that the same power provides "the surety of all art, all poetry, every mythic and aesthetic invention" (63). The "mana type" is the recourse of mythopoesis. What it "really is," is a blank where one sign is inscribed on another in the infinite project to make the vague more definite. "The notion of *mana* does not belong to the order of the real," he warns, "but to the order of thinking, which, even when it thinks itself, only ever thinks an object," even if it does not yet know what object it thinks (59). If all thought is in signs, and if signs facilitate the realization of the real, then the zero signifier is the theoretical starting point of an infinite process of growth, an ideal first sign.

Codrington supplies an example of the semiotic growth-process. When the agents of colonization come to the Melanesian islands, he remarks, they usually bring along a stock of signifiers of the mana type. Ironically, none of these signifiers is "mana" itself. European traders, for example, sometimes find it difficult to determine "the native name" for a place or a thing, so they traffic in counterfeit names instead. Similarly, they resort to the word "devil" whenever they encounter something unknown or unfamiliar. "The 'pigeon English,' which is sure to come in, carries its own deceits," Codrington adds, "'plenty devil' serves to convey much information; a chief's grave is 'devil stones,' the dancing ground of a village is a 'devil ground,' the drums are idols, a dancing club is a 'devil stick.'"[64] The floating signifier is not something inert. Instead it exercises a force of "mythic and aesthetic invention." The trade in counterfeit names yields a surplus of counterfeit things. If a missionary or visitor "expects to see idols," then "he sees them," and if "a Solomon islander fashions the head of his lime-box stick into a grotesque figure," it is not long before "it becomes the subject of a woodcut as 'a Solomon Island god'" (118). The floating signifier, whether "devil" or "idol," never floats for long. What it lacks in sense and reference, it supplements with a surplus of entelechy. To utter it not only produces real consequences but brings real objects into emergence: objects that do not emerge *until* they are misnamed.

Nor can Malinowski do without the entelechy of the mana type, not even after he expels the word "mana" from the anthropology of magic. In his 1925 essay "Magic, Science and Religion," he bluntly states that "this force as described by Codrington is almost the exact opposite of the magical virtue as found embodied in the mythology of savages, in their behavior, and in the structure of their magical formulas." [65] There is simply no such thing as mana. It is a signifier without a corresponding signified. Thus "mana" itself is a signifier of the mana type. The "real virtue of magic" resides, rather, "only in the spell and in its rite" (77), the effects of which are fixed by convention. Malinowski admits that "the very word" magic seduces the nonspecialist into believing in the existence of magical forces, for it carries a connotation of limitless potentiality: "Magic—the very word seems to reveal a world of mysterious and unexpected possibilities!" (69). Thus "magic" too is a signifier of the mana type. It signifies a potentiality that has not yet negated what it is the potentiality of, although the only place where such a potentiality exists, Malinowski claims, is discourse, especially poetry and myth. "Magic" really is magic there. As long as it confines itself to a circumscribed context, it remains "genuinely effective": "[the word] 'magic' seems to stir up in everyone some hidden mental forces, some lingering hopes in the miraculous, some dormant beliefs in man's mysterious possibilities. Witness to this is the power which the words *magic, spell, charm, to bewitch* and *to enchant*, possess in poetry, where the inner value of words, the emotional forces which they still release, survive longest and are revealed most clearly" (70). Malinowski explains the effectiveness of a spell and its rite as an effect of projection. The power we perceive in them is proportionate to the strength of the feelings we invest in them. And they echo our strongest hopes and fears: "a strong emotional experience, which spends itself in a purely subjective flow of images, words, and acts of behavior, leaves a very deep conviction of its reality, as if of some practical and positive achievement, as if of something done by a power revealed to man" (81). Ironically, Malinowski's analysis, which is based on his fieldwork in the Trobriand Islands, reproduces Tylor's hypothesis, which is distilled from archival study: those who trust in spells mistake relations between ideas ("emotional experiences") for relations between things ("reality").

Every utterance, however, carries a force of breaking with its present context. And that includes the spell too. Not even Malinowski can purge "modern anthropology" of the lingering forces of "poetry" and "myth." He casts mana out in "Magic, Science, and Religion" only to bring it back in the dedication to his 1925 lecture "Myth in Primitive Psychology." The dedication is addressed to "Sir James Frazer." Malinowski likens the act of uttering it to the performance of a spell. He stresses that it is part of a larger magical rite performed in celebration of his "tribe's" totem: Frazer's *Golden Bough*. When he utters it, he takes on the face and voice of a "magician in a savage tribe." [66] The spell is an auto-prosopopoeia:

> We are gathered here to celebrate the annual totemic festival of *The Golden Bough*; to revive and strengthen the bonds of anthropological union; to commune with the source and symbol of our anthropological interest and affection. I am but your humble spokesman, in expressing our joint admiration to the great writer and his classical works: *The Golden Bough, Totemism and Exogamy, Folklore in the Old Testament, Psyche's Task*, and *The Belief in Immortality*. As a true officiating magician in a savage tribe would have to do, I have to recite the whole list, so that the spirit of the works (their "mana") may dwell among us. (94)

The spell does not convoke Frazer's ghost. It summons up the force of his discourse. No matter what he says elsewhere, Malinowski suggests here that this force, which he describes as a spirit power, can only be called "'mana.'" He cites each of Frazer's titles individually, as if to suggest that uttering their names is a necessary step toward convoking their author's soul, for the soul resides not only in the name but in every text that bears it.

Why does Malinowski banish mana in one essay and call it back in another? One answer is that he is repaying an intellectual debt where no repayment is possible but nonpayment is unthinkable—and only a magical utterance has the power to actualize what exists impotentially. Another answer emerges at the end of "Magic, Science, and Religion," the essay that banishes mana from anthropological discourse. "Round every big magician," he remarks, "there arises a halo made up of stories about his wonderful cures or kills, his catches, his victories, his conquests in love. In every savage society such stories form the backbone of belief in magic, for, supported as they are by the emotional experiences which everyone has had himself, the running chronicle of magical miracles establishes its claims beyond any doubt or cavil." [67] Frazer, then, is the "big magician." Malinowski is the little magician who aspires to replace him. The list of Frazer's titles chronicles the big magician's "victories" and "miracles." When the little magician recites them, he catches some of the glow of the big magician's "halo," investing his own discourse with a dose of Frazer's power. Mana may not be mana in reality, but it "really is" mana among the members of Malinowski's "tribe." What he says elsewhere of mythology he says here of anthropology: "it is not an idle tale, but a hard-worked active force"— indeed a "living reality." [68] A mythopoeic utterance acts rather than means. It does not represent the world that already is but completes a world that never lost its potentiality to not-be.

Waitangi

If signifiers of the "mana type" intervene wherever a gap opens between symbolism and knowledge, then it is more than ironic that "mana" failed to be uttered in the one context of the nineteenth century in which it was the only word capable of spanning the gulf between what was irrevocably uttered and what was understood. In February 1840, an assembly of delegates representing the British Crown and several autonomous Māori tribes gathered at the village of Waitangi to negotiate the treaty that delivered the colony of New Zealand into being. A string of words inscribed on a blank page and read aloud achieved what magical spells are reputed to do: it made an idea real, inscribing a European society onto the space already occupied by the Māori societies. An illocutionary act of such force was several decades in the making.

Political relations between Great Britain and the Māori societies date back at least to 1769, when James Cook and his party began mapping the coast of Aotearoa.[69] In the 1790s, ships from Britain, the United States, and the colonies of New South Wales and Van Diemens Land came to hunt for whales and seals. The crews put in to local harbors to rest, barter for provisions, and cut timber for spars. Some whaling stations developed into permanent settlements (31–33). By the late 1820s, Māori and Europeans were conducting a substantial trade in timber and flax. European merchants settled along the coast, and Māori sailors joined the crews of whaling ships (32–34). Māori farmers cultivated staples for export to New South Wales and in return imported weapons, tools, clothing, and luxury goods (35). The Anglican Church Missionary Society established a mission in the Bay of Islands in 1814; the Wesleyan Missionary Society landed in Whangaroa in 1823; a Roman Catholic mission opened at Hokianga in 1838 (36–37). The missionaries helped with the diversification of Māori agriculture and translated Christian literature into Māori. Meanwhile Māori learned to read and write in their own language.

Māori and Europeans soon acknowledged that they needed a way to regulate these encounters. In the early 1830s Māori leaders twice appealed to

Great Britain to defend them from the abuses of European adventurers.[70] In 1831, the French warship *Favorite* visited the Bay of Islands, and there were rumors that France was about to annex New Zealand. A group of northern chiefs asked the king of England for protection (11–12). In 1830 the brig *Elizabeth* transported a war party to Akaroa, where they executed a chief and members of his family.[71] The chief's relatives protested to the governor of New South Wales, who advised the British government to establish a resident in New Zealand, "preferably supported with a warship" (12). The Colonial Office appointed James Busby, who arrived in New Zealand in May 1833 (12–13). In 1834 he convened a meeting of Māori chiefs to select a national flag, since without one, ships built in New Zealand were subject to seizure on the high seas. The delegates used the meeting to form "an embryonic Māori government" (19). In 1835 thirty-four chiefs issued a Declaration of Independence recognizing New Zealand as an autonomous state and requesting the protection of the king of England.[72] The signatories called themselves the United Tribes and affirmed that they continued to exercise "sovereign power" and "authority" over their traditional territories. In the Māori text, "sovereign power" is translated as *te kingitanga* (the English noun "king" combined with a Māori suffix meaning "-ship"); "authority" is translated as *te mana.*[73]

When war broke out among Māori groups in the Bay of Islands in 1837, British settlers and traders petitioned the Crown for "relief." At Busby's request, HMS *Rattlesnake* was dispatched from New South Wales under the command of William Hobson, who later advised the Colonial Office to establish trading "factories" in New Zealand and place them under British jurisdiction (23–24). Busby proposed a British protectorate instead (24–25). In May of 1837 the newly formed New Zealand Association, later the New Zealand Company, outlined a plan for aggressive colonization (28). Faced with the prospect of uncontrolled immigration, the Colonial Office intervened. Hobson was appointed "consul" in February 1839. He was instructed to "protect" the interests of Māori and to establish a self-governing British colony (28). Because the Crown had recognized New Zealand's independence in 1835, the secretary of state for colonies decided that Māori leaders would have to cede sovereignty before a colony could be established (30–31). Hobson sailed for New Zealand in August 1839 to negotiate cession, install a colonial administration, and oversee the purchase of land for settlement. New Zealand was to be a "dependency" of New South Wales (29–30). No provision was made for Māori self-government.

Hobson arrived in Sydney on Christmas Eve 1839, where he was sworn in as lieutenant governor of any territory he might annex in New Zealand.

He sailed into the Bay of Islands on January 29, 1840. The next day he informed a meeting of settlers that he was assuming the position of lieutenant governor. That is, he asserted Great Britain's authority before he secured Māori consent.[74] Māori leaders were invited to attend an assembly at Waitangi on February 5, 1840, to strike a treaty. First, however, the text of the treaty had to be drafted to the secretary's specifications. Hobson wrote a preamble and three articles with the aid of his secretary, J. S. Freeman. Then he fell ill. Busby produced another draft consisting of three articles and a postscript.[75] The English text of the treaty is thought to combine Hobson's preamble with Busby's draft, although Hobson later submitted several versions to the Colonial Office (37, 85). On February 4, a draft was entrusted to the Anglican missionary Henry Williams, who translated it into Māori with his son Edward. Neither of them was an experienced translator. Nor did they translate the treaty into the local Ngapuhi dialect (37–38). Instead they modeled the translation of the treaty on previous translations of English prayers, liturgies, and scriptures.[76] "The language of the Treaty of Waitangi," Ruth Ross observed in the 1970s, "is not indigenous Maori; it is missionary Maori, specifically Protestant missionary Maori."[77] The result was an illocutionary act of unconventional force.

Fifty years later, William Colenso, the printer for the Anglican mission, published an "eyewitness" account of the negotiations, which were conducted on the lawn of the resident's house. According to Colenso, Hobson opened the meeting by telling Māori leaders that the queen of England was offering them her "protection." He read the English text of the treaty aloud, and then Henry Williams read the shorter Māori translation.[78] Thus two versions of the treaty were tabled for negotiation. Both outlined the consequences of the illocutionary act of signing. The preamble to the English text says that the Crown intends to establish "a settled form of Civil Government" in New Zealand.[79] Article 1 says that in signing the treaty the chiefs and tribes of New Zealand agree "absolutely and without reservation" to cede sovereignty to the Crown. Article 2 affirms that, in signing, the chiefs and tribes retain full, undisturbed, and exclusive possession of their lands and estates, forests and fisheries, and other properties, whether owned individually or collectively, but grants the Crown a right of preemption over any land put up for sale. Article 3 promises to extend the rights and privileges of British subjects to all Māori. The Māori text, however, promised a different set of consequences.

After the two treaties were read aloud, Busby reassured Māori delegates that "the governor" had not come to take their land from them but to "secure them in the possession" of the lands they had not already sold.[80] "Sud-

denly," says Colenso, Te Kemara rose up and declared that settlers and missionaries had already stolen his ancestors' territory. He advised Hobson to
go home (17–18). The chiefs who spoke next were more favorably disposed
toward the treaty, but the debate was hampered by the difficulty of translating between English and Māori. Some members of the English-speaking
audience pointed out that Henry Williams was neglecting to translate what
some Māori were saying about the land purchases of missionaries, including those of Williams himself (19–21). The chiefs retired to consider their
response, and Hobson proposed to reconvene the assembly two days later,
on February 7.

The Māori delegation decided to resume negotiations the following
morning. By the time Hobson's party arrived at the hastily reconvened
assembly, some chiefs had already left. The Māori text of the treaty, copied onto parchment, was laid out on a table, and after further discussion
the chiefs agreed to sign. While Heke, the first signatory, was approaching
the treaty table, Colenso asked Hobson (or stages himself asking Hobson)
whether he thought the Māori delegates fully understood the illocutionary
force of "the articles of the treaty which they [were] now called upon to
sign."[81] Colenso reminds Hobson that Māori leaders are "quite children in
their ideas" and cannot be assumed "fully to comprehend a document of this
kind" (33). Busby, replying on Hobson's behalf, repeats a remark that Heke
made the day before: "The Native mind could not comprehend these things:
they must trust to the advice of their missionaries" (33). Colenso reminds
Busby that the locutionary act of stating the treaty's consequences must be
fully performed in order for the illocutionary act of signing to be considered
happily performed. "Yes," he tells him, "the missionaries should explain
the thing in all its bearings to the Natives, so that it should be their own
very act and deed. Then, in case of a reaction taking place," he continues,
"the Natives could not turn round on the missionary and say, 'You advised
me to sign that paper, but never told me what were the contents thereof'"
(33). Afterward Hobson's agents traveled to villages on the north and south
islands to persuade other chiefs to join the treaty. On May 21, 1840, Hobson
proclaimed British sovereignty over both islands, bringing negotiations to
an abrupt end.[82]

Mauss and Hubert predicted more than a century ago that "a closer analysis of New Zealand magic where *mana* plays a role . . . would provide similar conclusions to the studies carried out in Melanesia."[83] Nothing could be
further from the case. What stands out among the things that have been said
about mana since 1891 is the force of a text in which "mana" failed to be said
"correctly and completely." According to Claudia Orange, Hobson was well

aware "that unless a treaty were entered into 'intelligently' by the Maori, it would be a 'mere illusion and pretence which ought to be avoided.'"[84] But other scholars argue that the Māori translation failed to state the treaty's illocutionary consequences. The two versions of the treaty, therefore, produced one set of consequences for the colonizers and another for Māori.[85] The debate hinges on the way Williams and son translated, or rather failed to translate, the Māori word for political sovereignty. That word is mana. Ruth Ross opened the debate in 1972. She argues that the translation is the Treaty of Waitangi proper, for "it is the Maori text which was signed at Waitangi on 6 February 1840, and at other places on subsequent dates."[86] She offers compelling reasons for concluding that the copy is more original than the original itself. The English text of article 1 says that in signing, Māori leaders agree to cede "sovereignty" to the British Crown. The translation, however, renders "sovereignty" as *kawanatanga*, which was not "originally" a Māori word. Bruce Biggs explains that *kawana* is a Māori variant of the English "governor," whereas *-tanga* is a Māori suffix meaning "-ship."[87] Hence *kawanatanga* means "governorship." Missionaries coined the word in 1833 to translate the English "governance" and "kingdom" into Māori.[88] According to Biggs, neither of these words had a referent in precolonial Māori culture. Their referents were imported into Māori from English prayers and the English Bible. Thus *kawanatanga* was a zero signifier enlisted to fill the gap between Māori symbolism and English knowledge: "as there had never been any supra-tribal authority in New Zealand, there is no way that any Māori, who had not at least visited Australia or England, could have understood much of what Williams meant."[89] The appropriate translation for "sovereignty" is *mana*. Ross speculates that in the absence of this word, so extensively debated in other contexts, Māori signatories could not have fully gauged the treaty's force. The treaty told them they were ceding *kawanatanga*, governorship, but in signing what they ceded instead was *mana whenua*, sovereignty over land. When considered as a locutionary act, the treaty said one thing, but when considered as an illocutionary act, it did something very different. The meaning of the translation concealed the illocutionary force of the act of signing: "if the Maori concept of *mana* had been seen as a part of the European concept of sovereignty," Ross asks, "would any New Zealander have signed the treaty?"[90] Colenso suggests that when Kawiti, Hakiro, and Tareha signed, they understood that they were agreeing to the appointment of a British governor, not to the cession of sovereignty over land.[91] Tareha, for one, rejects the notion that a "foreigner" has the authority to govern him or his people: "We will not be ruled over. What! thou, a foreigner, up, and I down! Thou high, and I,

Tareha, the great chief of the Ngapuhi tribes, low! No, no; never, never" (24). In signing, he let the British governor rule with him, not over him. The cession of "governorship" entailed neither political subordination nor loss of territorial sovereignty. Ranginui Walker agrees that "if sovereignty had been translated as *mana whenua,* 'sovereignty over land,'" then the chiefs would not have misjudged the treaty's illocutionary consequences. And it is unlikely that they would have signed it. "That the Treaty did not appear to convey anything substantial to the Crown from the Māori viewpoint," he remarks, "is encapsulated in the comment [made in April 1840] by the Kaitaia chief Nopera Panakareao: 'The shadow of the land goes to Queen Victoria but the substance remains to us.'"[92]

The English text of article 2 acknowledges that Māori retain "full possession" of their lands and estates, forests and fisheries, and so forth. The Māori translation of the same article translates "full possession" as *tino rangatiratanga.* The word *rangatiratanga* is another missionary neologism.[93] *Rangatira,* however, is a traditional Māori word for "chief." The Māori translation of the Lord's Prayer, for example, uses *rangatiratanga* in place of "kingdom" in the phrase "Thy kingdom come." Thus *rangatira-tanga* means "chieftainship." Walker argues that although it is a neologism, *rangatiratanga* is not therefore a zero signifier since *rangatira* is conventionally associated with the concept of political sovereignty.[94] "Rangatiratanga over land," moreover, "is inseparable from the word mana."[95] I. W. Kawharu explains that *rangatira* signifies the potential for greatness. People are born to it, but they have to prove themselves worthy of it by performing great actions, which cannot be done without mana, the individual's capacity "to lead." Mana buttresses a chief's authority, and the chief's authority supplies the ground for the tribe's sovereignty: "[a] *rangatira* is a trustee for his people."[96] Walker points out that "from the Māori viewpoint, the guarantee of the rangatiratanga of their lands is equivalent to the guarantee of their sovereignty."[97]

He concludes that in signing the treaty, Māori leaders ceded governorship to the Crown, and the Crown agreed to protect Māori land tenure, social organization, and valuable possessions, including natural resources. The signing "confirmed" Māori sovereignty and gave the Crown "the right to establish a governor" who was to rule at the chiefs' "behest" and on their "behalf."[98] Kawhuru concludes that "for the Māori, power was to be *shared,* while for the Crown, power was to be *transferred,* with the Crown as sovereign and the Māori as subject."[99] Māori agreed to a restricted form of settlement, whereas the Crown agreed to enforce British law among settlers and to defend Māori territory from conquest by other nations.

From 1891, when Codrington started the craze, until 1950, when Lévi-Strauss brought it abruptly to a close, the discourse of anthropology could not stop speaking of mana. Yet the Treaty of Waitangi proved curiously incapable of uttering it between February 5 and May 21, 1840. The treaty generated a surplus of illocutionary force by occluding the word that in other, later contexts would come to signify the force of discourse.[100] When Māori leaders signed the treaty, it did not say what it was going to do, and after they signed, it did what they did not know it had said. Its constative failure endowed it with a rich performativity. The meaning it evoked was inversely proportional to the force it discharged. Only a notion of the "mana type" can explain how a text supplements its locutionary poverty with an illocutionary surplus. As long as scholars deny the possibility of a force that is neither entirely discursive nor entirely physical, it will go on escaping criticism at the very moment it sets to work.

Actual Ideas

Swann entertains the possibility of such a force even before Proust's narrator does. The child-savage discovers it in place-names. Swann encounters it in the "little phrase" from Vinteuil's sonata, which he associates with his unrequited love for Gilberte's mother, Odette de Crécy, later Madame Swann. When he hears the sonata during an evening concert at the home of the marquise de Saint-Euverte, it launches him into a meditation on the entelechy of musical discourse. His obsession with Odette has caused a minor scandal in his circle, where a "gentleman" is not supposed to fall in love with a "courtesan," and although the affair causes him genuine suffering (he knows that Odette does not love him), his friends and acquaintances dismiss it "as an insignificant" though regrettable "aberration."[101] The concert, however, is a rite. The performance of Vinteuil's "utterance" is a spell. The musicians who perform it are magicians. They conjure up a spirit: "the musicians were not nearly so much playing the little phrase as performing the rites [les rites] on which it insisted before it would consent to appear, and proceeding to utter the incantations necessary [incantations nécessaires] to procure, and to prolong for a few moments, the miracle of its apparition" (378/347). When the spirit-phrase finally arrives in answer to their invocation, she "speaks" to Swann about his censored love and accords it the dignity he feels it deserves.

Swann is an animist. The five-note phrase that comes to life before his ears and addresses him with a human voice is, paradoxically, an utterance that speaks. It is discourse personified. What it says has the same effect on

Swann that the sound of his daughter's name will later have on the narrator: "Swann felt its presence [*la sentait présente*] like that of a protective
goddess, a confidante of his love, who, in order to be able to come to him
through the crowd and to draw him aside to speak to him, had disguised herself in this sweeping cloak of sound" (378/348). Swann perceives no difference between the sequence of signs (the "cloak of sound") and its purported
referent (the "confidant of his love"). To perform the one is to convoke the
other. The performance actualizes what exists impotentially. His guardian
spirit may not be real, but she has a very real effect on him. She exercises a
force that is not quite discursive and yet not quite physical either, provok-
ing a scene of recognition that brings his struggle for recognition to an end:

> He felt that he was no longer in exile and alone since she, who addressed
> herself to him, was whispering to him of Odette. For he had no longer,
> as of old, the impression that Odette and he were unknown to the little
> phrase. Had it not often been the witness of their joys ? (378)

Her arrival is at once a statement and an action, locution and illocution. In
speaking to him of his state of feeling, which seems "trivial" to others but
is "serious" for him, she transforms it, drawing him out of his solitude and
dispelling his melancholy:

> For the little phrase, unlike them, whatever opinion it might hold on
> the transience of these states of soul, saw in them something not, as all
> these people did, less serious than the events of everyday life, but, on the
> contrary, so far superior to it as to be alone worth while expressing. It
> was the charms [*charmes*] of an intimate sadness that it sought to imi-
> tate, to re-create, and their very essence, for all that it consists in being
> incommunicable and in appearing trivial to everyone save him who ex-
> periences them, had been captured and made visible by the little phrase.
> So much so that it caused their value to be acknowledged. (379/348–49)

The phrase does not reflect his "sadness" but recasts it in a form that commands respect instead of ridicule. Hence she personifies the sort of discourse
that completes what it imitates: the living "presence" of general mimesis.

Proust's conjuration scene appears to confirm Malinowski's account of
the effectiveness of spells. Swann's jealousy and self-pity join to produce
"a strong emotional experience" that leaves behind a "deep conviction"
of reality, "as if of something done by a power revealed to man." Yet the
entelechy of music is not limited to the sphere of emotion. Swann's inter-

pretation of the phrase brings him into an encounter with a wider "world" of living signs. He conceives of them as "actual ideas": ideas that actualize what has the potential both to be and to not-be. Ever since "the love of music" had been "born in him," the narrator explains, "Swann had regarded musical *motifs* as actual ideas [*véritables idées*], of another world, of another order, ideas veiled in shadow, unknown, impenetrable to the human mind, but none the less perfectly distinct from one another, unequal among themselves in value and significance" (379–80/349). Swann's doctrine of actual ideas is closer to Peirce than to Plato. They are the sort of signs that proceed from the vague to the definite. Peirce calls them living generals. Swann credits them with "showing us what richness, what variety lies hidden, unknown to us, in that vast, unfathomed and forbidding night of our soul which we take to be an impenetrable void" (380). Peirce argues that the thoughts inscribed in this void, or blank space, are habits, and that habit determines the "suchness" of what exists. The limits of thought fix the limits of being. Sometimes, though, there occurs an event so unexpected, so "surprising," that it breaks thought's habits and thereby alters reality's limits. Yet the moment of surprise does not last long, for cognition quickly brings the new discovery into "order" by gathering it under a familiar idea. As one category crumbles, another forms in the ruins. Nevertheless every change in the order of thought precipitates a corresponding change in the order of being.[102] What was formerly "unknown" comes to emergence; what was "hidden" acquires definition. Peirce's term for the logic that brings anomalous events under general rules is "abduction." Others call it hypothetical reasoning. Abduction, furthermore, is how newness enters the world, making the "void" into the "solid" (380). And no possibility is excluded. Abduction assumes that every potentiality is a potential to be and to not-be. When we abduct, "there is not the slightest scintilla of logical justification for any assertion that a given sort of result will, as a matter of fact, either *always* or *never* come to pass."[103] Abduction actualizes what exists potentially and *im*potentially.

Swann mistakes the logic of abduction for the casting of a spell. He conceives of it, in classically animist fashion, as the crystallization of the ideal into the real: "In [Vinteuil's] little phrase, although it might present a clouded surface to the eye of reason, one sensed a content so solid, so consistent, so explicit, to which it gave so new, so original a force, that those who once heard it preserved the memory of it on an equal footing with the ideas of the intellect" (380). He not only endows the phrase with a "real existence" but ranks it "on the same footing as certain other notions without material equivalent, such as our notions of light, of sound, or perspective, of physical pleasure." [104] Peirce calls such notions "legisigns": general ideas, such as "light" and "sound," at work in events—hence not just actual but actualizing ideas. Swann shares Peirce's savage realism. He does not limit the interpretation of living signs to music. He extends it to natural events. Vinteuil is as daring an experimenter as "a Lavoisier or an Ampère," Swann thinks, because like them he had "the audacity" to investigate "the secret laws that govern an unknown force," discovering the general concept, or legisign, that determines the suchness of things (382). [105] Meanwhile Swann, even as others ridicule him, makes a discovery of his own. He finds a life force, or entelechy, at work in musical discourse. And the novel suggests he is right: "Swann was not mistaken when he believed in the real existence of this phrase"; he simply personifies a legisign as an anthropomorphic spirit (382). The narrator confirms that the rest of the audience experiences the force of Vinteuil's "utterance" as deeply as Swann does:

> Swann dared not move, and would have liked to compel all the other people in the room to remain still also, as if the slightest movement might imperil the magic presence, supernatural [le prestige surnaturel], delicious, frail, that was so soon to vanish. But no one, as it happened, dreamed of speaking. The ineffable utterance of one solitary man, absent, perhaps dead (Swann did not know whether Vinteuil was still alive), breathed out above the rites of those two hierophants [the violinist and the pianist], sufficed to arrest the attention of three hundred minds, and made of that platform on which a soul [une âme] was thus called into being one of the noblest altars on which a supernatural ceremony could be performed. (383/352–53)

Afterward, the comtesse de Monteriender, "famed for her imbecilities," informs him that the performance of the sonata is the most astonishing thing she has witnessed "since the table turning" (383–84). She is right to conclude that the story in which she is a character borrows its imagery from the discourse about animism. Her imbecility lies in trivializing it.

CHAPTER FOUR

Commodity Totemism

> Animism spiritualized the object, whereas industrialism objectifies the spirits of men.—*Theodor W. Adorno and Max Horkheimer, "The Concept of Enlightenment"*

Participation

Do things think? Only a hardcore animist would say so, but then only the animist knows how to talk to them. "There is no event or thing in either animate or inanimate nature," writes Walter Benjamin in "On Language as Such and on the Language of Man," an essay written in 1916 but unpublished in his lifetime, "that does not in some way partake of language, for it is in the nature of each one to communicate its mental contents [*geistigen Inhalt*]."[1] The young Benjamin discovers "mental being" (*geistig Wesen*) in "absolutely everything." How does he know that things think? He overhears them when they speak: "the fact" is, he explains, "that we cannot imagine a total absence of language in anything" (62). The "mental being" of things is not the idea we have of them, therefore, but the idea they have of themselves.

Benjamin affirms that "all expression" is the "direct expression" of mind: "What does language communicate? It communicates the mental being [*geistige Wesen*] corresponding to it" (63/142). After so much talk of spirits, it is impossible to ignore the connotations of the phrase *geistige Wesen*. The adjective *geistige* typically means "mental" or "intellectual," while the noun *Geist* means "mind" and "spirit" and even "ghost." Benjamin's English translator is correct to render *geistige Wesen* as "mental being," but the German also connotes, as a kind of ghostly surplus, the notion of "spirit-being." Kant says it is *Geist* in the "aesthetic sense": *Geist* defined not as mind, but as the "animating principle in the mind."[2] Thales, according to Aristotle, thought that "all things are full of gods."[3] Benjamin speculates that things are full of *Geist*. What language communicates are the souls of things. It has mana in Codrington's sense. By the standards of his day, then, the "young" Benjamin gives the philosophy of language a savage turn. He endorses the first principles of animism.

A thing's mental being—which is simultaneously its spirit-being—overlaps its linguistic being without remainder. "That which in a mental entity is communicable," says Benjamin, "*is* its language" (63). By "is" he means "is immediately" (63). The linguistic sign does not stand for a thought that corresponds to a thing. "This view," he cautions, "is the bourgeois conception of language" (65). He proposes an animist conception instead. Mental being, for the animist, is not an exclusive property of human beings. Nor is it limited to animals generally. Everything that is possesses *geistig Wesen*. And that includes "inanimate" things. Furthermore, mental being communicates itself *in*, not *through*, language. Language is not a vehicle of expression. It is the seat of both human and thingly self-consciousness. Benjamin considers it a question "of the highest metaphysical importance," whether "mental being—not only of man (for that is necessary) but also of things, and thus mental being as such—can from the point of view of linguistic theory be described as of linguistic nature" (66). His answer is that "mental being" is "identical" with "linguistic being": "Language is thus the mental being of things" (66). Not only does everything think, but all thought is in signs. What is more, the thing, insofar as it thinks, is itself a sign: "If mental being is identical with linguistic being, then a thing, by virtue of its mental being, is a medium of communication" (66). In communicating its linguistic being, it communicates its own self-consciousness. Language is the coming to presence of the spirits of things: a conjuration.

The "bourgeois conception" holds that language mediates between cognition and its object. When we want to state what we know about the thing, especially if the thing itself is not present, we take the detour of the sign.[4] The animist conception holds that language is the immediate mediation of one mental being with another. The animist sign is something "magical":

Mediation, which is the immediacy of all mental communication [*geistigen Mitteilung*], is the fundamental problem of linguistic theory, and if one chooses to call this immediacy magic, then the primary problem of language is its magic [*Magie*]. At the same time, the notion of the magic of language points to something else: its infiniteness. This is conditional on its immediacy. For precisely because nothing is communicated

through language, what is communicated *in* language cannot be exter-
nally limited or measured. (64/142–43)

Benjamin's solution to the "primary problem of language" dispenses with
the principle of noncontradiction and embraces what Frazer characterizes
as "the principles of primitive philosophy."[5] The "magic" of language lies
in its capacity to balance two opposing possibilities at once. It is, impossibly, both "mediation" and "immediacy." In a word, it is immediation.

Frazer discovers immediation at the core of homeopathic, or imitative,
magic. The "primitive philosophers" who speak from the pages of *The
Golden Bough* echo Benjamin's premise that spirit-being communicates itself *in*, not through, language. When you speak your name, they argue, you
hold your soul in your mouth. Each is immediately present in the medium
of the other. The soul, moreover, consists of two elements: it is both a self-
conscious, "mental being" and a living, bodily force. Hence if you speak
your name too freely, you risk not only losing your judgment but damaging
your "constitution":

> so these primitive philosophers may have argued, when a man lets his
> own name pass his lips, he is parting with a living piece of himself,
> and if he persists in so reckless a course he must certainly end by dis-
> sipating his energy and shattering his constitution. Many a broken-down
> debauchee, many a feeble frame wasted with disease, may have been
> pointed out by these simple-minded moralists to their awe-struck dis-
> ciples as a fearful example of the fate that must sooner or later overtake
> the profligate who indulges immoderately in the seductive habit of men-
> tioning his own name. (286)

The immediation of name and soul supplies magicians with a powerful homeopathic technique, for if you know what people call themselves, then
you can control how they conduct themselves:

> When the Sulka of New Britain are near the territory of their enemies
> the Gaktei, they take care not to mention them by their proper name,
> believing that were they to do so, their foes would attack and slay them.
> Hence in these circumstances they speak of the Gaktei as *o lapsiek*, that
> is, "the rotten tree trunks," and they imagine that by calling them that
> they make the limbs of their dreaded enemies ponderous and clumsy like
> logs. This example illustrates the extremely materialistic view which
> these savages take of the nature of words; they suppose that the mere

utterance of an expression signifying clumsiness will homeopathically
affect with clumsiness the limbs of their distant foemen. (288)

The "young" Benjamin agrees with Frazer's savage philosophers, who are
themselves creatures of discourse, that spirit-being resides in the name
more than in any other linguistic form. "The name is that *through* which,
and *in* which, language [the mental being of things] communicates itself
absolutely. In the name," he continues, in a deliberate tautology, "the mental entity that communicates itself is language."[6] Only people, however,
have proper names. And only people are permitted to say them aloud. The
language of things is "nameless" and mute (74). How can things communicate their mental being if they are forbidden to speak? "They can communicate to one another only through a more or less material community.
This community is immediate and infinite, like every linguistic communication; it is magical [*magisch*]," he argues, "(for there is also a magic [*Magie*] of matter)" (67/147). Benjamin, like Frazer's "primitive philosophers,"
takes an "extremely materialistic view" of language. Homeopathic magic
works on the premise that "like produces like."[7] The language of things
works on the premise that like communicates with like. Matter speaks.
Things themselves are signs, not linguistic signs, but likenesses: the sort of
signs that Peirce calls icons.[8] Things speak together by imitating each other.
"The communication of matter in its magical community," Benjamin repeats almost two decades later, in a 1933 fragment, "takes place through
similarity."[9] Similarity is a medium of immediate communication: an immediation. What it communicates is *geistig Wesen*: spirit-being.

Things communicate with each other by resembling each other, and
they resemble each other by mirroring something that none of them is. For
each is the medium of something they have immediately in common. As
Andrew Lang puts it in *The Secret of the Totem*, "things equal to the same
thing are equal to each other."[10] What is the ground of this immediation?
"In the things from which it shines back silently and in the mute magic of
nature," says the "mature" Benjamin, "God's word has become the communication of matter in magical community" (718). The mental being,
"if not the soul," of things is not language "as such" but the language of
God. Spirit-being is what survives of the divine word in things. One thing is
similar to another because all bear a trace of the absolute performative that
spoke them into being. They partake of one another insofar as they partake
of it. Benjamin assimilates animism to monotheism.

God's word enacts what it states. Benjamin conceives of it as an expenditure of pure actualizing energy, though he admits that "in presupposing

language as an ultimate reality," he is only repeating "what emerges of it-self" from the Bible, notably from the first chapter of Genesis:

> In individual acts of creation (Genesis 1:3 and 1:11) only the words "Let
> there be" occur. In this "Let there be" and in the words "He named"
> at the beginning and the end of the act ["And God said 'Let there be
> light.' . . . And God called the light Day"], the deep and clear relation of
> the creative act to language appears each time. With the creative om-
> nipotence of language it begins, and at the end language, as it were, as-
> similates the created, names it. Language is therefore both creative and
> the finished creation; it is word and name.[11]

In the beginning, language was a divine entelechy: a force of invention. After God had uttered his celebrated performative, though, he entrusted language, "which had served *him* as medium of creation," to his human creatures, who used it as a constative tool for understanding creation. The linguistic form with which God made things is the word; the form by which humans know them is the name. The pursuit of knowledge is a ceaseless "translation" from word to name, which aims at "the identity of the cre-ative word and the cognizing name in God" (70). We can name things, and thereby know them, "only" because God's word survives in them: "the cre-ative word in them is the germ of the cognizing name" (70). The name is like a seed. It does not stand for a thing, but grows out of the word that lingers in things. "In name," Benjamin argues, "the word of God has not remained creative; it has become in one part receptive, even if receptive to language. Thus fertilized it aims to give birth to the language of things themselves, from which in turn, soundlessly, in the mute magic of nature, the word of God shines forth" (69). Yet the word that survives in things is mute. Things utter it, but they do so silently, by resembling each other. The name, in contrast, is clamorous.

Things speak immediately of God. Humans speak mediately of God by imitating the sounds things make, for although things cannot say "the word" aloud, they do make nonlinguistic noises. "The incomparable fea-ture of human language," Benjamin maintains, "is that its magical com-munity [*ihre magische Gemeinschaft*] with things is immaterial and purely mental, and the symbol of this is sound" (67/147). Sound is the immedia-tion, or "magical" communion, of human language and that thing language in which "the word of God shines forth" (69). Benjamin rejects Saussure's principle of the arbitrariness of the linguistic sign and reverts instead to a "Cratylist" account of the origin and function of language: "if language, as is evident to the insightful, is not an agreed-upon system of signs," he argues in his 1933 essay "On the Mimetic Faculty," "we will, in attempting to approach language, be constantly obliged to have recourse to the kind of thoughts that appear in their most primitive form as the onomatopoeic mode of explanation."[12] The onomatopoeic explanation revives a possibility that Plato evaluates in the *Cratylus*. Hermogenes claims that "the correctness of names" is determined by "convention and agreement"; Cratylus responds that names express the essences of things by adapting sound to sense, using the letter *r* to imitate motion, for example, and *o* to signify "roundness"; Socrates adopts Cratylus's view and then pursues it until it collapses.[13] Plato's satire, however, did not dissuade Vico from reviving the Cratylist hypothesis in *The New Science*: "articulate language began to develop by way of onomatopoeia," Vico argues, "through which we still find children happily expressing themselves. By the Latins Jove was at first, from the roar of thunder, called *Ious*; by the Greeks, from the whistle of the lightning, *Zeus*; by the Easterners, from the sound of burning fire, he must have been called *Ur*, whence came *Urim*, the power of fire; and from this same origin must have come the Greek *ouranos*, sky, and the Latin verb *uro*, to burn."[14] Benjamin agrees that the name is already present in the sound of the thing (even if, like lightning, the thing makes no sound). The name and the thing are linked not by an "ideal and arbitrary association" but by a "real and substantial bond," for they partake of the same acoustic material.[15] Yet that is how savage philosophers are said to think about language.

In the *Course in General Linguistics*, Saussure points out that onomatopoeic words are "already partly conventionalised" because they only approximate the sounds they mimic. English dogs say "bow-wow"; French dogs, *ouaoua*; German dogs, *wauwau*.[16] Hence dog-speak is always arbitrary "to a certain extent." Benjamin concedes that, post-Babel, the same things have different names in different languages, but he nevertheless insists that the diversity of names can be traced back to an original "core" of resemblance: "if words meaning the same thing in different languages are arranged about that signified as their center, we have to inquire how they all—while often possessing not the slightest similarity to one another—are similar to the signified at their center."[17] Things that are equal to the same thing are equal to each other. Words that are "equal" to the same "signified" are equal to each other,[18] for they are different echoes of the same sound. That "every word—and the whole of language—is onomatopoeic," Benjamin adds, is obvious to anyone who has a gift for seeing the similarity between dissimilar things (721). This gift is the "mimetic faculty." It is the survival of a more "ancient," more primitive, capacity for reasoning by analogy: "the perceptual world of modern man contains only minimal residues of the magical correspondences and analogies that were familiar to ancient peoples" (721). Today the "residues" of magic survive almost exclusively in language, which for Benjamin is "the most complete archive of nonsensuous similarity: a medium into which the earlier powers of mimetic production and comprehension have passed without residue, to the point where they have liquidated those of magic" (722). He agrees with Tylor that language is an "old barbaric engine." But he breaks with him in his valuation of the barbaric. Tylor hopes to supersede it; Benjamin proposes to revive it. Language is the magic that comes after magic.

Why does Benjamin, against the grain of linguistic research, insist on an onomatopoeic hypothesis that Saussure had debunked and that Frazer had racialized? Why revive the argument that names grow out of things themselves, as if language were a self-producing force of nature? The maxim that opens the lasts paragraph of "On the Mimetic Faculty" points toward an answer: "To read what was never written." Benjamin is not merely concerned with reading what was never written *down*. He aspires to read what cannot be perceived. "Such reading," he says, "is the most ancient: reading prior to all languages, from entrails, the stars, or dances" (722). To read the language that comes before language requires a sense for the nonsensuous. For such a language speaks precisely by failing to speak. And its reader perceives it precisely by failing to perceive it.

In his 1910 monograph *Les fonctions mentales dans les sociétés inférieures* (translated into English under the only slightly less embarrassing title *How Natives Think*), Lucien Lévy-Bruhl argues that the art of perceiving the imperceptible survives today in the form of a "primitive mentality." He opens his study with a critique of the English school of anthropology, especially the work of its "head," E. B. Tylor. By comparing the writings of missionaries, travelers, and ethnographers, he argues, the English school discovered "extraordinary likenesses, and sometimes even exact resemblances" between "undeveloped peoples" from "the most distant quarters of the globe."[19] The fact that such different societies are so similar led Tylor and his followers to conclude that the human mind is "exactly the same at all times and in all places." At some point in its history, they for example argue, every society attributes changes in the natural world to the actions of spiritual beings because animism is the first, inevitable stage of mental development (18). Lévy-Bruhl remarks that if his own society suddenly lost the knowledge it has acquired over the centuries and "we were brought face to face with nature like the real 'primitives,'" then, by the logic of the English school, "we should be certain to construct for ourselves a 'natural philosophy,' which would also be primitive, and that philosophy would be a universal animism" (19). He accuses the English school of projecting the consciousness of the observer onto the object of observation, which, ironically, is what the English school says that savage philosophers do. The discourse of the English school does not represent the institutions, customs, and languages of other societies; the institutions, customs, and languages of other societies cast an inverted, mirror-image of the English school's discourse.

Lévy-Bruhl counters that the categories of savage thought—he rounds up the usual suspects: magic, mana, and totem—are "collective" rather than individual "representations," the invention of a "social group" rather than its "individual members" (13). Individual representations are objective. Collective representations are inventive. Individual representations distinguish cognition from its object. Collective representations project cognition onto objects, as if things themselves were capable of thought. Individual representations aim at enlightenment. Collective representations tend toward personification. Individual representations separate the real from the ideal. Collective representations fold them together. Individual representations bring "an image or idea of an object" before consciousness. Collective representations are charged with "emotions and passions." Individual representations distinguish the sensuous from the nonsensuous. Collective representations endow sensuous objects with nonsensuous qualities, which indicates "not only that the primitive actually has an image of the object in his mind, and thinks it real, but also that he has some hope or fear connected with it, that some definite influence emanates from it, or is exercised upon it. This influence," Lévy-Bruhl argues, "is a virtue, an occult power which varies with objects and circumstances, but is always real to the primitive and forms an integral part of his representation" (37–38). Collective representations are "mystic," he concludes, not in any "religious" sense but "in the strictly defined sense in which 'mystic' implies belief in forces and influences and actions which, *though imperceptible to sense,* are nevertheless real" (38, emphasis added). Mysticism is a sense for the nonsensuous, an art of reading what cannot be written. For it makes it possible to perceive nonsensuous similarities.

The savage mind finds nonsensuous forces at work in the most commonplace sensuous objects: "A road, like everything else, has its own peculiar mystic properties. The natives of Loango say of an abandoned path that it is 'dead.' To them, as to us, such an expression is metaphorical, but in their case it is fraught with meaning. For the path, 'in active existence,' has its secret powers, like houses, weapons, stones, clouds, plants, animals,

and men—in short, like everything of which the primitive has a group idea"
(43). Savage philosophers are once again incapable of metaphor because too
capable of lively metaphor. They believe that things having different sensuous properties are nevertheless similar to each other because they harbor the same nonsensuous forces. Still, the action of these secret powers is
most obvious in cases where there is an obvious similarity between things:
"It is a well-known fact that primitives, even members of communities
which are already somewhat advanced, regard artificial likenesses, whether
painted, carved, or sculptured, as real, as well as the individual they depict" (46). Things that look like each other act on each other in a visibly
invisible way.

Roland Barthes was a "primitive" philosopher in Lévy-Bruhl's sense. In
Camera Lucida he revives the notion that some "likenesses" are as alive as
the people they portray—even if those people are dead. He recalls that after
the death of his mother, he sorted through a collection of photographs of
her until he "suddenly" came across one, taken when she was a child, that
restored her to him "in a flash." It was as if he had received a visit from her
ghost. Or as if this singular portrait were as real as the person it resembled:
"All the photographs of my mother which I was looking through were a
little like so many masks; at the last, suddenly the mask vanished: there
remained a soul, ageless but not timeless."[20] The photograph of the mother-
child is an instance of immediation: the copy is bound to the "soul" of the
original. For Barthes, however, the hypothesis of immediation is not a survival of savage philosophy. It is a basic premise of postscholastic "realism."
Just as savage philosophers perceive a substantial yet imperceptible bond
between people and their names, realists find a "magical" yet imperceptible
"community" between people and their images: "the realists do not take
the photograph for a 'copy' of reality, but for an emanation of *past reality:*
a *magic,* not an art" (88). The discourse about magic is here a recourse of
realism in a nominalist world order.

What Barthes calls realism, though, Lévy-Bruhl calls mysticism.[21] Its
first principle is that the sign takes part in its object. A collective representation draws its forces from "whatever" it represents, whether "living
beings, inanimate objects, or articles manufactured by man" (75–76). The
connection between representations, objects, and forces is not fixed by convention. It is governed by the "law of participation." Lévy-Bruhl warns that
it is "difficult to formulate this law in abstract terms," so he describes it as
an injunction to read what was never written: "in the collective representations of primitive mentality, objects, beings, phenomena can be, though in
a way incomprehensible to us, both themselves and something other than

themselves. In a fashion which is no less incomprehensible, they give forth
and they receive mystic powers, virtues, qualities, influences, which make
themselves felt outside, without ceasing to remain where they are" (76–77).
The notion of participation is "incomprehensible" because it endows perceptible objects with imperceptible properties, yet only a theory of participation can explain how things that are sensuously different can be nonsensuously similar. To "us" a name is merely a "label" that distinguishes one
thing from another; to the savage philosopher it is an event that mobilizes
the forces at work in the thing named (53).

But who could understand such a discourse? Who could read a language
of signs that can be neither spoken nor heard, neither written nor read?
Benjamin proposes a technique for the perception of the imperceptible in
his doctoral thesis, published in 1920 as *The Concept of Criticism in German Romanticism.* His name for this technique is "magical observation"
(*die magische Beobachtung*). Like all things said to be magical, it obeys a
law of participation. The things the critic says about the object of observation echo the things that the object says about itself.[22] The critic does not
come to know the object from the outside but discovers what it already
knows about itself on the inside. The discourse of magical criticism is immanent in the object. The critic distills understanding from the object's
self-understanding. "To observe a thing," Benjamin proposes, "means only
to arouse it to self-recognition" (148). Magical observation is a magical communion between the spirit-being of the critic and the spirit-being of the
object: another case of immediation.

The object does not begin to see itself, though, until it sees it is being
observed by another, whether a person or a thing, who looks upon it as if
through its own eyes: "observation fixes in its view only the self-knowledge
nascent in the object; or rather it, the observation, *is* the nascent consciousness of the object itself" (148). I recognize myself in the object, and the
object recognizes itself in me. We understand each other insofar as we participate in each other, and we participate in each other insofar as we resemble each other, for "every being knows only what is like itself and is
known by beings that are like it" (145). The object and I are both ourselves
and something other than ourselves, for we have self-consciousness in common. We are equal to each other because we participate equally in this third
thing. But the similarity between us remains strictly nonsensuous.

The magical community of the observer and the observed allows for the
reflection in the subject of the object's reflection of itself, for "no knowledge is possible without the self-knowledge of what is to be known" (147).
There can be neither cognition nor recognition where no self-consciousness

is present. Yet it need not be a human self-consciousness. "All knowledge is self-knowledge of a thinking being," Benjamin affirms, "which does not need to be an 'I'" (145). In order for one thing to know another, it has only to mirror the gaze that the other turns toward itself. When I, a human observer, come to know a thing in this way, I discover what it knows about other things too:

> It is not only persons who can expand their knowledge through intensified self-knowledge in reflection; so-called natural things can do so as well. In their case, the process has an essential relation to what is commonly called their "being-known." That is, the thing, to the extent that it intensifies reflection within itself and includes other beings in its self-knowledge, radiates its original self-knowledge onto these other beings. In this way, too, the human being can participate [*teilhaftig werden*] in this self-knowledge of other beings . . . a knowledge that is at bottom the self-knowledge of their reflectively produced synthesis. (146/57)

Magical observation annuls the distinction between the animate and the inanimate world, and suggests that things are as capable of the discourse of reason as people are: "Everything that is in the absolute, everything real, thinks" (144). Hence everything real has mental being. In coming to know a thing, I discover that it reflects our common self-consciousness back to me:

> Accordingly, everything that presents itself to man as his knowledge of a being is the reflex in him of the self-knowledge of the thinking in that very being. Thus, there exists no mere being-known of a thing; just as little, however, is the thing or being limited to a mere being-known through itself. Rather, the intensification of reflection in it suspends the boundary that separates its being-known by itself from its being-known by another; in the medium of reflection, moreover, the thing and the knowing being merge into each other. (146)

There can be no production of knowledge unless the subject of knowledge participates in the object of knowledge. The "medium of reflection" is their *im*mediation. Seeing the object, I see myself; the thing, seeing me, glimpses its own image, which is a vital part of it. What we find in each other is a "spirit" that runs through us both. Magical observation, whether directed to art or nature, "consists not in any reflecting *on* an entity," Benjamin concludes, "but in the unfolding of reflection—that is . . . the unfolding of spirit [*des Geistes*]—*in* an entity" (151/66).

Inversion

In a 1921 fragment, Benjamin proposes a study comparing religious icons with paper money: "a comparison between the images of the saints of the various religions and the banknotes of different states." The study would proceed on the lines of magical observation. The self-conscious spirit of the human observer would discover its own speaking portrait in the money-text: "The spirit [*Geist*] that speaks [*spricht*] from the ornamental design of banknotes."[23] How did the money-text come to be endowed with a spirit capable of speech? Benjamin does not say. He did not complete his study. In the first volume of *Capital*, however, Marx explains that money, like every commodity, is a "sensuous" thing that possesses "suprasensible" properties.[24] Considered as something sensuous, the money-text is either paper or metal; considered as something nonsensuous, it is something "social" (165). Money is the sort of thing that can be both itself and something other than itself. The "spirit" that speaks from the money-text has something to tell the critic of political economy about the relations of capitalist production, but what it says is imperceptible to the senses. It invites the critic to read what was never written, and nowhere is such an interpretation more necessary than in the case of money that makes money: interest-bearing capital. Later, in the third volume, Marx observes: "In interest-bearing capital, the capital relationship reaches its most superficial and fetishized form. Here we have $M–M'$, money that produces more money, self-valorizing value, without the process that mediates the two extremes."[25] The "capital relation" pits a class that owns the capacity to work against a class that owns the means of work. The workers sell their labor power to capitalists in order to be able to work at all, and they produce more value in the form of commodities than they receive in the form of wages. A portion of surplus value pays the interest on the capital borrowed to purchase the means and materials of production. Yet the formula for interest-bearing capital omits the workers' role in producing value and suggests instead that money grows from money, as if finance capital had an intrinsic capacity for self-production, indeed as if banknotes had souls. The critic who discovers traces of the "capital relation" in the money-text affirms the existence of forces that "though imperceptible to the sense, are nevertheless real."

Marx enters into a dialogue with the money-spirit in the third section of his *Economic and Philosophical Manuscripts* of 1844. Money, he observes, is the object most worth having because it lets its owner purchase all other objects.[26] It is the pure potential for appropriation. Hence it is the most powerful kind of spirit there is. Marx sardonically calls it "an omnipotent being" (375). What the money-god buys becomes not only my own, but my "own-ness." I am what I appropriate: "That which exists for me through the medium of *money*, that which I can pay for, i.e. which money can buy, that *am I*, the possessor of the money" (377). The money-sign behaves as if it were a living, self-producing force. If I have it, I possess the strength of a dozen people. "The stronger the power [*Kraft*] of my money," Marx maintains, "the stronger am I. The properties of money are my, the possessor's properties and essential powers [*Wesenskräfte*]. Therefore what I *am* and what I *can do* is by no means determined by my individuality. . . . As an individual I am lame, but money procures me twenty-four legs" (377/564). But I pay a premium for my prosthesis. Money grants me its "properties" on the condition that I let it have my mind, indeed my spirit (*Geist*), in return. As long as I have money, though, I can always buy a new one: "I am *mindless* [*geistlos*], but if money is the *true mind* [*wirkliche Geist*] of all things, how can its owner be mindless? What is more, he can buy clever people for himself, and is not he who has power over clever people cleverer than them? Through money I can have anything the human heart desires. Do I not therefore possess all human abilities?" (377/564–65). Although money is a "mere thing," still in some ways it is more human than I am. I possess only some human potentialities. Money possesses them "all." How did it come to have more "human abilities" than humans do? And how did we trade places with a thing? The answer is that the spirit that speaks to us from the money-text is a human soul trapped in an inanimate body.

"Often," says Frazer, "the abduction of a man's soul is set down to demons."[27] Marx sets down the abduction of human potentiality to a god. He does not level the accusation in his own voice, though, but rather borrows the voice of "Shakespeare's" Timon, who, at the height of his misanthropy, delivers an animating address to gold, speaking to the money-text as if it were capable of speaking back to him: "Thou *visible god*, / That solder'st close *impossibilities*, / And mak'st them kiss! That speak'st with every tongue / To every purpose!" (376).[28] Marx regards money as a "god" of inversion. It has the potential to turn everything into its opposite, folding opposites together and making even "impossibilities" possible. "It is the visible divinity," he says, "the transformation of all human and natural qualities into their opposites, the universal confusion and inversion [*die Verwechslung und Verkehrung*] of things" (377/565). Money is expert at inverting the terms of one binary opposition more than any other: "the difference between *being* and *thinking*, between a representation which merely *exists* within me and one which exists outside me as a *real object*" (378). The money-spirit (*Geldgeist*) inverts fictions into facts and confuses signs with things. Marx concludes that it is "the external, universal *means* and *power* . . . to turn *imagination into reality* and *reality into mere imagination*" (378). Predictably, it fuels the work of inversion by stealing actualizing energy from nature and giving it to discourse, turning "*real human and natural powers* into purely abstract representations" and, conversely, "*real imperfections and phantoms*—truly impotent powers which exist only in the individual's fantasy—into *real and essential powers* and *abilities*" (378). Money inverts impotentialities into potentialities and potentialities into impotentialities, enriching the sign ("abstract representation") with an intrinsic principle ("power and ability") of self-production.

Marx has no doubt about where the money-god—or, perhaps, the money-titan—got its forbidden power of invention. He accuses it of stealing it from the human body. Money's divinity is the inversion of a uniquely human potentiality, indeed of a human nature: "the *divine* power [*die göttliche Kraft*] of money lies in its nature as the estranged and alienating *species-essence* [*Gattungswesen*] of man which alienates itself by selling itself. It is the alienated *capacity* [*Vermögen*] of *mankind*" (377/565). Only human beings are permitted to shift the principle of change from nature to art, for human labor occupies the fold between them. We are the only natural force that can change nature's course, including our own human nature, for we alone make signs grow into their objects, inverting the ideal into the real. "At the end of every labor process," Marx explains two decades later, in the first volume of *Capital,* "a result emerges which had already been conceived by the worker at the beginning, hence already existed ideally. Man not only effects a change of form in the materials of nature; he also realizes his own purpose in those materials. And this is a purpose he is conscious of."[29] Nature accords humans the "sovereign" privilege of remaking nature in their own image. It is this privilege, indeed this sovereignty, that the money-demon usurps.[30]

The Marx of 1844 is like a detective investigating a theft, and as he pursues his suspect, he is careful to obey the cardinal rule of magical observation: "every being knows only what is like itself, and is known by beings that are like it." He takes up the culprit's trail in his "Excerpts from James Mill's *Elements of Political Economy,*" in which he discovers that money's theft of the characteristically human capacity for inversion has the form of an inversion of tropes. The money-text turns "the personification of things" (*die Personifizierung der Sachen*) into "the reification of the relations of production" (*die Versachlichung der Produktionsverhältnisse*), taking "will," "activity," and even "tongue" from those who have them and granting them to objects that lack them.[31] Human capacities become the properties of things; the properties of things become human capacities. Hence the inversion of prosopopoeia and reification conforms to the structure of a third trope, chiasmus. The money-form is structured like a discourse:

> The nature of money is not, in the first instance, that property is externalized within it, but that the *mediating function* or movement, human, social activity, by means of which the products of man mutually complement each other, is *estranged* and becomes the property of a *material thing* external to man, viz. money. If a man himself alienates this mediating function he remains active only as a lost, dehumanized creature. The *relation* between things, human dealings with them, become the operations of a being beyond and above man. Through this *alien mediator* man gazes at his will, his activity, his relation to others as at a power independent of them and of himself—instead of man himself being the mediator for man.[32]

The owner of money has a paradoxically immediate relation to the "alien mediator." Money, the medium that acts in my place, is immediately me, and I, the medium who speaks in money's place, am immediately it. Our immediation finds its condition of possibility in the law of participation. Money and I take part in each other because we share a life—namely, my life—in common. When I work, I fix a portion of my life force in the products of my labor, and when I sell them, I exchange potentialities with money, which precipitates an inversion. My capacity to act passes into the bodies of paper, silver, and gold, and their capacity to signify passes into me. I grant them not just activity, but life—"for what is life but activity [*Tätigkeit*]?"[33]—and in return they grant me sense and reference. Money becomes a "humanized creature"; human creatures become living signs.

Marx weighs the consequences of the inversion while commenting on Mill's analysis of interest-bearing capital. "Credit," he argues, "is the *economic* judgement on the *morality* of a man" (264). When I borrow, the lender interprets my appearance to determine whether I can repay the loan. My "flesh" stands not only for my economic potential, which is my capacity for productive labor, but for my moral potential, which is my capacity to adopt a relation to the future. I am capital and interest incarnate. The money-form is me reified; I am the money-form personified. I am simultaneously myself and the living, breathing sign of myself. "In the credit system," Marx explains, "*man* replaces metal or paper as the mediator of exchange" (264). I do not stand for a quantity of "metal or paper." I am myself money. My work habits and "social virtues" personify a sum that reifies me, which is equal to a portion of my future labor. The "alien mediator" is immediately me:

> Money has not been transcended in man within the credit system, but man is himself transformed into *money*, or, in other words, money is *incarnate* in him. Human individuality, human *morality*, have become both articles of commerce and the *material* which money inhabits. The substance, the body clothing the *spirit of money* [*der Körper des Geldgeistes*] is not money, paper, but instead it is my personal existence, my flesh and blood, my social worth and status. Credit no longer actualizes money-values in actual money but in human flesh and human hearts. (264/449)

I do not own the "money-soul" (*Geldseele*) that possesses my flesh and blood (262). Instead it owns me. The reification of my human activity "is immediately" the personification of another's capital. First the "money-spirit" (*Geldgeist*) steals my soul from me. Then the credit system gives it my body too.

If I lived in a "true community," however, I would be able to alienate the products of my labor without becoming alienated from them. I would give them up without giving them away. Although they would no longer be my property, they would not therefore become somebody else's. They would instead belong to a community that I would help to produce, and the community, since it would be the incarnation of my own labor power, would have an immediate relation to me: "this *true community*," Marx insists, "does not come into being as the product of reflection" but is immediately the individual's life, activity, and wealth, for it "arises out of the *need* and the *egoism* of individuals, i.e. it arises directly from their own activity" (265). My body would be home not to the money-soul but to a social soul. If I needed something, it would be mine, for it would belong "directly" to a "social being" that would immediately be me. I would participate in the product of your labor, and you would participate in mine. If you needed something I have made, I would give it to you without demanding anything in return, for the bare fact that you are human would entitle you to have it: "your human nature necessarily implies an intimate relationship with my human production" (275). A true community rests on the immediation of producers. "Men," Marx argues (by "men" he means "people"), "not as abstractions, but as real, living, particular individuals *are* this community. *As* they are, so it is too" (265). In a true community, our creations no longer confront us as "alien powers" because the immediation of producers entails the immediation of products.

Even within the money system, the fact that we need each other's products indicates that we stand in "another *essential* relation" to them "than that of private property." This other relation is one of participation. Says Marx, "the felt need for a thing is the most obvious, irrefutable proof that that thing is part of *my* essence, that its being is for me and that its *property* is the property, the particular quality peculiar to my essence" (267). If you need it, my property is immediately yours, just as if I need it, yours is immediately mine. When we meet in the marketplace, though, we cannot speak of our needs directly. The alien mediator speaks of them on our behalf. Our exchange does not proceed in a human language but in the language of things. "Naturally," Marx observes, "as a human being you have a human relation to my product: you have *need* of my product. It exists for you, therefore, as an object of your desire and your will. But your need, your desire and your will are impotent as far as my product is concerned" (275). You cannot ask me for my product unless you offer me something of yours in return. Thus it falls to your product to represent the need you cannot utter: "The thing that gives your need for my possessions a *value*, a *worth* and an *effect* in my eyes is simply and solely your *possession*, the *equivalent* of my possession" (276). My product, meanwhile, does not just signify yours (as if to say, "this is worth that"); it commands it (as if to say, "to get this, surrender that"). "Our mutual product," Marx continues, "is the *means*, the *mediator*, the *instrument*, the *acknowledged power*, of our mutual needs over each other" (276). We do not speak of our needs directly. Our products speak of them in our place: "The only comprehensible language we have is the language our possessions use together. We would not understand a human language and it would remain ineffectual" (276). Still we dare not ask them to be silent. If you have nothing to offer me in return for my product, then you can only beg me for it, and, as Marx points out, "such a language" humiliates the speaker and strikes the hearer as either impertinent or insane. Yet we respond to the language of things as if it were the discourse of reason: "We are so estranged from our human essence that the direct language of man strikes us as an *offence against the dignity of man*, whereas the estranged language of objective values appears as the justified, self-confident and self-acknowledged dignity of man incarnate" (276–77). The act of exchange is a variation on the inversion of capacities. We invest our life force in things, and things respond by speaking in our place. What do they say to each other in our stolen voices?

There are two schools of thought on this question. They agree that commodities speak to each other about value but disagree about the origin and nature of value. The first school draws its members from "people and governments." They believe that a commodity's value is equal to a sum of money. The "abstract relation" of private property to private property assumes a "real existence," according to this view, in the money-form. To "have" value, they claim, is to be "worth" money. Marx dismisses this line of argument as a "primitive superstition": "the primitive [rohe] economic superstitions of people and governments cling to tangible, palpable and visible bags of money and hold that the sole reality of wealth lies in the absolute value of the precious metals and in the possession of them" (261/447).[34] The second school consists of the more "enlightened" economists. They acknowledge, rightly, that money is a commodity like any other but assume, wrongly, that "its value, like that of any other commodity, depends on the relations between the costs of production and supply and demand" (261–62). They see through "the *sensuous* superstition which believes that [the] essence [of money] exists exclusively in precious metals" but cannot explain why the exchange value of one commodity is equal to that of another. Marx accuses them of "replacing a crude superstition" with "a sophisticated one." "The existence of money in metal is [for them] only the official, visible expression of the money-soul [*Geldseele*]," he argues, "which has percolated all the productions and movements of civil society" (262/447). In short, their theory is a survival of animism. They conceive of value as a soul that wanders from one commodity-body to another but cannot say whence it came. But how do the products of labor come to be "besouled" in the first place?

Soul Migration

When Marx resumes the analysis of the commodity form in *Capital*, he replaces the "sophisticated superstition" of the economists with a more sophisticated "superstition" of his own. Briefly, he exchanges one soul dogma for another. The economists affirm that the money-form is a living incarnation of the *Geldseele*. Marx deduces the general law of its *Seelenwandrung*.[35] This word is translated into English as "metempsychosis" but taken literally means something like "soul trekking." Tylor, when he discusses the theory of the soul's existence after death, speaks of "transmigration." Let us therefore translate *Seelenwanderung* as "soul migration." The later Marx puts the money-soul in its walking shoes, and as he follows its footprints, it leads him from the theory of alienation to the theory of surplus value.

The members of the commodity world (*die Warenwelt*) speak a language of resemblances. Marx calls it a commodity language (*ein Warensprache*)

(143/66). A commodity speaks only with what resembles it. And what resembles it is every other commodity. One commodity is the same as another because all commodities share a soul in common. Indeed the soul is all they talk about. It is the nonsensuous social essence behind their various sensuous appearances. To deduce the law of its motion, Marx eavesdrops on a conversation between the linen and the coat. The two commodities recognize that they are alike. Between them there is immediation. The linen sees "a splendid kindred soul" in the coat, and Marx interrupts to point out that it is "the soul of value [*Wertseele*]" (143/66). What is this "value-soul"? That is exactly what the two commodities are discussing. But they say nothing that Marx has not heard before: "everything our analysis of the value of commodities previously told us is repeated by the linen itself [*sagt die Leinwand selbst*], as soon as it enters into association with another commodity, the coat. Only it reveals its thoughts in a language [*Sprache*] with which it alone is familiar, the language of commodities [*der Warensprache*]" (143/66). Commodities speak. The production process is a prosopopoetic event that endows them first with a face, then with a mouth, and finally a voice. When they meet in the circulation process—they are commodities insofar as they are exchanged (131)—the coat speaks to the linen about value. Marx records their conversation: "20 yards of linen = 1 coat or = 20 coats or = x coats" (141). What the coat says to the linen, on the linen's behalf, is that although their bodies are sensuously different, their souls are nonsensuously similar, indeed "as like as two peas" (144).

Marx suggests that the commodity possesses a mimetic faculty. Hence it has a double identity and leads a double life. It is a use value (*Gebrauchswert*) when it satisfies some "human need" and an exchange value (*Tauschwert*) when it signifies the proportion in which use values are exchanged. But a use value does not express its exchange value directly. Rather it confers its face and voice on a use value that speaks in its place (140/63). Use value acts as "the material bearer" of exchange value. "A given commodity," Marx explains, "a quarter of wheat for example, is exchanged for x boot-polish, y silk or z gold, etc" (127). The use value is a signifier; the exchange value, a signified. The correlation between them—the exchange relation—is a sign. The commodity sign is not arbitrary, however, but mimetic. The body of one mirrors the soul of the other. A sensuous "appearance" reflects a nonsensuous "essence."[36]

Say that 20 yards of linen = 1 coat (139/63). The linen, or signified, is the relative value-form. The coat, or signifier, is the equivalent form. The sign, or simple value-form, expresses their similarity in the mode of difference, affirming what the linen is worth by comparing it to what it is not, the coat. What the coat says about the linen, as if with the linen's voice, is that though they differ both in quality and in quantity, they are nevertheless "equal to a third thing, which in itself is neither the one nor the other" (127/51). This "third" is the value-soul (143/66), the sort of spirit that animates commodity-bodies (*Warenkörper*) (126/50). To separate the value-soul from the value-body, Marx performs a labor of abstraction. First, he "disregards" the "sensuous characteristics" that make a commodity a use value (128). "It is no longer a table, a house, a piece of yarn or any other useful thing," he explains. "Nor is it any longer the product of the labour of the joiner, the mason or the spinner" (128). Then he isolates the imperceptible "residue" that the linen has in common with the coat:

> Let us now look at the residue [*Residuum*] of the products of labor. There is nothing left of them in each case but the same phantom-like objectivity [*gespenstige Gegenständlichkeit*]; they are merely congealed quantities of homogeneous human labor, i.e. of human labor-power [*Arbeitskraft*] expended without regard to the form of expenditure. All these things now tell us is that human labor-power has been expended to produce them, human labor is accumulated in them. As crystals [*Kristalle*] of this social substance, which is common to them all, they are values—commodity values [*Warenwerte*]. (128/52–53)

The "common factor" in the exchange relation—what makes sensuously different things nonsensuously similar—is human labor power. "A use-value, or useful article," he continues, "has value only because abstract human labour is objectified [*vergegenständlicht*] or materialized in it" (129). Although different kinds of commodities contain different kinds of labor, what they have in common, and what gives them value, is labor power considered without regard to its sensuous form: abstract, nonsensuous labor power. A commodity is a portion of the total labor power, or actualizing energy, of a society. Its value is equal to the quantity of labor it contains, and the quantity of labor is measured by the time the average worker takes to perform it, namely, "socially necessary labor-time"(129).

The linen and the coat are two perceptible crystals of a single, imperceptible social substance. Each is a "mirror" (*Spiegel*) of the other because each "is immediately" the other. They participate in each other. Indeed they participate in all commodities, for every "commodity-body" (*Körperform*) is "the visible incarnation [*die sichtbare Inkarnation*], the social chrysalis state, of all human labour," which is itself invisible (159/81). The simple value-form can therefore be extended to infinity: 1 coat = 10 lb. coffee =

1 quarter of corn = 2 ounces of gold = ½ ton of iron = 20 yards of linen, and so on (155/77). Nevertheless one commodity is especially well suited to embody the values of all. This commodity is gold, which wins the job of "universal equivalent" because it is uniform and can be readily divided into equal quantities, and because it is dense and can represent a large value in a small volume.[37]

What the commodity, speaking in its commodity language, confides to Marx is that it is both itself and something other than itself, something both "objective" and "phantom-like." It invites him to entertain the possibility that commodity values are material abstractions or, as he says in 1844, "real brain-phantoms" (die wirklichen Hirngespinste).[38] "Labor power" (Arbeitskraft) is the only commodity the capitalist can buy that possesses an intrinsic principle of change. It occupies a position between nature and the commodity world. Marx defines it as a "living" (lebendige), "self-acting" (sich betätigende), "self-objectifying" (sich wertschaffende), hence "natural" force (Naturmacht).[39] Only labor power can actualize in reality what exists potentially as a sign. Hence only labor power can set the means of production in motion and submit the materials of production to a transformation. The capitalist purchases this "living, form-giving fire" (lebendige, gestaltende Feuer) from the worker on the labor market, and the worker fixes it in the bodies of commodities in the labor process.[40] The worker is living labor personified. The commodity is living labor reified: "dead, objectified labor" (tote, vergegenständlichte Arbeit).[41] Production effects the inversion of personification and reification, taking a soul from the living human body and investing it in a living-dead commodity body: "so that living labor appears as a mere means to realize objectified, dead [todte] labor, to penetrate it with an animating soul [mit belebender Seele] while losing its own soul to it."[42] Afterward the worker takes on the attributes of a thing—her soul is a commodity for sale—while the commodity takes on the attributes of a person, for not only does it speak to other commodities but it "begins to work" in the worker's place, like an "animated monster" (beseeltes Ungeheuer).[43] Marx conceives of the event of "inversion" (Verkehrung) as a transmigration of souls. The worker's life force enters production in a "fluid" state (im flüssigen Zustand) and leaves in a "coagulated" state (in geronennem Zustand), passing from the worker's body to the commodity-body, where it awaits the moment of its resurrection (142/65). If the commodity-body is consumed as a use value, then its value-soul dies with it, but if it is consumed in the production of other commodities, then its value-soul is reincarnated in other, newer commodity-bodies.

Marx repeatedly states that capital is not a thing but "a movement": a ceaseless death and resurrection of value-souls. Its "circulatory process" is governed by a law of transmigration.[44] Only a select population of souls, though, are chosen to rise from the dead. They are the souls fixed in the means and materials of production. Living labor dies producing commodities that grant life, and add value, to other commodities. A portion of the loom passes into the linen; a portion of the linen, into the coat. Because it is forever giving it away to its products, the "animated monster" is always hungry for more labor power:

> A machine which is not active in the labor process is useless. In addition, it falls prey to the destructive power of natural processes. Iron rusts; wood rots. Yarn with which we neither weave nor knit is cotton wasted. Living labor [die lebendige Arbeit] must seize on these things, awaken them from the dead [sie von den Toten erwecken], change them from merely possible into real and effective use-values. Bathed in the fire of labor, appropriated as part of its organism, and infused ["bespirited," begeistet] with vital energy for the performance of functions appropriate to their concept and to their vocation in the process, they are indeed consumed, but to some purpose, as elements in the formation of new use-values, new products, which are capable of entering into individual consumption as means of subsistence or into a new labor process as means of production.[45]

Capital grows by adding value to itself: "its valorization is therefore self-valorization [Selbstverwertung]" (255/169). But it does not grow out of itself as natural things do. Rather it feeds on the worker's life force, which alone has the power to resurrect the souls of past labor and infuse them into new products. The worker is the hinge joining nature to capital and potentiality to actuality: "Through the exchange with the worker, capital has appropriated labour itself; labour has become one of its moments, which now acts as a fructifying vitality [als befruchtende Lebendigkeit] upon its merely existent and hence dead objectivity [todte Gegenständlichkeit]."[46] Capital is not just any animated monster though. It is a vampire. It achieves life after death by abducting souls from their living owners. Marx says it sucks. Repeatedly. It sucks in the Grundrisse: "But capital obtains this ability [to change form and thereby outlive itself] only by constantly sucking in living labor [die lebendige Arbeit] as its soul [als Seele], vampire-like [als ein Vampyr]" (646/2:530). And it still sucks in Capital: "Capital is dead labor [*verstorbne Arbeit*] which, vampire-like [*vampyrmäßige*], lives only by sucking living labor [*sich . . . belebt durch Einsaugung lebendiger Arbeit*], and lives the more, the more labor it sucks."[47] The labor sucked from the worker's body is incarnated in one commodity-body after another. But capital does not hunt for labor on its own. Instead it takes possession of the capitalist's body, which acts in its place. It is the capitalist—who is "capital personified": "His soul [*Seele*] is the soul of Capital [*Kapitalseele*]" (342/247)—who brings living labor into constant contact with dead labor. It is the capitalist who gets the monster its daily, indeed hourly, fix: "By turning his money into commodities which serve as the building materials for a new product, and as factors in the labor-process, by incorporating living labor [*lebendige Arbeitskraft*] into their lifeless objectivity, the capitalist simultaneously transforms value, i.e. past labor in its objectified and lifeless [*tote*] form, into capital, value which can perform its own valorization process, an animated monster" (302/209). The compulsion to "besoul" the products of past labor risks de-souling the producer. So remorseless is "the vampire thirst for the living blood of labor" (*den Vampyrdurst nach lebendigem Arbeitsblut*) that by the 1860s the British bourgeoisie had implemented a twenty-four-hour workday divided into shifts (367/271). Capital is the kind of parasite that kills its host, for it "usurps the time for the growth, development and healthy maintenance of the [living] body" (375–76).

Marx does not invoke the soul dogma as a metaphor for the labor process. Rather he models the labor process in metaphor's image. Aristotle did not yet fully distinguish physics from rhetoric. Neither does Marx. Aristotle argues that a force of actualization, whether *energeia* or *entelekheia*, is at work in nature and metaphor alike. Marx argues that the labor process, where humankind confronts nature as a force of nature, actualizes what exists potentially in signs by animating the means and material of production with stolen human souls, transforming a mere potentiality into a real and effective use-value. Living labor raises past labor from the dead. Every workday, therefore, is resurrection day: "in so far as labour is productive activity [*produktive Tätigkeit*] directed to a particular purpose, in so far as it is spinning, weaving or forging, etc., it raises [*erweckt*] the means of production from the dead [*von den Toten*] merely by entering into contact [*Kontakt*] with them, infuses them with life [literally, "bespirits them," *begeistet sie*] so that they become factors of the labor process, and combines with them to form new products."[48] It is not *as if* the "means and materials" of production come to life on contact with "living labor." They are, immediately, on contact, "reanimated" (*beseelt*).[49] Capitalist production is a forced migration of souls and depends on the producer's participation in the product: *"living labor [die lebendige Arbeit] makes instrument and material in the production process* into the body of its soul *[zum Leibe ihrer Seele macht]* and thereby resurrects them from the dead."[50] Marx does not graft an abstract, rhetorical "form" onto a material, social "substance." Metaphorical animation is really operative in the labor process. The movement he calls "capital" is at once a vivification that objectifies and an objectification that vivifies. Iron is mined, smelted, and dies; three days or three years later the soul of living labor rouses it from the dead and embodies it in rails. Capitalist production is at once an animating and a crystallizing event.

If the commodity is capital's sensuous "form of appearance," then soul migration is the unacknowledged, nonsensuous "essence" of its motion. Yet the general formula for capital (M–C–C'–M'), like the abbreviated formula for interest-bearing capital (M–M'), shelters the soul's travels from the economist's gaze, "as if by magic."[51] The capitalist invests a sum of money (M) in the purchase of labor power and the means and materials of production; labor power sets the means of production in motion and invests value in the materials of production (C'); the surplus congealed in the products of labor is realized when they are sold in the circulation process (M'). Because it omits the production process, the general formula suggests it is the act of sale that generates surplus value. Nowhere does it mention that surplus value is a surplus portion of the worker's life force, a surplus of soul, or that workers produce more value when they make things at work than they consume when they reproduce their labor at home. Nowhere does it mention that the worker is a self-producing *Naturmacht*. Instead it displaces the worker's entelechy onto the product, as if capital were capable of growing by itself, out of itself, indeed as if valorization were a natural event. "What is [thus] brought to fulfillment here," Marx famously concludes, "is the fetishism *[Fetischismus]* peculiar to bourgeois economics, which transforms *[verwandelt]* the social, economic character that things are stamped with in the process of social production into a natural character arising from the material nature of these things."[52]

It is ironic that he chooses the word "fetishism" to denote the error of the political economists. In 1871, fours years after the publication of the first volume of *Capital*, Tylor argues that fetishism is the theory that certain sensuous, "material objects" embody, and convey the influence of, immaterial, nonsensuous spirits.[53] That is how Marx conceives of the commodity. He says it is a concrete, sensuous body that harbors an abstract, nonsensuous soul. And he is not indulging in "mere" metaphor. His account of

the commodity-text, which he opposes to the fetishism of "bourgeois economics," is itself a "fetishism" in Tylor's sense. But the irony does not end
there. When he says "fetishism," what Marx in fact means, by the standards
of late nineteenth-century anthropology, is totemism. Frazer outlines the
conventional distinction between a "fetich" and a "totem" in the opening
paragraph of his 1887 monograph *Totemism*:

> A totem is a class of material objects which a savage regards with su-
> perstitious respect, believing that there exists between him and every
> member of the class an intimate and altogether special relation. . . . As
> distinguished from a fetich, a totem is never an isolated individual, but
> always a class of objects, generally a species of animals or of plants, more
> rarely a class of inanimate natural objects, very rarely a class of artificial
> objects.[54]

Marx's account of "fetish" falls under Frazer's definition of "totem." A "fetich," according to Frazer, is an "isolated individual," whereas a totem is a
genus. The commodity, according to Marx, is not an individual, such as a
coat, a table, Karl's labor power, or a loaf of bread; it is a generic "class" of
use values that act as the material bearers of exchange values. He replaces
the commodity fetishism of bourgeois economics with a commodity totemism of his own. It amounts to substituting one version of soul migration for
another.

Frazer's critic Lévy-Bruhl remarks that in a totemic system, "every individual *is* both such and such a man or woman, alive at present . . . and at the
same time he [or she] *is* his totem, that is, he partakes in mystic fashion of
the essence of the animal or vegetable species whose name he bears."[55] But
Frazer agrees. Everybody, he says, is "one" with the totemic group because
everybody is descended from the same "common ancestor." One individual
is nonsensuously similar to another because both are sensuously similar to
a third. They give their nonsensuous similarity a sensuous form by adopting the ancestor's name: "The clan totem is reverenced by a body of men
and women who call themselves by the name of the totem, believe themselves to be of one blood, descendants of a common ancestor, and are bound
together by common obligations to each other and by a common faith in
the totem."[56] Andrew Lang explains the "rapport" between the name, the
totem, and the individual, as follows: "if the *name* is the soul of its bearer,
and if the totem also is his soul, then the name and the soul and the totem
of a man are all one!"[57] Totemism hinges on the immediation of souls and
names.

Marx argues that in societies in which the capitalist mode of production prevails, every producer is both such-and-such a man or woman, and at the same time he or she *is* the average, abstract labor congealed in the commodity. The producer "partakes in mystic fashion" of the product's social "essence": homogeneous labor power. The commodity is both a class of material products and a social relation between producers. Every member of the commodity totem, or proletariat, embodies a portion of the total labor power of society. Every worker is a "descendant" of the universal worker. Yet the commodity signifies the producer's participation in the product in an imperceptible form. Indeed, by a logic of inversion, it presents the opposite relation to perception. To interpret the commodity-text therefore means reading what was never written.

Frazer finds totemic societies in almost every region of the globe. Lévy-Bruhl, following Spencer and Gillen, locates the paradigm of the totemic society in Australia. Long before others were to project it beyond Europe's limits, however, Marx finds totemism at work in nineteenth-century England, which he considers Europe's most economically "developed" society.[58] He invents a totemism that comes before totemism and names it fetishism. Thus "totemism" is a theory of European social relations before it becomes a theory of "savage" ones. Only by a long detour does it return to Europe bearing the traits of savage philosophy.

Marx's account of the commodity is, above all, the prototype for Émile Durkheim's account of "primitive" religion,[59] which brings the commodity-totem back to Europe from Australia in the inverted form of the Arunta *churinga*. In *The Elementary Forms of the Religious Life*, drawing on the fieldwork of Spencer and Gillen, Durkheim observes that the "Australian tribes" are organized into exogamous clans not, as Frazer claims, because "they have definite blood connections with one another" but, as Lang and Lévy-Bruhl claim, because "they are collectively designated by the same word" (122). The clan name, like the commodity form, is the sensuous form assumed by a nonsensuous social relation. Durkheim says it is borrowed from a "species of material things," such as plants and animals, or from the seasons and planets, water and fire. This species is the *totem*. The members of the clan consider it sacred (124–25). They are forbidden to touch it, eat it, or harm it except in rare and highly ritualized circumstances (150–55). They consider fellow clanspersons equally sacred. "This personal sacredness," he explains, "is due to the fact that [a] man believes that while he is a man in the usual sense of the word, he is also an animal or plant of the totemic species" (156–57). Durkheim's primitive philosophers are Proustian. The name, for them, is not an arbitrary correlation between a signifier and a signified; rather it partakes of the thing named: "the name, for a primitive, is not merely a word or combination of sounds; it is part of the being, and even something essential to it" (157). What he calls "primitive" thought is the racialized inversion of European realism. The clan name is the perceptible form of an imperceptible being-in-common. When a "member of the Kangaroo clan calls himself a kangaroo," therefore, he affirms that he is "in one sense, an animal of this species" (157). The name "kangaroos" the one it names. It *is* rather than represents its object.

There is more than one way, however, to denote a totem: "the totem is not merely a name," Durkheim maintains; "it is an emblem, a veritable coat-of-arms" (134), and the emblem, like the name, partakes of the thing it signifies. The members of the clan inscribe it on utensils, houses, and tombs and tattoo it into their skin. Durkheim points out that the societies of central Australia have built a complex system of "rites" around one class of objects in particular. These are the *churinga.* They are distinguished from other objects because they bear the clan's design: "They are pieces of wood or bits of polished stone, of a great variety of forms, but generally oval or oblong. Each totemic group has a more or less important collection of these. *Upon each of these is engraved a design representing the totem of this same group*" (140). The word *churinga,* used as either a substantive or an adjective, means "sacred." In fact the name of a churinga is "so sacred" that it cannot be shared with "a stranger" (141). The clan stores these precious objects "in a special place" and conceals the entrance, although even when they are shut away they continue to discharge a force so powerful that it electrifies its surroundings (142). "Women and the uninitiated" are forbidden to approach the churinga, but men use them to heal wounds and diseases, to ensure the reproduction of the totemic species, and to reinforce the social bond (142–43).

Curiously, the totem itself has no power. Durkheim insists it borrows its effectiveness from the totemic design: "The figures of all sorts which represent the totem are surrounded with a respect sensibly superior to that inspired by the very being whose form these figures reproduce" (155). Totemism is a case where the sign is "more actively powerful" than its object (156). Yet it has power over its object only insofar as it *fails* to represent it correctly: "Although the Australian may show himself sufficiently capable of imitating the forms of things in a rudimentary way, sacred representations generally seem to show no ambitions in this line" (148). The design partakes of the thing because both are nonsensuously similar to another "substance," that is not a thing, or an animal, or a person, but "an anony-

mous and impersonal force, found in each of these beings but not to be con-
founded with any of them" (217). This "force" cannot make itself directly
present to the senses, so it embodies itself in a sensuous substitute:

> the Australian . . . has been led to conceive it under the form of an ani-
> mal or vegetable species, or, in a word, of a visible object. This is what
> the totem really consists in: it is only the material [hence sensuous] form
> under which the imagination represents this immaterial [hence nonsen-
> suous] substance, this energy diffused through all sorts of heterogeneous
> things, which alone is the real object of the cult. . . . Thus the universe,
> as totemism conceives it, is filled and animated by a certain number of
> forces which the imagination represents in forms taken, with only a few
> exceptions, from the animal or vegetable kingdoms. (217–18)

Just as for Marx the commodity-body is the sensuous form assumed by a
nonsensuous social relation, the totemic sign is for Durkheim "the material
form" assumed by an "immaterial energy." And just as the commodity-
body, once animated, appropriates the producer's capacity to make the ideal
real, the totemic sign is an ideal form that can induce real, "physical effects"
on the human body: "Does an individual come in contact with them without having taken proper precautions? He receives a shock which might be
compared to the effect of an electric discharge" (218). Yet Durkheim warns
that only the primitive mind would believe that signs are really operative in
nature. The force of the totemic emblem, like that of the animated monster
named capital, is the estranged form of a social substance, and so although
it "appears to be outside of the individuals" belonging to the social group,
it "can be realized only in and through them" (253). The totemic design is
the reified mirror image of the group's own activity, its labor, just as the
value of the commodity, which appears to reside in its bodily properties, is a
congealed quantum of the total labor power of society. Durkheim concludes
that the "totemic principle" embodied in the totemic design is "nothing
else than the clan itself, personified and represented to the imagination under the visible form of the animal or vegetable which serves as totem" (236).
The totem, like the commodity, emerges from the inversion of personification and reification. Hence it is at once an animating and a crystallizing
event. The clan's physical and mental activity is reified in the sign, and,
paradoxically, the sign personifies the physical and mental activity of the
clan. The totemic design, like the commodity-text, is the discursive body
of a social soul.

Alarm Clock

In "On the Concept of History," Benjamin proposes to enlist "theology" in the service of a "puppet" he calls historical materialism.[60] What sort of theology is fit for the task? In 1916 he proposed a totemism of mono-theism, which discovered the residue of God's word in both animate and inanimate things. At the end of the 1920s, he suggests a totemism of labor power, which is attuned to the participation of producers in the products of their labor. He grafts the theory of commodity totemism from the discourse of ethnology to the discourse of Marxism. Somewhere on its journey from England to Australia and back, however, the concept of the value-soul has been racialized. What was once an account of European social organization now passes itself off as a paradigm of savage philosophy.

Among the vast crowd of citations that populate his *Arcades Project*, Benjamin makes a point of including the following passage on the ownership of commodities: "The collector actualizes latent archaic representations of property. These representations may in fact be connected with taboo, as the following remark indicates: 'It . . . is . . . certain that taboo is the primitive form of property[. . . .] To appropriate to oneself an object is to render it sacred and redoubtable to others; it is to make it "participate" in oneself.'"[61] The commodity, like Durkheim's version of the churinga, harbors a charge powerful enough to communicate a shock to its new owner, and this charge is what remains in the product of the producer's labor power: a capitalist mana. Upon taking possession of the commodity, the buyer exorcizes it and replaces it with his or her own taboo-making life force. The commodity is like a rechargeable battery: it is "besouled" in production and "resouled" in consumption. Its electrical sanctity keeps thieves and adventurers away, making it "redoubtable" to anyone who lacks the authority to touch it. Guterman and Lefebvre ground the right of property in the notion of soul migration. But what compels Benjamin to conserve this particular morsel of their discourse? What significance does it have for his thought?

In a 1928 review of Julien Green's novel *Mont-Cinère*, Benjamin calls for a "practical criticism" of the objects that fill the interior of the bourgeois home. Practical criticism is the successor, in Benjamin's canon, to magi-cal observation. "One of the profoundest, most legitimate features of the new schools of architecture," he remarks, "may well be seen in their efforts to liquidate the magical powers that we are inevitably and unconsciously subject to in the rooms and furniture of our dwellings. These efforts strive to transform us from the inhabitants of houses into their users, from proud owners into practical critics."[62] Practical criticism does not yield a body of positive knowledge about household commodities. Instead it resurrects the forces that slumber in them: "'To dwell': Does this still mean barely having a roof over one's head, a process full of fear and magic, one that was perhaps never so voracious as it has been under the cover of civilization and the small-minded bourgeois-Christian world? For beneath the surface," he warns, "things glow and smoulder; the cold flames of miserliness lick at the walls of the icy house. When at the end a fire lights up its windows and blazes from the roof, it will have been properly warm for the first time" (152). Benjamin's portrait of the commodity-totem is fashioned in the image of Durkheim's account of totemic religion—but with a twist. The scene in which the "magical powers" of things glow and smolder is the bourgeois interior rather than a so-called primitive society. When it comes home from the market, the commodity continues to speak of the social relations that govern the sale and purchase of value-creating labor power. To interpret it is to arouse the collective worker's dormant soul. Meanwhile the miser's house burns because he treats a social energy as if it were his private property and locks up a force that explodes its container.

Nobody, according to Benjamin, has done more to advance the practical criticism of the commodity world than the Surrealists, who made "the monuments" of the "primal history of the nineteenth century . . . ever more audible" (152). The Surrealists transposed "the philosophical realism of the Middle Ages . . . from the logical realm of ideas to the magical realm of words."[63] A word is "magical" if carries "mystic," nonsensuous forces. André Breton discovered such forces in commodities and so prepared commodity totemism for integration into Benjamin's revolutionary messianism. Breton takes the "energies" that smolder beneath the surface of the commodity world as portents of revolution, for revolution is the resurrection of the souls objectified in the products of labor past: "He can boast an extraordinary discovery: he was the first to perceive the revolutionary energies that appear in the 'outmoded'—in the first iron constructions, the first factory buildings, the earliest photos, objects that have begun to be extinct, grand pianos, the dresses of five years ago, fashionable restaurants when the vogue has begun to ebb from them. The relation of these things to revolution—no one can have a more exact concept of it" (210).

In 1940 Benjamin suggests that revolution is the sudden arrival of a messiah.[64] The gate opens for this messiah when the members of the commodity totem recognize that they participate in the products of each other's labor and thus cease to be alienated from them. A messianic potential for redemption slumbers in every commodity-body in the form of a collective soul. Benjamin's monotheism "is immediately" a pantheism. The souls congealed in the products of labor have the potential to awake in an instant of revolutionary "explosion": "Breton and Nadja are the lovers who convert everything that we have experienced on mournful railway journeys (railways are beginning to age), on godforsaken Sunday afternoons in the proletarian neighborhoods of great cities, in the first glance through the rain-blurred window of a new apartment, into revolutionary experience, if not action. They bring the immense forces of 'atmosphere' concealed in these things to the point of explosion" (210). Benjamin asks Breton's readers to entertain the conventionally savage hypothesis that the products of labor give out and receive "mystic powers," that they are at once "themselves and something other than themselves," for only on this hypothesis can we go savage enough to experience the nonsensuous yet "revolutionary energies" congealed in them. The critic who denies the hypothesis of participation finds it "incomprehensible" that the observation of things could prime them to explode. But if we learn to see our own faces looking back at us from the faces of commodities, then, by the inversion of personification with reification, we trade "the play of human features for the face of an alarm clock that in each minute rings for sixty seconds" (218). Revolutionary experience, "if not action," is the resurrection of a dormant social soul.

CHAPTER FIVE

Allegories of the Sun, Specters of Excess

I used to think that if I could talk to the spirit world, I'd get some answers. Ha bloody ha. I wish the dead would just come out and say what they mean instead of being so passive-aggressive about the whole thing.—*Eden Robinson,* Monkey Beach

Ghost Theory

In the opening paragraph of Eden Robinson's novel *Monkey Beach*, the "half-awake" narrator hears a murder of crows speaking to her from a plum tree. Birds do not usually talk to people in a human language. Is she still asleep? Does she ever wake up? These questions cannot be decided. The narrator is skilled in the art of dreaming while awake. She is named Lisa-marie after Elvis Presley's daughter. An "Elvis clock" stands on her bedside table. The effigy of the King is supposed to grind his hips when the alarm goes off, but the clock is secondhand, and he does not dance any more. Perhaps he never could: "The Elvis clock says the time is seven-thirty, but it's always either an hour ahead or an hour behind. We always joke that it's on Indian time."[1] Lisa observes that he is "caught in mid-gyrate." Like the personification of time, she too is suspended between past and future, balancing every hour gained with an hour lost. The "Indian," in Robinson's novel, is an allegory of repetition.

It was Lisa's brother Jimmy who gave her the clock. He recently joined the crew of a fishing trawler, but it is missing at sea. She was up late the previous night waiting for news. It never comes. She speaks from a present that goes neither forward nor backward in time, "caught in mid-gyrate" between a past she remembers in flashbacks and a future she anticipates with muted dread. The action of the novel lasts less than two days, about as long as it takes to read it. It is as if everything has been compressed into now-time.

After she wakes up, if she wakes up, Lisa lights a cigarette and looks out her bedroom window. What she sees and hears now, at the start of the novel, repeats in advance the things she will see and hear at the end. Her narration is a ghost event, both "repetition *and* first time,"[2] although the pattern of haunting can only be grasped on rereading: "The crows are tiny black dots against a faded denim sky. In the distance, I hear a speedboat. For the last week, I have been dreaming about the ocean—lapping softly against the hull of a boat, hissing as it rolls gravel up a beach" (2). Her parents fly south to be nearer the place where the trawler went missing. They phone the next morning to say that the Coast Guard has located a life raft. It is empty. Distraught, she decides to join them but finds it hard to get moving. She lives in Kitamaat Village, a Haisla community on the north coast of British Columbia. There are no direct flights south from there, and the road is one long detour. So she takes to the open ocean in her father's speedboat. But her passage from rest to motion is brief. She stops to rest at Monkey Beach, but as soon as she lands she is accosted by a crowd of resident ghosts. When she tries to climb back into her boat, she falls drowsily into the waves, as if she were half asleep. The hull strikes her on the head and pushes her under-water. She continues her narration beyond this point, but it is impossible to tell whether she has drowned or whether she is now, on page 374, dreaming the dream that she recounts on page 2. The novel itself is "caught in mid-gyrate" between its opening and closing scenes:

> Early evening light slants over the mountains. The sky is faded denim blue. Somewhere above my head, a raven grumbles as it hops between the branches of the tightly packed trees. . . . I lie on the sand. The clam-shells are hard against my back. I am no longer cold. I am so light I could just drift away. Close, very close, a b'gwus howls—not quite human, not quite wolf, but something in between. The howl echoes off the mountains. In the distance, I hear the sound of a speedboat. (374)

The denim sky, the gravel beach, the hissing of the waves, the noise of the speedboat: Lisa begins by saying that she dreams these sounds. When she hears them in the novel's closing paragraph, is her narration coming to an end, or is it about to start over from the top? Is this the dream she was dream-ing before she awoke and began speaking? Does the novel come full circle? Has she been dreaming the whole time? Or is it "something in between"?

There is one obvious difference between the two scenes. She hears the howl of the b'gwus at the novel's end but not at its start. Does it offer a clue? The b'gwus, or wild man of the woods, is better known today as the Sasquatch. He is the sort of creature who lives "in between" appearance and reality. Lisa's father used to tell stories about him when she and Jimmy were children. Once the *World Weekly Globe* offered a reward to anyone who successfully photographed him. There is only one place, though, where a creature of the in-between can cross out of one genre of mimesis, narrative, and pose for another, photography. It is Monkey Beach. Jimmy bought a camera and begged their father to take them there:

> Jimmy squirmed. "Please, Dad. Please. It's important."
>
> "Jimmy," Dad said, "Sasquatches are make-believe, like fairies. They don't really exist."
>
> "But Ma-ma-oo says they're real," Jimmy said.
>
> "Your grandmother thinks the people on TV are real," Dad said, then glanced at me, rolling his eyes. (9–10)

To prove the b'gwus has the power to pass from representation to reality, Jimmy cites the authority of his father's mother, Ma-ma-oo. In response, his father jokes that his mother often mistakes relations between signs for relations between things. That is what Tylor says children and savages do. Freud agrees that it is the principle of magical thought.

Not only does the novel haunt itself, then, but it is haunted by the ghosts of discourses past. Yet it repeats them as if uttering them for the first time. Compare the father's joke with Herbert Spencer's account of how the savage mind experiences mimesis. The excerpt comes from the 1893 edition of *The Principles of Sociology*:

> That we may understand better the feelings with which a savage looks at a representative figure, let us recall the feelings produced by representations among ourselves.
>
> When a lover kisses the miniature of his mistress, he is obviously influenced by an association between *the appearance* and *the reality*. Even more strongly do such associations sometimes act. A young lady known to me confesses that she cannot bear to sleep in a room having portraits on the walls; and this repugnance is not uncommon. In such cases the knowledge that portraits consist of paint and canvas only, fails to expel the suggestion of something more. The vivid representation so strongly arouses the thought of a living personality, that this cannot be kept out of consciousness.

> Now suppose culture absent—suppose there exist no ideas of attri-
> bute, law, cause—no distinctions between natural and unnatural, pos-
> sible and impossible. This associated consciousness of a living presence
> will then persist. No conflict with established knowledge arising, the
> un-resisted suggestion will become a belief.[3]

The "vivid representation" is something real for Spencer's "savage." It not
only evokes a likeness but, through an overexpenditure of discursive energeia, conjures up "something more": a "living presence." Even Spencer falls
under its spell. He speaks of his portrait of the "young lady" as if it were the
woman herself, as if she were immediately present before him, affirming in
her own voice that she prefers not to sleep with pictures. Then he takes the
further step of letting her living portrait speak for an otherwise mute savage
philosopher. It says aloud what the "savage" thinks but cannot say. Spencer
does what Lisa's father accuses his mother of doing: he thinks the verbal
pictures he paints are real.

More than one ghost of discourse past haunts the pages of Robinson's
novel, however. If Lisa's Ma-ma-oo reproduces the characteristic traits of
Spencer's savage philosopher, then Lisa herself is fashioned in the image of
Nietzsche's "man of the ages of barbarous primordial culture," for she lives
in two equally real worlds at once.[4] One day when she was a child, she came
across a dog lying in a roadside ditch. Too young to understand it was dead,
she reached down to pet it. A voice stopped her in midmotion:

> Someone tsk-tsked. I looked up, and a little, dark man with bright red
> hair was crouching beside me.
>
> "Your doggy?" I said.
>
> He shook his head, then pointed towards my house. (19)

Afterward she tells herself he was a dream, for only in dreams are apparitions permitted to speak and act as if they were realities (20). The next
time he visits her, though, he makes a point of asserting his living presence—and effectivity—in the waking world: "The next time was when I
was six. I woke up with the eerie feeling that someone was staring at me"
(20). Just as she is falling back to sleep, she hears something drop to the
floor: "I jolted awake, heart thudding so hard I couldn't breathe. My jew-
elry box's tinkling, tinny music played, but I heard it only somewhere in
the distance because I was staring open-mouthed at the red-haired man
sitting cross-legged on the top of my dresser" (21). He leaves by stepping
through the wall—a classic ghost maneuver—but the box's fall confirms that

he has the capacity to move "material objects" in obedience to nature's laws. He is something abstract, a mere appearance, yet he is nevertheless active among concrete, physical things: another case of "something in between."

When Lisa reports him to her mother, however, she receives an introductory lesson on the difference between "ideal" and "real" actions. "Some dreams," her mother tells her, "feel very real," just as some portraits, according to Spencer, are so vivid they seem alive (21). Lisa's mother does not teach her how to live "in between" ideality and reality. She instructs her to decide between them. Do not say, "I saw him," she tells her daughter; say rather, "I dreamed I saw him." The mother's lesson echoes Spencer's account of the "savage" theory of dreams. "If, now . . . we ask what must happen when a dream is narrated by a savage," he speculates, "we shall see that even supposing he suspects some distinction between ideal actions and real actions, he cannot express it. His language does not enable him to say—'I dreamt that I saw,' instead of—'I saw.' Hence each relates his dreams as though they were realities."[5] Savage thought, as Spencer understands it, operates on the principle of catachresis. Savage philosophers do not distinguish the real from the ideal because they can speak of the ideal only "in terms of" the real: a "use of words" that "with us is metaphorical," he explains, "is, with the savage, not distinguished from the literal" (133). Savage philosophers, as usual, are incapable of metaphor because too capable. Nothing is metaphorical because everything is. Their discourse does not describe things. It is active among them. Whatever is vivid, lives. The sense of animation yields an actuality effect.

When Lisa is older, her grandmother takes her into the bush to gather plants that protect against haunting.[6] One is a toxic root she calls *oxasuli*; the other is the cedar bough. Her grandmother leaves tobacco at the base of the cedar in return for each bough she takes. Lisa points out that trees do not smoke. Her grandmother answers that her gift is not for the tree itself but for the cedar-tree spirit:

> "What do the spirits look like?"
> She paused, looking up into the top of the cedar tree. "I don't know. Never seen one. The chief trees—the biggest, strongest, oldest ones— had a spirit, a little man with red hair. Olden days, they'd lead medicine men to the best trees to make canoes with." (152)

Lisa confesses that she has seen the "little man." Her grandmother tells that her she has inherited a "gift" traditionally granted to women on her mother's side of the family: a capacity to speak with ghosts and, sometimes, to foresee events before they happen. Lisa's mother has it too. So why did she neglect to tell her about it? Her grandmother asks the same question:

> She eased herself down onto a stump, then patted the space beside her. "Here, sit." She frowned. "Your mother never said anything?"
>
> "She just said he was a dream."
>
> "Hmmph," she grunted. "He's a guide, but not a reliable one. Never trust the spirit world too much. They think different from the living." (153)

How "different," exactly, do spirits think? Among other things, they ignore the principle of contradiction. They personify possibilities that, as Spencer puts it, the "cultivated members of civilized communities" consider "mutually destructive."[7] Spirits are apparitions that have the force and the density of real things. They are dead, yet they assume the faces and voices of the living. They are "natural and unnatural, possible and impossible" at once. They require Lisa to say, at the same time and with equal conviction, both "I saw them" and "I dreamed that I saw them." Spencer concedes that paradox is a characteristic, if baffling, procedure of savage logic: "It is difficult to picture them [though all he does is "picture" them] as thinking that the dead, though buried, come back in tangible shapes. And where they assert that the duplicate goes away, leaving the corpse behind, there seems no consistency in the accompanying supposition that it needs the food and drink they provide, or wants clothing and fire. For if they conceive it as aëriform or ethereal, then how can they suppose it to consume solid food?" (169–70). Ma-ma-oo has no such difficulty. One day she takes Lisa to the Octupus beds to celebrate her grandfather's birthday. But there is only one problem. Her grandfather is dead. So Ma-ma-oo lights a fire and offers a sacrifice to his ghost, incinerating a bottle of scotch, a pack of cigarettes, and a box of Twinkies:

> "But he's not here," I said.
>
> "Yes he is," she said, "You just can't see him, because he's dead."
>
> I frowned. "Can you see him?"
>
> "She gets it from you," Ma-ma-oo said to the air again. "No, I can't see him. He's dead. He can come to you only in dreams. Be polite and say hello when you give him food." (79)

Spencer has already framed the questions that Lisa repeats more than a century later. How can spirits be visible to one observer but invisible to others? How can they be "aëriform" enough to walk through walls yet "solid" enough to accept a gift of booze, smokes, and junk food? How can they be and do opposite things at once?

Traditionally, the "civilized" scholar is not supposed to ask such questions. "A traditional scholar does not believe in ghosts," Derrida observes, "nor in all that could be called the virtual space of spectrality." When a scholar like Ma-ma-oo speaks with them, she revives the forbidden art of reconciling "irreconcilable conceptions," which requires her to break a fundamental rule of western European logic. "There has never been a scholar," Derrida explains, "who, as such, does not believe in the sharp distinction between the real and the unreal, the actual and the inactual, the living and the non-living, being and non-being . . . in the opposition between what is present and what is not, for example in the form of objectivity. Beyond this opposition, there is, for the scholar, only the hypothesis of a school of thought, theatrical fiction, literature, and speculation."[8] Do not conclude that spirits are absent, Lisa's Ma-ma-oo tells her, just because they are not present. Nor that they are unreal just because they are not real. Nor that they are dead just because, as Derrida puts it, they are "non-living." What kind of scholar is Ma-ma-oo? What kind was Derrida? According to a long tradition, the scholar who respects the opposition between contradictory ideas is praised as "civilized," while the one who collapses it is condemned as either "savage" or "uncultured."[9] The one who upholds the principle of contradiction belongs to a superior race; the one who flouts it belongs to another, inferior race. For it is not just a logical principle but a racializing one. Derrida's list of binary oppositions—real and unreal, living and nonliving, being and nonbeing—is comprised of racialized concepts.

So what compels scholars to talk about spirits at all? Traditionally, the "ghost theory" comes in answer to the question What causes change? The animist says that spirits do. Spirits are personified causes. What they personify, moreover, is the potentiality for impotentiality. The scholar who speaks of them, and with them, affirms that it is impossibly possible for immaterial, nonsensuous events to produce material, sensuous consequences:

With the development of the ghost-theory, there arises an easy way of accounting for all those changes which the heavens and earth hourly exhibit. Clouds that gather and presently vanish, shooting stars that appear and disappear, sudden darkenings of the water's surface by a breeze, animal-metamorphoses, transmutations of substance, storms, earthquakes, eruptions—all of them are now understood. These beings to whom is ascribed the power of making themselves visible and invisible

at will, and to whose other powers no limits are known, are omnipresent. Explaining, as their agency seems to do, all unexpected changes,
their own existence becomes further verified. No other causes for such
changes are known, or can be conceived; therefore these souls of the
dead must be the causes. (1:217)

The "ghost theory" shares a premise with the doctrine of illocutionary
forces. Both affirm that there exists a potential for change in which cause
and effect are not *in pari materia*. In the ghost event, an apparition is really
operative in actuality; in the illocutionary act, the act of saying something
entails consequences that "are usually not the *saying* of anything." [10]

Sometimes the ghost event takes the form of an utterance that describes
nothing that is but invites the emergence of something that is not. Derrida
calls it a conjuration: "the appeal that causes to come forth *with the voice*
and thus . . . makes come, by definition, what *is not there* at the present
moment of the appeal. This voice does not describe," he argues, "what it
says certifies nothing; its words cause something to happen." [11] To say that a
conjuration "causes to happen" presupposes a "fundamentally different
sense of cause" from the one "used in physical causation." [12] The art of
conjuring produces a "spectrality effect." One way of achieving nondiscursive consequences by discursive means is the act of citation. A ghost, after
all, is a citation of itself. It arrives for the first time "*by coming back.*" [13]
To conjure is always, in a sense, to cite. Derrida suggests it is a kind of
originary citation, an event that happens for the first time by happening
again. Yet it is precisely by repeating itself that it makes itself effective.
In repetition, there is a potential for the "effectivity" of the ineffective.
A citation's potentiality to act is simultaneously its *im*potentiality to act.
But there is no contradiction between them: "*What is* a ghost? What is the
effectivity or the *presence* of a specter, that is, of what seems to remain as
ineffective, virtual, insubstantial as a simulacrum? Is there *there*, between
the thing itself and its simulacrum, an opposition that holds up? Repetition
and first time, but also repetition *and* last time, since the singularity of
any *first time* makes of it also a *last time*. Each time it is the event itself, a
first time is a last time" (10). The event of citation happens not just *in* time
but *to* time (77). Its "effectivity" depends on its capacity to fold back over
the original until it precedes it. An event cannot precede itself unless it is
always already divided from itself. Yet the citation does not have to be fully
present to be effective. Indeed the force of the citation depends on its ability
to break with the context of its occurrence, whether past, present, or future.
"Before knowing whether one can differentiate between the specter of the

past and the specter of the future, of the past present and the future present, one must perhaps ask oneself whether the *spectrality effect* does not consist in undoing this opposition, or even this dialectic, between actual, effective presence and its other" (39–40). Robinson gives the name "Indian time" to the present that folds back over the past to interrupt the arrival of the future. Her novel suggests that the "Indian" emerges on the surface of discourse today as a citation of what was said about savage philosophers in discourses past. But savage thought is "by definition" what recurs. The specter of savagery is a specter of repetition: "always either an hour ahead or an hour behind." Robinson summons up the ghosts of discourse past not to endorse what they say but to affirm a mode of being that, hovering in between appearance and reality, hinges on being repeated.

A Great Day for Spirits

The question recurs: How can the same statement be repeated, and remain valid, from one historical context to another? "In other words," Derrida asks, "how can it come back and present itself again, anew, as the new? How can it be there, again, when its time is no longer there" (49)? Do the ghosts of discourse past have a history? Does history have a place for them? Or a time? "Is there a present of the specter? Are its comings and goings ordered according to the linear succession of a before and an after, between a present-past, a present-present, and a present-future" (39)? Hegel makes the definitive attempt to exorcize the specter of repetition from history in the introduction to the *Philosophy of History*, a series of lectures given in the winter of 1830–31. The writing of history, he suggests, hinges together two mutually incompatible modes of time. Events follow one another in a linear series—a succession from a present-past, through a present-present, to a present-future—although this line is not straight, but curved, because history's end is already contained in its beginning. Hegel's unit for measuring circular, historical time is the day. The day itself, however, is a point. It goes neither forward nor backward in time. It can only repeat itself in the present. Every day is a horizon for the emergence of something new. Yet today is no different from the day before. The course of history advances from one present to the next, but the present itself, like the Elvis clock, Robinson's personified reification of time, stays "caught in mid-gyrate." To sublate the difference between circular time and day time, history and repetition, Hegel resorts to an allegory.[14] He compares history's course to the sun's passage across the sky. History happens *in* a day *as* a day. The sun, however, is a figure of repetition. Its passage is supposed to stand for an unrepeatable series of events, but it keeps coming back day after day. Hegel's effort to conjure repetition from history remains, even today, an allegory of its own impossibility.[15]

The allegory of the sun receives its fullest treatment in the chapter "The Classification of Historical Data," which connects Hegel's introduction to "The Philosophy of History" proper. He speaks of it as if it were something that we, his readers, have already read. It is both a citation and the original. Hence it performs the sort of repetition that it is supposed to forestall. Hegel invites us to recall the "picture" of a "blind man" who is granted sight and watches the sun rise for the first time.[16] For a while the man is astonished; gradually, though, he begins to contemplate the world outside him; then he turns his attention to the world inside him, his own consciousness; at last he sets to work remaking the outer world in his inner world's image, endowing nature with a human form. The blind man's progress represents history's course. Historical peoples make actual in the world what exists potentially in consciousness, and as history draws to a close, they find their image looking back at them from the products of their labor. They have delivered humankind to self-consciousness:

> Imagination has often pictured to itself the emotions of a blind man suddenly becoming possessed of sight, beholding the bright glimmering of dawn, the growing light and flaming glory of the ascending Sun. The boundless forgetfulness of his individuality in this pure splendor, is his first feeling—utter astonishment. But when the Sun is risen, this astonishment is diminished; objects around are perceived, and from them the individual proceeds to the contemplation of his own inner being, and thereby the advance is made to the perception of the relation between the two. Then inactive contemplation is quitted for activity; by the close of day man has erected a building constructed from his own inner Sun; and when in the evening he contemplates this, he esteems it more highly than the original external Sun. For now he stands in a *conscious relation* to his Spirit, and therefore a *free* relation. If we hold this image fast in mind, we shall find it symbolizing the course of History, the great Day's work of Spirit.[17]

Hegel maintains that reason, which is at once infinite form and infinite matter, takes part in the production of historical events. History is therefore "a rational process" (9). Determined as form, reason is spirit (*Geist*), a principle of change. Determined as matter, reason is nature, a principle of repetition and thus the "very contrary of change" (55). Spirit makes itself actually what it is potentially. It is an idea that realizes itself. Nature remains what it always was. Its potentiality to be is balanced by its potentiality to not-be. Spirit tends toward self-consciousness. It knows what it is when it sees what it has done. Nature already is all that it will ever become. There is no organic evolution. Spirit is constantly at war with itself and strives to overcome itself. Nature rests in "peaceful growth" (55). Spirit lifts itself up. Nature recurs: "The changes that take place in Nature—how infinitely manifold soever they may be—exhibit only a perpetually self-repeating cycle; in Nature there happens 'nothing new under the sun,' and the multiform play of its phenomena so far induces a feeling of *ennui;* only in those changes which take place in the region of Spirit does anything new arise" (54). History, for Hegel, is a dialectic of change and repetition, which aims to sublate the difference between them. The circular series of present moments tends toward an eternal present of self-contemplation. Out of the strife between spirit and nature, change and repetition, comes spirit-nature: changeless self-repetition.

The sun reaches its zenith over the "German Nations" of western Europe, bathing them in the light of self-conscious, "self-repeating," freedom. Meanwhile, to the west of the West, the indigenous civilizations of the Americas flicker dimly in history's shadows and are extinguished: "Of America and its grade of civilization, especially in Mexico and Peru, we have information, but it imports nothing more than that this culture was an entirely national one, which must expire as soon as Spirit approached it" (81). The dawn does not astonish "this culture." It incinerates it. The Americas are home to a spirit lacking in entelechy. Its "grade of civilization" is "self-repeating" nature. Hence it is a nature-spirit. As the sun advances westward, European entelechy sweeps it into history's shadow: "America has always shown itself physically and psychically powerless, and still shows itself so. For the aborigines, after the landing of the Europeans in America, gradually vanished at the breath of European activity" (81). Ironically, the specters of repetition return to life a few lines later, as if to suggest that repetition is not just the "matter" but the "form" of universal history: "In the United States of North America all the citizens are of European descent, with whom the old inhabitants could not amalgamate, but were driven back. The aborigines have certainly adopted some arts and usages from the Europeans, among others that of brandy-drinking, which has operated with deadly effect" (81). The specters of repetition come to an end by coming back. No matter where they recur, they mimic the utterance that conjures them into being: an utterance that Hegel's discourse carries along but cannot carry forward, a survival that he cannot sublate, that is resistant to change, and that keeps coming back, although each time it returns, it appears in the guise of the new, as if it were valid for all times in which it is possible to say "our time."

Hegel says it was because the "aborigines" were "physically and psychically powerless" that others "had" to be brought to the Americas to do history's work. Do not blame Europeans for the institution of slavery, he suggests, blame Native Americans: "The weakness of the American physique was a chief reason for bringing the negroes to America, to employ their labor in the work that had to be done in the New World" (82). Only nature has the energy to fuel spirit's "self"-actualization. When the American nature-spirit proved to be too "weak" to work, Europe had no choice but to replace it with the African nature-spirit. The colonization of the New World puts the European spirit in an embarrassing situation. It is supposed to achieve self-consciousness by realizing its aims in the products of its *own* labor; in the Americas, though, it is constrained to realize its aims in the products of African labor. Europe's "self"-emancipation depends on Africa's enslavement. The historical world borrows its principle of change from the self-repeating, natural world.

Hegel divides this world into three regions: North Africa, which is "European," the Nile valley, which is connected "with Asia," and "Africa proper," which "lies south" of the Sahara desert (91). The sun of history never shines down south: "Africa proper, as far as History goes back, has remained—for all purposes of connection with the rest of the World—shut up; it is the Gold-land compressed within itself—the land of childhood, which lying beyond the day of self-conscious history, is enveloped in the dark mantle of Night" (91). The "proper" African (the non-European, non-Asian, that is, black African), like the "aborigines" of the Americas, personifies the sort of spirit that lacks the energy to raise itself from self-repetition to self-consciousness. "The Negro," Hegel maintains, "exhibits the natural man in his completely wild and untamed state" (93). The wild man is rich in entelechy. Thus he is capable of enormous activity. But he is poor in ideas. Hence he is incapable of directing his activity toward a purpose. What he lacks, in particular, is any idea of the future. So he makes nothing that lasts. Instead he spends the day passing now as if it were the only day he has: "Every idea thrown into the mind of the Negro is caught up and realized with the whole energy of his will; but this realization involves a wholesale destruction. These people continue long at rest, but suddenly their passions ferment, and then they are quite beside themselves. The destruction which is the consequence of their excitement, is caused by the fact that it is no positive idea, no thought which produces these commotions;—a physical rather than a spiritual enthusiasm" (98). The specters of repetition are specters of excess. They balance every act of creation with an act of destruction. Sometimes they explode into action, but even then they do no work. They spend all of their energy now and save none for later. Although they grow, they do not develop. That is why they have no history. Hegel says of "Africa proper" what he has already said of nature: "This condition is capable of no development or culture, and as we see them at this day, such have they always been" (98). Hegel's proper Africans are "caught in mid-gyrate": always one hour ahead *and* one hour behind in history's course. He claims that if Europe had not taught them how to fix their labor power in durable goods, they would have spent the rest of time wasting it in spontaneous acts of expenditure. Work shall make the slave free. But not yet. Hegel regards slavery as a necessary "phase" of Africa's "education." "Slavery is in and for itself *injustice*," he admits, "for the essence of humanity is *Freedom*; but for this man must be matured. The gradual abolition of slavery is therefore wiser and more equitable than its sudden removal" (99). Best to wait until spirit's work in the Americas is done.

Slavery, for Hegel, is Africa's only connection to Europe and, through Europe, to history: "it is no historical part of the World; it has no movement or development to exhibit" (99). So after he has issued his call for "gradual abolition," he is free to conjure the specters of repetition from history: "At this point we leave Africa, not to mention it again" (99). He refuses to be haunted, whether by repetition or by "injustice."

Yet as soon as he bans it—indeed at the very "point" at which he bans it—repetition returns in the form of the allegory of the sun. Hegel conjures it back in the very act of conjuring it away:

> What we properly understand by Africa, is the Unhistorical, Undeveloped Spirit, still involved in the conditions of mere nature, and which had to be presented here only as on the threshold of the World's History.
>
> Having eliminated this introductory element, we find ourselves for the first time on the real theatre of History. It now only remains for us to give a prefatory sketch of the Geographical basis of the Asiatic and European world. *Asia* is, characteristically, the *Orient* quarter of the globe— the region of origination. It is indeed a Western world for America; but as Europe presents on the whole, the centre and end of the old world, and is absolutely the *West*—so Asia is absolutely the *East*.
>
> In Asia rose the Light of Spirit, and therefore the history of the world. (99)

Projecting a two-dimensional, linear succession of events onto the three-dimensional surface of the globe, he observes that just as the "light" rises in the east and travels to the west, so history "originates" in Asia and comes to its proper "end" in Europe. But his allegory involves the philosopher of the *Aufhebung* in a contradiction he cannot sublate.

The dawn of history breaks over "the nomadic tribes" of the Asian Upland. Hegel situates them "in between" repetition and development. They balance the "calm *habitual* life" of the shepherd, who personifies nature, with the "wild and restless" life of the warrior, who personifies spirit (101). The rising sun shines next on "the river-plains" of China, India, and "Babylonia." The peoples of the plains liberate spirit from the self-repeating present of unproductive expenditure and instill it with the "foresight and solicitude" necessary for productive labor. Because they have no access to the sea, though, they remain "shut up within themselves" (101). The sun leaves them behind and passes on to "Anterior Asia," which consists of Syria, Asia Minor, and Arabia. Here the warlike energy of the uplands joins with the future-oriented industry of the plains, producing the negation of the negation. Anterior Asia does not keep the results of its world-historical labor for itself, however, but transmits them "to Europe," which alone has the potential to finish what Asia begins (101). Still, the world spirit does not find the "means of realizing" its potential—which is self-conscious freedom—until it arrives over the "German World"—principally France, Germany, and England—where freedom and necessity, reason and nature, are finally reconciled in the constitution of the nation-state (26, 109).

It is here, at the limit where history's origin passes into its end, that the allegory of the sun spins out of Hegel's control. The sun's journey across the sky "symbolizes" a course that, although circular, cannot be repeated. Yet a circular motion is better suited to serve as an allegory of repetition than as the allegory of a one-way development. In the morning the sun rises and in the evening it sets. Then it does it again the next day. Every rising of the sun, like every visit of a ghost, is a repetition and a first time. Hegel admits that when the sun of history finishes its journey from Asia to Europe, it will carry the light of self-conscious freedom from Europe to the Americas— "America is therefore the land of the future, where, in the ages that lie before us, the burden of the World's History shall reveal itself" (86)—but as it advances westward, the sun will eventually travel so far west that it will arrive in the east again, where it will inevitably repeat its daily journey, and when night finally settles on the Western world, Asia will rise above Europe on the trajectory of the world spirit's self-development.

Hegel foresees that his allegory threatens to summon the specter of repetition back into the historical field, so like a latter-day Joshua warring against the Amorites, he commands the sun to stop in its tracks at the westernmost limit of the west. He concedes that "east" and "west" are defined in opposition to each other and therefore "relative," but he nevertheless imposes an "absolutely" eastern beginning and "absolutely" western end on the sun's journey across history's sky. The difference between Asia and Europe is one dialectical opposition that he refuses to sublate: "The History of the World travels from East to West, for Europe is absolutely the end of History, Asia the beginning. The history of the World has an East $\kappa\alpha\tau'$ $\dot{\epsilon}\xi o\chi\acute{\eta}\nu$ [kath'heauton, "per se"]; (the term East in itself is entirely relative), for although the Earth forms a sphere, History performs no circle around it, but has on the contrary a determinate East, viz., Asia." (103). East and west may be "relative" terms in other contexts, but they are "determinate," and therefore fixed, in Hegel's allegory of history. If he let the sun rise again in the east after it sets in the west, then Asia would usurp Europe's place, and the end of history would simultaneously be its repetition. But it is the privilege of the end to contain the origin. The origin cannot be permitted to eclipse the end. Asia gives history to Europe, and at the end of the day, Hegel declines to give it back, even though by arresting the sun in midcourse he brings dialectics to a standstill as well.

Nothing New under the *Sun*

Fifty years later, the allegory of the sun returns, as if for the first time, in Spencer's theory of superorganic evolution, which holds that natural life grows "by insensible steps" into social life. Hegel admits that the sun is a figure for history. Spencer does what he says savage philosophers do. He takes a figure for a fact. In violation of Darwin's laws of the variation of species, he argues that the sun is really active in the production of organic and social forms.[18] Indeed it is their common principle of development. Spencer's sun is governed by the prodigality principle. It spends its forces without reserve, keeping nothing for itself. Yet it always has more to give.[19] Organic life, in contrast, is governed by the parsimony principle. It stores the sun's energy in myriad life-forms. And the more energy the sun spends, the more complex life becomes. Single-cell organisms develop into multicellular ones. Multicellular organisms gather into social aggregates. There are "communities" of birds and a "governmental organization" of bison.[20] The most complex aggregates, though, are human ones. Spencer conceives of them as vast stores of "solar radiation." But the sun does not distribute its riches equally. It discriminates on the basis of distance. Societies located either too far from or too close to the sun remain caught, in midgyrate, on the threshold of superorganic development: "We must therefore say that solar radiation, being the source of those forces by which life, vegetal and animal, is carried on; and being, by implication, the source of the forces displayed in human life, and consequently in social life; it results that there can be no considerable social evolution on tracts of the Earth's surface where solar radiation is very feeble" (20). The societies of the poles—"the Esquimaux" to the north and "the Fuegians" to the south—lack "a sufficient surplus-power" to build a complex civilization (17–18). Indeed they are so poor in energy that they are forced to waste what little they do have, balancing absolute scarcity with absolute excess. The "Esquimaux," because they lack heat, consume "vast quantities of blubber and oil" (18). The "still-more-miserable Fuegians" are so cold that they devote all their forces to "preserving the vital balance" (18). At the poles, there is nothing left over to fuel the growth of the aggregate. Superorganic evolution can only occur in between the extreme north and the extreme south. Since it requires more energy to create a social organism than to sustain one, however, "the first considerable societies arose, and the primary stages of social development were reached, in hot climates" (19). Only later did superorganic life "take root and grow" in the "temperate regions," although it is there, he insists, that "societies have evolved most, both in size and complexity" (19–20).

Spencer argues, anachronistically, that the human body is a balance of humors: cold and hot, moist and dry. The sun regulates the balance between them. Where its heat is scarce, it makes bodies cold and moist. Where its heat is excessive, it makes them hot and dry. Furthermore the balance of humors is responsible for producing that most privileged signifier of racial difference: the color of the skin. If your climate is poor in heat but rich in moisture, Spencer claims, you are destined to be black. If your climate is poor in moisture but rich in heat, you are destined to be white. Your race is a function of your body's relation to the sun. He cites a list of authorities in support of his racial hypothesis: "Speaking of the varieties of negroes, Livingstone says—'Heat alone does not produce blackness of the skin, but heat with moisture seems to insure the deepest hue'; and Schweinfurth remarks on the relative blackness of the Denka and other tribes living on the alluvial plains, and contrasts them with 'the less swarthy and more robust races who inhabit the rocky hills of the interior': differences with which there go differences of energy" (23).

Yet Spencer resorts to more than one strategy for explaining the origins of racial difference. Race is also, he suggests, the body's moral evaluation of the soul, and the body evaluates the soul's morality according to an economic standard. The color of your skin indicates whether you incline toward prodigality or parsimony, that is, whether you tend to accumulate or to squander value. Parsimony is, predictably, noble; prodigality is base. If you are white, it is because your body accumulates the sun's forces and holds them in reserve for future-oriented works of productive labor. If you are black, it is because your body squanders the sun's forces in present-oriented acts of "physical enthusiasm." If historically the "lighter" races tend to dominate the "darker" ones, Spencer argues, it is because the souls of light bodies use solar radiation more productively and more responsibly than the souls of dark bodies do. History rewards those who save and punishes those who spend. Social domination is a natural part of the solar cycle:

> I note this fact for the purpose of suggesting its probable connexion with the fact that the lighter-skinned races are habitually the dominant races. We see it to have been so in Egypt. It was so with the races spreading south from Central Asia. Traditions imply that it was so in Central America and Peru. Speke says:—"I have always found the lighter-coloured savages more boisterous and warlike than those of a dingier hue." And if, heat being the same, darkness of skin accompanies humidity of the air, while lightness of skin accompanies dryness of the air, then, in this habitual predominance of the fair varieties of men, we find further evidence that constitutional activity, and in so far social development, is favored by a climate conducing to rapid evaporation. (23)

Where there is accumulation, there is "development"; where there is expenditure, inertia. The "lighter-skinned races" personify the moral-economic virtue of industry; darker-skinned races, the moral-economic vice of indolence. The accumulation of solar radiation makes the light and dry races active, future-oriented, and anxious to build complex social forms; the expenditure of solar radiation makes the hot and humid races passive, present-oriented, and forgetful of social development. Spencer cautions, though, that "dark" bodies often grow "lighter" after they move from a humid to a dry climate, just as "light" bodies grow "darker" after they move from a hot and dry to a hot and humid climate.

The allegory of the sun, whether taken as a figure or as a fact, discharges a race-giving, race-forming force. It brings racial differences into emergence on the surface of discourse. By 1886, the sun of history, ignoring Hegel's injunction to halt over Germany, has traveled as far west as Vancouver Island, so far west that it is about to return to the east, where it is about to resume its unrepeatable course. Following in its path, Franz Boas has traveled from

Berlin to the frontier city of Victoria, where he has set about studying the languages and cultures of the northwest coast of the Americas. He records his impressions of the western limit in a letter-diary addressed to his parents. In an entry dated September 27, 1886, he muses that it is as if historical time has come to stop here. What he writes today repeats what he wrote the day before: "This diary affords little variety. It always tells the same story: that I went to visit Indians and that I returned home; that I am told stories and that I copy them, etc."[21] When he writes about "Indians," he can only copy "stories" he has copied before. Today, which is the "same" day as yesterday and tomorrow, he visited two women he has already visited, and one of them recited a story he has already heard. Naturally, it is a story of the sun: "This morning I visited the Tsimsian woman, who told me a long story, and in the afternoon the Wikiano [Wikeno] woman told me the story of the origin of the sun" (27). The "story of the sun" is inevitably a story of origins. To recite it is both a repetition and a first time.

Boas's letter-diary is one of those media that supply its time with a "techno-tele-discursive" surface for the emergence of events. Yet what emerges there, for the first and last time, is neither physical nor nonphysical, "neither living nor dead, present nor absent." His diary, rather, is the sort of medium that conjures up specters, as if the only way to write about the limit between east and west is to repeat what was written the day before. Derrida points out that any "techno-tele-discursive" surface can serve as a medium that "spectralizes."[22] A spectral medium is one that traffics in spirits, and a scholar who hopes to account for its "effectivity" has to return, against the current of intellectual history, to the hypotheses of animism and revive them, for animism is the philosophy of spirits. Derrida, like any other savage philosopher, affirms that ghosts and specters, indeed spirits of all sorts, are principles of change. Today, though, change is more than ever the actualization of what exists *im*potentially, and "power," the capacity to produce change, achieves its most hegemonic "effects" by the most spectral techniques. Nonetheless, scholars continue to labor under the prejudice that ghosts are incapable of producing material consequences:

> As it has never done before, either to such a degree or in these forms, the politico-economic hegemony, like the intellectual or discursive domination, passes by way of techno-mediatic power. . . . Now, this power, this differentiated set of powers cannot be analyzed or potentially combated, supported here, attacked there, without taking into account so many *spectral* effects, the new speed of *apparition* (we understand this word in its ghostly sense) of the simulacrum, the synthetic or prosthetic image,

and the virtual event, cyberspace and surveillance, the control, appropriations, and speculations that today deploy unheard-of powers. (53–54)

Derrida dares today's scholar to return to the forbidden study of specters, appearances, and idealities, giving them their due and acknowledging their force. But when did scholars stop trafficking with ghosts? What, in other words, is the temporal horizon of Derrida's "never before"? For more than two centuries, scholars have displaced the potentiality of impotentiality onto the figure of a savage philosopher who insists that "the similitude can take the place of the model" and that "a double [is] equally material with the original."[23] Living with ghosts is what savage philosophers do. It is what they have always done. They emerge into discourse already equipped with the knowledge that the simulacrum not only reproduces the image, but carries the force, of the original. Boas is alarmed to find himself copying a copy of a story of origins. Savage philosophers have no such qualms. Derrida asks us to mimic them, copying the copies that traditional scholars located at the origin of our intellectual development. Only by going savage can a society that exercises domination by techno-mediatic techniques come to terms with its own barbarism. Only conventionally savage philosophers can teach supposedly civilized scholars how to live in a spectral world order.[24]

At the end of *Monkey Beach*, just before she circles back to the beginning, Lisa receives a cryptic lesson in the importance of learning to live with ghosts. After she drowns, while she hovers between life and death, her grandmother returns from the ghost world and urges her to finish her education in the "unheard-of powers" of specters: "'You have a dangerous gift,' she says. 'It's like oxasuli. Unless you know how to use it, it will kill you.'" The lesson is lost on Lisa. There is nobody, living or dead, who can instruct her in the art of impotentiality. The novel leaves her suspended in between ignorance and knowledge: "'I still don't understand,' I say."[25] She makes an appeal for instruction, and although a voice from the ghost world urges, "Tell her," the call goes unanswered. A spectral discourse murmurs all around her, but she lacks the skill to interpret it. Indeed she does not even have words of her own: "I want to yell for help, but nothing comes out" (373). Her narrative is an allegory of what befalls the scholar who fails to learn to live with ghosts.

Lisa's encounter with specters ends where Derrida's begins. He opens the *Exordium* to *Specters of Marx* with a stage direction: "Someone, you or me, comes forward and says, *I would like to learn to live finally*."[26] Lisa comes forward too late, and when she does, she cannot even find the words to ask for help. But who is the "someone" who asks for instruction in Derri-

da's text? He says it could be anyone: "you or me." Perhaps it is the anonymous murmur of "our time" that calls us—you *and* me—to learn to speak
with the ghosts of discourse past, especially the ghosts conjured back daily
on the "tele-techno-discursive surfaces" of the media. It is as if "the media"
have taken over the role of "the medium," a conjurer skilled in the convoca-
tion of spirits. They traffic in ghosts of discourse. The rest of this chapter is
devoted to a single, though substantial, case of "techno-mediatic" conjuration. But it is not just any example. It demonstrates the effectivity of the
specters of discourse and underlines the necessity of learning just how "different" they think and act "from the living."

In the 1990s the government of Canada and the province of British
Columbia negotiated a comprehensive land claims agreement with the
tribal council of the Nisga'a First Nation. The land at the center of the
negotiations fell within the region traditionally located between repetition
and history, the region where events are said to begin by coming back: the
northwest coast of North America. Between 1995 and 2000, the British
Columbia media tried more than once to discredit the Nisga'a claim. One
of its favored techniques was to conjure up the specter of savage excess.
One mediatic surface where the specter kept returning, like the nothing
that is always news, was the *Vancouver Sun*, one of the province's oldest
newspapers.

When the *Sun* was first published on February 12, 1912, the editors
called for the swift and just resolution of aboriginal land claims.[27] The
Nisga'a nation had been claiming title to a territory bordering the Nass
River, to the south of the Alaska Panhandle, since the 1880s. Good-faith
negotiations did not begin, however, until 1991. In February 1995, the *Sun*
reported that it had obtained information about a pending agreement in
principle. Stewart Bell and Justine Hunter asked conservative "critics" to
review it and published their comments under a front-page banner headline:
"Nisga'a offer too much, Reformers say." The headline can be read in two
ways. If "offer" is taken as a noun, it says that the governments of Canada
and British Columbia are about to concede too much to the Nisga'a nation. If "offer" is taken as a verb, then it is the Nisga'a who are giving too
much away and the provincial and federal governments that are offering
too little in return. The article sets the upper and lower limits of the coming debate: surplus and scarcity. The "Reformers"—members of the now-
superseded, neoconservative Reform Party—conjure up the specter of excess, as if it were the one thing fit for every time in which it is possible to
say "our time":

A land-claims settlement offered to Nisga'a native Indians in northwestern B.C. is overly generous and sets a dangerous precedent, opposition
politicians charged Wednesday.

Critics said they were shocked to learn Ottawa and Victoria had
offered $125 million and 1,900 square kilometres of land to the 6,000-
member Nisga'a Tribal Council last July.

"I find it incredible that a package like this could be offered to that
many people," said John Duncan, the Reform party's aboriginal-affairs
critic.[28]

Excess is not only the article's theme but its mode of emergence. To speak
of "native Indians" is itself an act of excess. Verbs expand the actions they
denote: the proposed settlement does not surprise critics but "shocks"
them. Nouns are burdened with intensifying adverbs and adjectives: the
settlement is not just generous but "overly" generous, and it "sets" not
just a precedent but a "dangerous" one. Everything is big. On the inside
page, Mike Scott, the member of Parliament for Skeena, the federal riding
that includes the Nisga'a territory, remarks that the negotiations threaten
the "whole" economy of northwestern British Columbia: "I'm really concerned"—not just "concerned," but "really" concerned—"because our
whole economy in the northwest is primarily driven by forestry and when
we talk about 15.5 million cubic metres [the amount of timber allegedly
included in the agreement in principle], that would almost certainly have
an impact on the existing sawmills in the area." Scott convokes the ghost
of the improvident savage who squanders the future by spending a surplus
of resources now.

The three parties to the negotiations did not in fact strike an agreement
in principle until February 15, 1996. It was signed in the Nisga'a village of
New Aiyansh on March 22. The following week Stewart Bell returned to
the *Sun* with a story about the cost of land-claims negotiations in British
Columbia. The expenditures, he suggests, are potentially limitless. To date,
the government of British Columbia has spent three million dollars; the government of Canada, six million. However it is the Nisga'a who have made
the largest expenditures: twenty million. Bell asks a Liberal member of British Columbia's Legislative Assembly to comment. First he paraphrases the
member's reply: "Liberal critic Mike de Jong said it's a hefty sum when you
consider the Nisga'a deal is just one of dozens of treaties being negotiated
across the province."[29] Then he quotes it: "'It's a lot of money,' said de Jong,
'When you multiply that over the 50 or 60 sets of negotiations that are

taking place it becomes a staggering amount of money.'" The statement
on savage excess has a self-expanding form. When first stated, the amount
under discussion is "hefty"; when repeated, it is "a lot of money"; when
repeated again it is "a staggering amount." The discussion of fiscal inflation
obeys a law of discursive inflation.

The agreement in principle was a long time coming. Indeed it took almost 120 years: an excess of time. The British Columbia reserve commissioner Peter O'Reilly arrived in the Nisga'a village of Kincolith in October
1881, where he spent two weeks visiting Nisga'a territory and setting aside
land for reserves. The rest of the land was to be thrown open for settlement
and resource extraction. The Nisga'a insist that O'Reilly did not explain
the purpose of his visit.[30] Nor did he survey the land before carving it up. It
has been estimated that the reserve system reduced Nisga'a tribal territory
from 14,830 square kilometers—roughly the size of New Jersey—to 76: a
reduction of 99.5 percent (74–75). In 1881 Chief Mountain and Charles Russ
traveled to Victoria in the company of two missionaries to discuss the land
question with the federal Indian superintendent for British Columbia, I. W.
Powell. Russ remarked afterward that Powell did not appear to give them
a fair hearing.[31] In 1886 surveyors for the Indian Reserve Commission arrived on Nisga'a territory to begin mapping the boundaries that O'Reilly had
sketched five years before. The Nisga'a expelled them.[32] Nisga'a chiefs met
with chiefs from the Tsimshian village of Port Simpson in the same year,
and the two parties agreed to send a joint delegation to Victoria to ask the
provincial and federal governments for a treaty.[33] The meeting took place in
the winter of 1887. Federal and provincial officials belittled the concerns of
the Nisga'a and Tsimshian delegation but agreed to appoint a joint federal-
provincial commission to investigate the land question.[34] In the fall of 1887,
Clement Cornwall, representing the dominion, and Joseph Planta, representing the province, held public hearings in the north coast villages of Kincolith,
Nass Harbor, and Port Simpson. The attorney general of British Columbia
instructed Planta to "discountenance" any suggestion that the First Nations
had a title to their territory; this instruction would remain the province's
policy for more than a century.[35] The commissioners recommended enlarg-
ing reserves and advised the federal government to appoint an Indian agent
for the north coast, a proposal that Nisga'a and Tsimshian chiefs rejected.[36]
In 1907 the Nisga'a established the Nisga'a Land Committee to pursue their
claim,[37] and in 1913 the committee issued "Statement of the Nisga'a Nation
or Tribe of Indians," which reaffirmed that the Nisga'a held title to territory
in the Nass valley and affirmed that aboriginal title in western Canada had
been established by the Royal Proclamation of 1763.[38] In May 1913 the com-

mittee submitted a petition to the Privy Council of Great Britain, asking for a treaty, recognition of title, and self-government. The Imperial government referred the matter to the government of Canada.[39] In 1916 the committee made a submission to the McKenna-McBride commission, which had been established in 1913 to adjust the boundaries of reserves in British Columbia. The commission recommended that the size of reserves be increased but let the more valuable reserve lands be "cut off" and sold to settlers, speculators, and municipalities. In 1923 the Nisga'a requested compensation for the loss of land and resources. In 1927 the Parliament of Canada, at the urging of Indian Affairs administrators, added section 141 to the Indian Act, making it illegal to raise funds for the pursuit of land claims.[40]

In 1942 the Native Brotherhood of British Columbia opened a branch in the Nisga'a village of Greenville. The secretary was Frank Calder.[41] After the Second World War, the Indian Act was amended and the ban on fund-raising removed. The four clans and four villages of the Nisga'a nation gave Calder "consent" to form a tribal council, which renewed the Nisga'a claim (122–23). In 1969 the Nisga'a Tribal Council petitioned the supreme court of British Columbia for "a declaration" that Nisga'a title to lands in and around the Nass River valley, Observatory Inlet, Portland Inlet, and the Portland Canal had "never been lawfully extinguished." Calder was first on the list of plaintiffs, and the suit came to be known as the Calder case. In October 1969 the province's supreme court ruled that the Crown had asserted its undisputed sovereignty over British Columbia by performing a series of thirteen "legislative events" between 1858, when the mainland colony of British Columbia was established, and 1871, when the colony of British Columbia joined the Canadian confederation.[42] These illocutionary acts came to be known as the Calder Thirteen. In May 1970, the British Columbia court of appeal ruled that the Nisga'a had been too "primitive" at the time of settlement to have had any civilized "notions of private property." No government, the court concluded, could reasonably be expected to recognize rights of a primitive "kind."[43] The case was appealed to the Supreme Court of Canada in November 1971, and seven judges ruled in January 1973. One group of three judges held that even if the Nisga'a had held title to the land and its resources, it had been extinguished by the illocutionary force of the Calder Thirteen. Another group of three found that aboriginal title to lands and resources is a "burden"—effectively a white man's burden—on the underlying title of the Crown, that this title could be surrendered only to the Crown, and that it could be extinguished only by an act of Parliament. That had never been done. Title was unextinguished.[44] The seventh judge noted that provincial law required the plaintiff to secure the province's consent before bringing a suit against it. The Nisga'a Tribal Council had not done so. The Calder case was quashed on a technicality.

The next day Frank Howard, member of Parliament for Skeena, rose in the House of Commons in Ottawa and asked whether Prime Minister Pierre Trudeau would agree to meet with the Nisga'a Tribal Council to discuss the longstanding claim, and on February 7 Trudeau made his now famous concession: "perhaps you have more legal rights than we thought you had." [45] On August 8 the minister of Indian Affairs and Northern Development issued a statement that the federal government was now ready to negotiate unresolved land claims with First Nations across the country but would negotiate one claim at a time in each province or territory. [46] An Office of Native Claims was established to supervise the process. The Nisga'a submitted their claim in 1974, and negotiations with the federal government began in 1976. The province agreed to attend as an observer (191, 206–7). In 1981 the federal government implemented a comprehensive claims procedure, and the Nisga'a claim was one of seven accepted for negotiation. [47] The government of British Columbia agreed to join the negotiations in 1990, in part because aboriginal people had been protesting by mounting blockades on provincial roads since 1983. [48] At the urging of the First Nations Congress, later the First Nations Summit, the province appointed the British Columbia Claims Task Force to devise a negotiating process. The task force recommended that a treaty commission be established to settle outstanding claims. The commission was appointed in April 1993, too late to include the Nisga'a claim. [49]

The public debate that flared up around the negotiations in the late 1990s distributed the Nisga'a nation and settler society onto two sides of an inverse ratio. Its logic runs as follows. When one side of the ratio increases by a certain amount, the other shrinks by an equal, opposite amount. What one gains the other loses. Tom Spicer articulates the law of the inverse ratio in a letter to the *Sun*'s editor, published on September 19, 1995: "our governments continue to give large tracts of land and huge amounts of money to the very small number of native Indians (less than three per cent of the population), while expecting ordinary taxpaying Canadians to foot the bill." [50] Every quantum added to the small side of the ratio, the "minority," takes a quantum from the large side, the "majority." The small, "very small," side consists of "native Indians"; the large side, of "ordinary" people. The exact ratio between them is 97:3. Yet Spicer insists that the minority poses a threat to the majority: 3 is larger than 97. "We" have given "them" not just land but "large tracts of it," not just money but "huge amounts of it." The threat to "us" is inversely proportional to the magnitude of "them."

Hegel, who "is *also* the thinker of irreducible difference,"[51] points out that an inverse ratio is a *qualitative* quantum. A quantum is qualitative when it marks a limit. The inverse ratio in fact marks a double limit. It distributes a finite quantum, 100, between two opposing sides, 97:3. The distribution, moreover, determines the essence of each side. Each *is* what the other does not *have:* 97 is 100 minus 3; 3 is 100 minus 97. As Hegel explains, "the quantum is, *first,* an immediate magnitude as a *simple* determinateness, the *whole* as a quantum simply affirmatively present." In Spicer's ratio, the simple determinateness, or "whole," is 100. "But secondly," Hegel adds, "this immediate *determinateness* is also a *limit;* for that purpose the quantum is differentiated into two quanta which in the first instance are mutually related as others."[52] In Spicer's ratio, the two "mutually related" quanta are 97 and 3. If one ceased to exist, the other would lose the means to exist. Without the 3, there is no 97. When one side appropriates the whole, the other is reduced to zero. The one that has all ceases to be what the other does not have. Hence neither of them can *be* at all. Instead they join to become 100, a whole number, not a ratio (319). Hegel's account helps to explain why the discourse about the land question in British Columbia aims not toward resolution but toward infinity. One side can appropriate almost all of the whole, but if it were to seize the whole of the whole, then both sides would lose the means to exist. The inverse ratio brings them into being by drawing a limit between them. It is not supposed to be resolved. It is geared instead for eternal recurrence.

In a guest editorial published on February 20, 1996, Owen Lippert, writing for the Fraser Institute, a conservative lobby group, warns that signing the agreement in principle commits the federal and provincial governments to transfer "substantial land and cash to the Nisga'a."[53] Seldom does he utter a noun without adding an adjective of quantity, and each time he quantifies, he inscribes a limit between two races. The inverse ratio, like the allegory of the sun, is a race-giving, race-forming force. What is at stake in the agreement in principle, he says, is not just "bucks" but "*big* bucks," and he predicts it will set a pattern for all the treaties to be negotiated by the British Columbia Treaty Commission: "The negotiations, themselves, will see ever more expansive demands. The Nisga'a deal [even though it was negotiated outside the commission's mandate] becomes the starting point, not the upper limit." For Lippert, even the lower limit is too high. Even small is too big. "They" are about to take away "our" side of the ratio. Yet "we" would not exist without "them."

In December, Stewart Bell reported on a speech delivered by George Erasmus, then cochair of the Royal Commission on Aboriginal Peoples.

Erasmus argues that the agreement in principle puts the Nisg̲a'a on the racialized ratio's lower limit. The problem is not that it gives away too much
land and money to the Nisg̲a'a but that it "doesn't transfer enough powers"
from settler governments "to the tribal government."[54] Far from impover-
ishing the large side of the ratio, it brings the small side a little closer to the
vanishing point. Three days later Bell reported that "a provincial government study" had concluded that the agreement in principle would make the
small side larger and the large side smaller. He arranges the two sides into
separate paragraphs. The first records a loss, the second a gain:

> Lumber mills and fish plants in the region could be forced to cut staff if
> the Nisg̲a'a build their own processing facilities. Stores in towns such as
> Terrace may also suffer if the Nisg̲a'a use some of their money to start
> their own businesses.
>
> But in the long term, the settlement of the long-standing land claim
> should increase economic activity in the North Coast region while im-
> proving the standard of living of the 5,500 Nisg̲a'a Indians in the remote
> Nass Valley, the study says.[55]

The first paragraph suggests that one side of the ratio can increase by a given
amount only if the other decreases by the same amount. The Nisg̲a'a are
what settler society does not have. The second paragraph gives back what
the first took away. Both sides will get bigger because the whole quantum
is going to grow.

The logic of the inverse ratio operates as a historical a priori. It structures the emergence of events but is not structured by them. Hence it enters
into history by subtracting itself from history. That is why it can recur, and
remain valid, in every time in which it is possible to say "our time." Hegel
says it possesses a spurious infinity. It cannot be sublated. It can only be
displaced. One way to gauge its force of breaking with its present context
is to compare the 1996 debate about the agreement in principle with the
transcript of the 1887 meeting between Tsimshian and Nisg̲a'a chiefs and
representatives of the governments of Canada and British Columbia.

John Ryan, speaking for the Tsimshian, opened discussions in the premier's residence on February 3, 1887. He adopts the position most readily
available to him in the discourse of colonial administration: the position
of the child-savage. "You know how children are," he says. "First they do
not see anything or know anything when they are quite youngsters. After
a while when they get a little bigger they open their eyes, begin to know
things, and have more thought than when they were youngsters." Children

are born blind, he suggests, echoing Hegel's allegory, but as they grow up, they open their eyes, begin to contemplate their surroundings, and turn from contemplation to activity and from activity to self-consciousness. Ryan adds that "their father" usually rewards his children for reaching enlightenment.[56] What the "children" specifically ask of their "father" is the "gift" of "a bigger coat" to wear: "I want this coat to go on me that you have given me. This coat I cannot get on; and I ask you to give me a little bigger one so that I can wear it" (253). William Smithe, the premier of British Columbia, pretends not to understand Ryan's allegory (253), so "John Wesley," speaking for the Nisga'a, supplies a gloss: "We want you to cut out a bigger reserve for us, and what we want after that is a treaty" (255). Already, in 1887, the treaty question is framed by the logic of the inverse ratio. The Nisga'a and Tsimshian nations want something "more," he explains, something "bigger." But Smithe pleads ignorance: "What do you mean by a treaty" (255)? Wesley explains that they want land set aside for their exclusive use and their title recognized in law: "I have mentioned after a certain amount of land is cut out for the Indians, outside of that we want such a law as the law of England and the Dominion Government which made a treaty with the Indians" (255). Smithe answers that the Nisga'a can make a gain only if they are willing to incur a loss. The dominion and the province are ready to "give" them larger village sites, but they will have to give up the lands where they "hunt" and "gather":

> If your reserve on the Naas is too small, it can be made larger, and both the Dominion and the Provincial Governments will be perfectly willing to give you additional land for your purposes. But when, in addition to that, you want hunting grounds, it becomes a very different question. Now, why do you want those hunting grounds? It seemed to me to be the desire of everybody—both the Indians and their teachers—to raise the Indians out of the position which they have held in the past, when they were little better than wild animals that rove over the hills, when they required a large extent of land to gather berries from, or for hunting over. (256)

The comparison of aboriginal people to "wild animals" made Smithe one of the villains of the province's history. Aboriginality, in his view, is an inverse ratio. "Indians" enjoy a surplus of land but suffer a scarcity of resources. Civilization, in contrast, is an equation. It replaces difference—which opposes the "more" to the "less"—with sameness. Smithe urges Wesley to leave the ratio and join the equation: "it seems to me far better to be contented to accept the same position as a white man in that regard; to be the same in the eyes of the law; to ask no more and to take no less" (256). The people of the Nass can have what they want, he promises, so long as they cease to be who they are. There is no qualitative difference between the two sides of Smithe's equation. It is a formula for assimilation.

Charles "Burton," who translated at the meeting, reminds Smithe that a Nisga'a chief has jurisdiction over both "a fishing ground" and a "hunting ground" (257).[57] Reserve Commissioner O'Reilly answers that if the province were to recognize every chief's double jurisdiction, the whole quantum would gravitate to the "Indian" side of the ratio. The Tsimshian and Nisga'a control only a "little" of the disputed territory. It is irrational, he maintains, for them to claim "all":

> They each have a *little* spot which they are in the habit of calling their own. *Every* inlet is claimed by some one, and were I to include *all* these [in reserve lands], it would virtually declare the *whole* country a reserve. . . . To lay out *all* the inlets pointed out and claimed by them, would be impossible. They were given the right to *all* streams which run through their reserves, and *every* fishing ground pointed out by them, of *every* sort or kind, was reserved for them. . . . But to declare *every* inlet, nook, and stream an Indian reserve would be virtually to declare the *whole* country a reserve. (257, emphasis added)

How can the small side, O'Reilly asks, claim ownership of the large side? How can the "less" and the "little" act as if they were "more" or "the whole"? Simply to ask for a treaty is in his view excessive. Indeed a treaty is by definition too much because it breaks with the principle of sameness and convokes the possibility of difference. "Any reasonable request made with regard to the reserves," explains Alex Davie, attorney general for British Columbia, "or in regard to any of those fishing stations being included in the reserves, it is only necessary to mention to obtain. But if you go beyond that and speak about treaties, and think that this government, or the Dominion Government, are going to say that all the land belongs to the Indians it is a very different thing" (262). "Indians," in Davie's discourse, are those who go "beyond" reason's limits and aim at "more" (262). Indeed they aspire to "all." They personify the danger of an irrational and unassimilable excess.

One hundred and ten years later, in the fall of 1996, the government of British Columbia appeared to have resumed the colonial-era policy of refusing to strike treaties with the specters of excess. An election returned the New Democratic Party to power under a leader who, according to the

Vancouver Sun, showed "little interest" in reaching a final agreement. In April 1997 Justine Hunter reported that federal officials were pressing their provincial colleagues to resume negotiations. "And in the last five weeks," she adds, "Premier Glen Clark . . . has also given his negotiators a fresh mandate to settle."[58] The pressure intensified in December 1997, when the Supreme Court of Canada handed down a long-awaited decision in the case of *Delgamuukw v. British Columbia.* The case had been working its way through the courts for years.

In 1977 the Gitxsan and Wet'suwet'en First Nations filed a declaration of ownership and jurisdiction over traditional territories in the province's northwestern interior. The government of Canada accepted the declaration as a basis for negotiation; the government of British Columbia did not.[59] In 1984 the Gitxsan and Wet'suwet'en took the province to court. Fifty-one hereditary chiefs of the Gitxsan and Wet'suwet'en First Nations claimed ownership of, and the right to govern, ninety-eight separate Gitxsan territories bordering the watersheds of the Skeena, Nass, and Babine rivers, and thirty-five separate Wet'suwet'en territories bordering the watersheds of the Bulkley and Fraser-Nechako rivers. Some chiefs claimed these territories individually; some, on behalf of their houses or the members of their houses. The area amounted to 35,420 square kilometers. The first plaintiff named in the action was a Gitxsan chief named Earl Muldoe; his Gitxsan name was Delgamuukw.

The suit went before the British Columbia supreme court in May 1987. The hearing ended on the last day of June 1990. The trial judge, Chief Justice McEachern, delivered an "inordinately long" decision on March 8, 1991.[60] Indeed it fills almost five hundred pages of volume 79 of the *Dominion Law Reports.* If he is prolix, he explains, it is because the trial consumed a surplus of time—it was "a long trial"—and generated a surplus of discourse: 318 days of evidence, 56 days of argument, 61 witnesses who gave evidence at trial, 15 witness who gave evidence on commission, 53 territorial affidavits filed, 30 deponents cross-examined out of court, 23,503 pages of evidence given at trial, 5,898 pages of argument, 9,200 exhibits filed at trial (199). "The parties adduced such enormous quantities of evidence, introduced such a huge number of documents, and made so many complex arguments," he sardonically remarks, "that I have sufficient information to fuel a Royal Commission" (202). Yet he says the land in dispute suffers a surplus of lack. It is a "vast" territory, he remarks, but it is "empty." Inevitably, he distributes it onto the two sides of an inverse ratio: "The most striking thing that one notices in the territory away from the Skeena-Bulkley corridor," he says, "is its emptiness" and lack of "Indians" ("very few Indians are to be seen

anywhere except in the large river corridors"). Doubtless because the specter of excess is a specter of repetition, he repeats the point at the end of
the same paragraph: "As I have mentioned, the territory is, indeed, a vast
emptiness" (207).[61] What emerges after these remarks is nothing new under
the sun.

Although "inordinately long," the judgment can be reduced to a single
sentence from paragraph 28 of the "Summary of Findings and Conclusions":
"It is the law that aboriginal rights exist at 'the pleasure of the crown,' and
they may be extinguished whenever the intention of the crown to do so
is clear and plain" (197). This finding is a ghost of judgments past. The
chief justice upholds the Supreme Court of Canada's 1973 minority opinion
that if an aboriginal title had existed prior to colonization, it was clearly
and plainly extinguished by the illocutionary force of the Calder Thirteen,
which accordingly gave settler society an "unburdened title" to British Columbia (197). In addition, the judge found that the plaintiffs had failed to
prove that they had occupied their hunting and fishing grounds prior to
contact with Europeans, although they were unable prove occupation partly
because he gave little weight to oral history.[62]

In their appeal, the plaintiffs modified their claim for ownership and
jurisdiction to a claim for aboriginal title and self-government and simpli-
fied the claims made by chiefs on behalf of themselves and their houses
into two communal claims on behalf of the Gitxsan and Wet'suwet'en First
Nations.[63] On June 25, 1993, the British Columbia court of appeal ruled
that the plaintiffs' aboriginal rights had not "all" been extinguished by the
Calder Thirteen but noted that those rights do not include an unfettered,
fee-simple ownership of the land.[64] The court urged the parties to define
the contents of aboriginal rights by negotiation. The Gitxsan nation ad-
journed its appeal to the Supreme Court of Canada for a year to work out
an agreement with the federal and provincial governments.[65] The province
broke off talks early in 1996, and the appeal went ahead. On December 11,
1997—just when the Nisga'a final agreement was starting to look like a
dead letter—the Supreme Court threw out the trial judge's findings and ordered a new trial. The court found two errors in the 1991 decision. First,
the trial judge was wrong to exclude oral history as evidence of traditional
occupation and use of the land. Second, aboriginal title does indeed exist
but is unique in kind because it can be alienated only to the Crown and is
based on systems of aboriginal law that predate the common law's arrival
in North America.[66] Henceforth, if governments refused to reconcile Crown
sovereignty with aboriginal title, the courts would have the authority to
rule in favor of aboriginal plaintiffs. British Columbia reached a final agree-

ment with the Nisg̱a'a Tribal Council and the government of Canada in August 1998.

On December 19, Owen Lippert rose once more with the *Sun* to warn that the Supreme Court's ruling "practically gives control of 95 per cent of the B.C. land mass to about 5 per cent of the population."[67] He has revised his weighting of the inverse ratio from 97:3 to 95:5, as if to suggest that "they" are gaining on "us." The recognition of aboriginal title promises to "escalate" the "costs" of resource extraction, he claims, while making "profit margins shrink." Land will lose value too. Worse, the "definition of aboriginal title [as a sui generis interest in the land itself] creates the prospect of very generous court judgements." First nations, he warns, now have little incentive to negotiate outstanding land claims: "Why would any aboriginal leader bother with long and tedious negotiations that are based on the assumption that no more than five per cent of Crown land would be transferred when the chief justice of the land has said, implicitly, the prize is *infinitely* bigger" (emphasis added). Yet the Nisg̱a'a had been trying to negotiate a treaty for more than a century. What "aboriginal leaders" is Lippert talking about? Or is he haunted by the "infinitely" repeatable specter of savage excess?

On February 2, 1998, the *Sun* ran a headline warning that the province's First Nations were poised to claim fully 100 percent of the inverse ratio: "B.C. Indian Chiefs lay claim to entire province, resources." Rick Ouston reports that the First Nations Summit, an intervener in the Delgamuukw case, has asked the provincial and federal governments to freeze development on disputed lands until outstanding claims are settled. Yet that is not how he frames the issue. "B.C.'s native Indians," he writes instead, "are laying claim to every tree, every rock, every fish and every animal in the province."[68] Ouston predicts an economic apocalypse, for when an inverse ratio reaches unity, it vanishes, taking both sides with it: "In an unprecedented set of demands, the province's reserve Indians are brandishing a recent Supreme Court of Canada decision they say grants them unfettered control of the entire B.C. land mass, including forests, mines and fish." Neither the claim to aboriginal title nor the rhetoric of excess is "unprecedented" here. What is perhaps new is the assertion that the specters of excess are claiming more land and resources than the province contains:

Various native groups have staked their claims to portions of B.C. over the years. The borders of the individual claims—representing areas where native bands historically fished, hunted, gathered or traded— overlap, covering the entire province.

But the natives have, until now, never demanded land or profit from land in private hands. And for the first time they are speaking in a united voice to demand, simply, legal title to B.C.

In its judgment, the Supreme Court reaffirmed the long-standing principle that aboriginal title is a "burden" on the Crown's underlying title and found that aboriginal title may be infringed for a long list of reasons, such as "the development of agriculture, forestry, mining, and hydroelectric power, the general economic development of the interior of British Columbia, protection of the environment or endangered species, the building of infrastructure and the settlement of foreign populations to support those aims."[69] First nations are entitled to be involved in decisions about the development of lands not yet included in treaties and to be compensated whenever an unextinguished title is infringed. Although the specters of excess threaten to appropriate "the entire province," they control almost none of it.[70]

In an opinion piece published on the same day, Joe Gosnell, the president of the Nisga'a Tribal Council, suggests it is time to stop speaking of aboriginal people as beings without limits: "however emboldened Indians may be feeling," he cautions, "they have reason to act with restraint. Compensation claims that would beggar the governments will get nowhere. To prove aboriginal title to specific territory they would have to go to court, which is time-consuming and costly. Negotiating a land and cash settlement might mean settling for less land, but assuming control over the resources sooner."[71] It is still necessary, in 1998, to repeat that aboriginal people are capable of both "reason" and restraint—hence that they can control the exuberance that has long been said to govern them.

On April 16, four months after the Court's decision, the *Sun*'s editors declared that the province's economic development had been suspended in now-time: "Four months may be the blink of an eye from the perspective of First Nations people, who have been trying to establish their claim to land for more than a century. But it is an eternity for other people who are trying to create or expand businesses and add to the province's threadbare economy."[72] The whole "economy," by this argument, is caught in mid-gyrate. The reader might be forgiven for concluding that it is the Nisga'a who cannot wait for the treaty question to be settled. The editors, however, assume that all time is the same time for the inhabitants of the now. One hour more or less makes no difference when you live in "Indian time." It is "other people," those who stock up present labor for future gain, for whom every moment wasted is a quantum of value lost.

On June 18, Andrew Coyne opines that the Court's judgment goes "a *long* way" toward defining the concept of aboriginal title, but "does so at the cost of creating *much* greater uncertainty in society at *large*" (emphasis added).[73] A gain on the small, "aboriginal" side of the ratio inflicts a loss on the "large" side, the side of "society." What is more, the judgment is a threat to future-oriented time itself, for it suspends the province in a present that neither advances nor recedes: "not only is the whole future economic development of the province up in the air, but so presumably, is the past." Two days later, Stewart Bell stresses that the negotiators "have agreed that land claim negotiations must be speeded up . . . accelerated . . . [and] move quickly" because the process is generating a surplus of economic "uncertainty."[74] The Nisg̱a'a, it bears repeating, had asked for a treaty early in 1887. Exactly who, then, tends to get caught in midgyrate?

On July 17, 1998, Vaughan Palmer reported that the governments of Canada and British Columbia had offered the Nisg̱a'a nation "an additional $70 million worth of contributions" to secure an agreement.[75] An editorial printed on the same page claims that these "additional contributions" constitute "a disturbing escalation" because they are likely to increase the cost of other treaties.[76] Yet Palmer admits that some of the "cash cost" will not actually be paid in cash:

> The initial agreement, signed in 1996, provided $190 million in cash and almost 2,000 square kilometers of provincial land valued at about $125 million. The province gave up an amount of timber representing $36 million in revenues, plus the two governments provided $24 million to fund fishery measures.
>
> The $70 million that was tossed into the kitty this week pushes the total value of the settlement to $445 million, shared equally between the two governments.[77]

The province agreed to pay the Nisg̱a'a a further "$60 million" in cash, but the bulk of its share of the $445 million consists of "foregone revenue," namely, taxes that might have been paid on resources that might be extracted from the land included in the agreement. What the province spent, then, was not cash, but potentiality. It gave up a part of its claim to the future.

Chapter 11 of the Final Agreement recognizes the Nisg̱a'a nation's right to self-government and its authority to make laws.[78] Palmer predicts this provision is likely to "generate extensive debate" in the province, adding a further surplus to a discourse already determined as a ratio of surplus and lack. A day earlier, he had warned that the agreement gives the Nisg̱a'a an excess of legislative authority: "it sounds as if the treaty will provide the

Nisga'a with a form of government that is more powerful than a munici-
pality and may—on matters of resource management—approach that of a
province."[79] He convokes the specter of a surplus government that will not
just be "powerful" but "more" powerful than the governments of cities and
towns. Gordon Campbell, leader of the Liberal Party of British Columbia,
later remarked, "That's a lot of government."[80]

Yet an editorial published on July 23 suggests there is no basis for arguing that the Nisga'a will enjoy more "duties, rights and privileges" than
"we" do. Palmer's statement refers to nothing that is. "The fear that the
Nisga'a will end up with more power than non-Nisga'a British Columbians
may be unjustified," the editors concede, "but the prospect is unsettling."[81]
The "fear" of ghosts persists even after ghosts are shown to be "make-
believe." If the editors know their concerns are "unjustified," and even un-
just, then why do they voice them at all? Why do they find "the pro*spect*"
of aboriginal self-government "unsettling" even when they say it is not? Do
they mean that the *specter* is "unsettle*ring*" or even "unsettle*menting*"?
The specter of excess is the sort of "make-believe" that makes itself real.
That is precisely its spectrality effect.

Delegates representing the Nisga'a nation and the governments of Canada and British Columbia signed the final agreement in New Aiyansh on
Tuesday, August 4, 1998. Joe Gosnell delivered a speech at the signing ceremony, and the *Sun* published it the next day. He situates the final agreement where it has always been: in between a quantum "too much" and a
quantum "too little": "We have detractors—oh, yes. Naysayers who say our
interests should continue to be ignored. Those who say Canada and British Columbia are 'giving' us *too much.* And there are others, particularly
within the aboriginal community, who say we settled for *too little.*"[82] Like
the sun of history, the discourse that conjures up aboriginal people as specters of excess continues to go in circles even after it is ordered to stop. It
begins and ends at what is traditionally the westernmost limit of the West,
forever suspended between the two sides of an inverse ratio. What results is
a scandal of repetition: the scandal of a discourse that remains stalled in the
now even as it is carried forward into the future.

The Means to Continue

For a long time, the societies of the northwest coast supplied anthropology
with its paradigm of the culture of excess. "It is an anthropological truism,"
writes Philip Drucker in the introduction to *Indians of the Northwest Coast,*
"that development of complex or 'high' culture among primitive peoples is

linked with, or, better, results from the notable increase in economic productivity that accompanies the invention or acquisition of agricultural techniques, and within limits, the domestication of animals."[83] The societies
of the northwest are an anomaly, he argues, because they built a "unique
and *rich*" civilization without learning to farm first: "it *was* a civilization
of the so-called 'hunting-and-gathering type,'" he continues, banishing that
civilization to the past, "without agriculture (except for a few instances of
tobacco growing), and possessing no domesticated animals other than the
dog" (2, emphasis added). How did it manage to do more with less? Drucker
attributes its spectacular "development" to nature's "abundance." The
First Nations of the Northwest are nature's gift to culture. They personify
culture in the state of nature. They are, he concludes, a natural culture and
a savage civilization:

> That they were able to attain their *high* level of civilization is due *largely*
> to the *amazing wealth* of the natural resources of their area. From the
> sea and rivers, fish—five species of Pacific salmon, halibut, cod, herring,
> smelt, and the famous olachen or "candlefish" (this last *so rich* in oil
> that a dried one with a wick threaded through it burns like a candle), and
> other species *too numerous* to mention—could be taken *in abundance*.
> Some of these fish appeared only seasonally, but were easy to preserve.
> The sea also provided a *tremendous quantity* of edible mollusks; "when
> the tide goes out the table is set," as the saying goes. *More spectacular*
> was the marine game: hair seal, sea lion, sea otter, porpoise and even
> whale. On shore, land game too *abounded*. Vegetable foods were *less*
> plentiful, although *many* species of wild berries were *abundant* in their
> season. In other words, the *bounty* of nature provided that which in most
> other parts of the world man must supply for himself through agricul-
> ture and stock raising: a *surplus* of foodstuffs *so great* that even a dense
> population had an *abundance* of leisure to devote to the improvement
> and elaboration of its cultural heritage. (2, emphasis added)

A savage civilization achieves by indolence what civilized civilizations accomplish by toil. Nature works so that culture does not have to, granting its
chosen people not just "wealth" but "amazing" wealth, not just "leisure"
but "an abundance of leisure." The sea yields a surplus so "tremendous,"
so "spectacular," that it beggars description, while the land "abounds" with
game and berries without limit. It as if food jumped into the mouth fully
cooked.

Drucker's introduction dates from 1955. Surely the rhetoric of excess is outdated by now. Scholars know better today, right? Yet the same pattern repeats itself differently in Paul Tennant's indispensable book *Aboriginal Peoples and Politics*, published in 1990. Like Drucker, Tennant marshals the rhetoric of excess early, so that it acts as the threshold that "aboriginal people" have to cross in order to emerge into scholarly discourse—not a datum of history but a rule for the formation of statements. In a breathtaking reduction, Tennant attributes the achievements of the northwest coast societies to the largess of "the giant red cedar tree," one of many "gifts" the "coastal environment" has granted them. The cedar made it possible to build "dugout canoes," allowing the coastal First Nations to exploit local resources, and "large plank houses," allowing the household to become the basic unit of social organization. "Had the cedar tree not existed," he concludes, "the coastal peoples could not have created their complex and sophisticated civilizations."[84] The specters of excess do not make their own history. They receive it as a gift from natural forces they neither understand nor control.

A majority of Nisga'a voters elected to ratify the final agreement in a plebiscite held on November 6, 1998. Barbara Yaffe warned the *Sun*'s readers on November 10 that soon the rest of the First Nations of British Columbia would be asking the provincial government for similar bounty: "we're now one step further along the road to increasing expectations of all native Indians in B.C. that the Nisga'a deal will be fully implemented and stand as a template for their own situations."[85] She evokes a sense of inflation by yoking nouns to intensifying adverbs and adjectives. Not only does the agreement transfer *"huge* sums of cash" to the Nisga'a nation, she warns, but it was signed amid *"so much* public ignorance" about its "implications" and leaves such *"huge* issues of contention outstanding" that it even poses a threat to public order (emphasis added). Two weeks later she complains that the text of the final agreement itself contains an excess of discourse: "did you know the Nisga'a treaty document is 252 pages long, with appendices totaling another 462 pages. That's a lot of words and numbers to interpret."[86] Could this be the most fearful specter of all? The final agreement exposes settler society to an infinite labor of interpretation. It asks its readers to become scholars.

It is the lot of the specter of excess to recur a lot, to signify a lot, to be cited a lot, but never to refer to anything that is. How is it possible to interrupt a discourse that comes to an end precisely by beginning again? "The search for the means to put an end to things, an end to speech," a voice warns, "is what enables the discourse to continue."[87] The Nisga'a Final Agreement Act was tabled in the Legislative Assembly of British Columbia on November 30, 1998. The next day, on the front page of the *Sun*, Jim Beatty reported that the session had opened with an "emotional" ceremony as "about 200" Nisga'a delegates entered the legislature's public gallery to witness the introduction of the bill for debate.[88] The editors remark that the *Sun* welcomes the tabling of the act but considers the "hoopla" an unjustifiable excess.[89]

The New Democratic government resumed debate on the final agreement after the Christmas recess. In April 1999, after further delay, the bill was peremptorily advanced to its third and final reading. The leader of the opposition, Gordon Campbell, declared that the government's attempt to limit debate was "the most menacing, autocratic, undemocratic assault . . . on the B.C. legislature, in the history of the province."[90] Even as it drew to its close, the discourse of savage excess found the means to continue. The agreement passed into provincial law on April 22. Months later the *Sun*'s editors still found it necessary to remark that "half the treaty's 22 chapters had been discussed in what amounted to 120 hours worth of consideration on the treaty, the longest such debate in the province's history."[91] The government, they argue, put excessive limits on a scarcity of debate that consumed an excess of time. The specter's return lasts far too long and yet never long enough.

When bill C-9, an act to ratify the Nisga'a Final Agreement, was introduced into the Parliament of Canada in early December 1999, the Reform Party, which had the support of conservative voters in western Canada, tabled 348 amendments in order to stall the bill's passage, and the discourse of savage excess was compelled to begin all over again. Mike Scott explained his party's strategy to the *Sun:* "We as official opposition must use every option available to us to try to extend the debate."[92] Within days, the number of amendments had increased. "The 471 amendments," the government's house leader remarked, "are probably the largest number to one bill ever put before Parliament."[93] It took forty-two hours for the House of Commons to dismiss them. Members of Parliament took turns voting around the clock. "Time not only dragged," Rick Mofina and Kelly Cryderman reported on December 9, "it actually stood still."[94] The bill left Parliament caught in midgyrate. "Under House of Commons procedure," they explain, "on the day when Commons business hours are extended, as they were for Reform's Nisga'a amendments, the Commons calendar freezes" and begins moving again "on the day regular business resumes." The bill was signed into law on April 13, 2000. But still the discourse around it did not find the means to end. "The Nisga'a treaty," the *Sun* promised two days later, "is not yet a done deal."[95]

The *Solaris* Hypothesis

At the next stage, the idea becomes flesh and blood. That's all.—*Stanislaw Lem*, Solaris

What has become of the hypotheses of magical criticism? After the closing of the colonial frontier, scholars are less likely to sketch a portrait of "the savage mind" in order to entertain the possibility that discursive forces have more-than-discursive consequences. The horizon for the displacement of general mimesis is narrower now. Sometimes it finds shelter under the broad banner of postmodernism, though at the risk of revealing that a supposedly characteristic trait of contemporary Western culture used to be attributed to premodern, pre-Western cultures. Stanislaw Lem found another solution half a century ago. His novel *Solaris* transports general mimesis into deep space, opening a new and infinite horizon for a hypothesis that used to be reserved for savage philosophy.[1] The rule of displacement, which dictates that discursive energy can only be named by taking the name of something else—facilitation, energeia, entelechy, soul power, mana, spectrality—finally ejects it from the earth's surface. To study discursive forces, after Lem, is to make contact with an alien intelligence.

The novel is narrated from the point of view of Kris Kelvin, a psychologist, who pauses on three occasions to review the literature of Solaristics. Specialists agree that the planet Solaris is a living, thinking organism—intelligent life, though not in human form. Its surface is covered by an ocean of liquid protoplasm "dotted" with islands and charged with electromagnetic current (16). The "ocean-brain" is the savage mind divorced from its racialized body and projected into space, where it continues to be perceived as an impediment to the advancement of knowledge (22).

Researchers quickly found that this ocean has an advanced capacity for general mimesis. It does not mirror the things it imitates, but completes them, producing copies that augment their originals: "The first attempts at contact were by means of specially designed electronic apparatus. The ocean itself took an active part in these operations by remodeling the instruments" (21). Solaris is a reservoir of depersonified mimetic forces. Because the object of observation participates in the act of observation, Solaristics is a case of magical criticism. "What exactly," Kelvin asks, "did the ocean's 'participation' consist of" (21)? He finds an answer in a volume of Solariana titled *The Little Apocrypha*.

The volume includes documents relating to the disappearance of Fechner, a physicist who fell into the ocean on an ill-fated research mission.[2] One of the pilots dispatched to find him briefly got lost in the ocean's "colloidal" fog and returned to base presenting symptoms of "nervous shock" (78, 41). Afterward he refused to leave the base or even look out the window (41). He later told the commission of enquiry that as he was flying near the ocean's surface, he encountered three impossible works of imitation. The first was a stylized garden, complete with trees, hedges, paths, and an apiary. The second was the enormous, twitching likeness of a human child, two or three years old. He refused to divulge the third (79, 81). The commission concluded that what he had seen were hallucinations induced by "atmospheric poisoning" (85). However, one of the commission's members, A. Messenger, offered a dissenting opinion. It was not the pilot's brain that mistook ideas for things; it was the ocean-brain that made ideas—Fechner's ideas—into things, creating living images. "The source of all the various forms observed by [the pilot]," Messenger confides in an apocryphal letter, "is Fechner—or rather, Fechner's brain, subjected to an unimaginable 'psychic dissection' for the purposes of a sort of re-creation, an experimental reconstruction, based on impressions (undoubtedly the most durable ones) engraved on his memory" (87). The pilot's name is "André Berton," a play on the name of André Breton, who, in his "Manifesto of Surrealism," affirms "the superior reality of certain forms of previously neglected associations" of ideas.[3] Solaris enjoys the forbidden power to actualize "neglected associations," such as a "crazy daydream" or "an obsession."[4] It is a Promethean planet. Kelvin discovers that it exerts its omnipotence when he sleeps (26).

He arrives at the Solaris research station in a spacecraft named, none too subtly, the *Prometheus*. There are three scientists on board: Snow ("Snaut" in the French translation of the novel and in Andrei Tarkovsky's film adaptation), Sartorius (transformed into Gordon in Steven Soderbergh's film

adaptation), and Kelvin's mentor Gibarian. Snow promptly informs Kelvin
that Gibarian has killed himself but does not say why. Then he offers Kelvin
some advice: "Be prepared to meet . . . anything. It sounds impossible I
know, but try" (10). Kelvin does not meet just "anything." After visiting
Gibarian's cabin, he glimpses a figure walking down the corridor. What kind
of figure? A walking stereotype: "A giant Negress was coming silently towards me with a smooth, rolling gait. I caught a gleam from the whites of
her eyes and heard the soft slapping of her bare feet. She was wearing nothing but a yellow skirt of plaited straw; her enormous breasts swung freely
and her black arms were as thick as thighs" (30). The woman in the grass
skirt walks into Lem's novel in much the same way as the "apparition of a
woman" walks out of the "wilderness" in that other romance of failed first
contact, Conrad's *Heart of Darkness:* "She walked with measured steps,
draped in striped and fringed cloths, treading the earth proudly with a slight
jingle and flash of barbarous ornaments. She carried her head high, her hair
was done in the shape of a helmet, she had brass leggings to the knees,
brass wire gauntlets to the elbow, a crimson spot on her tawny cheek, innu-
merable necklaces of glass beads on her neck, bizarre things, charms, gifts
of witch-men, that hung about her, glittered and trembled at every step."[5]
This "wild and gorgeous" figure is said to personify the "wilderness" itself:
she is "the image" of its "soul" (60). The woman in the grass skirt is a
survival of discourse past. Her passage through Lem's novel marks a displacement, confirming that what it used to be possible to say of the savage
mind can now be said of a far-off planet. The one is a successor to the other
in the history of discourses. Perhaps that is why Lem's portrait of wildness
is silent. She has conferred her voice on her substitute. Just as the savage
philosopher is said to be suspended in the present, she spends the rest of the
novel draped over Gibarian's corpse in the cold-storage room, not gone but
forgotten.[6] She is frozen in now-time—literally. Both Tarkovsky, in his 1972
film, and Soderbergh, in his 2003 remake, tactfully omit her.

How did Gibarian's "visitor" get on board the station? Kelvin finds out
as soon as he falls asleep. Or rather as soon as he wakes up. He opens his
eyes thinking he has just dozed off—has he too entered now-time?—and
sees that he is being watched: "The curtains were half-drawn, and there, opposite me, beside the window-pane lit by the red sun [Solaris has both a red
and a blue sun], someone was sitting. It was Rheya" (52). He takes comfort
in the thought that he is dreaming, because his wife Rheya ("Harey" in the
French translation; "Hari" in Tarkovsky's film) had killed herself ten years
earlier. He holds himself responsible for her suicide. However, it rapidly
becomes apparent that he is doing what savage philosophers used to be said

to do. He is dreaming while awake. Solaris has conjured his lover back to life on the border of sleep. Indeed that is how it summons all of the station's visitors. "They only come," Snow informs Kelvin later, "as we wake up, which suggests that the ocean is especially interested in our sleeping hours, and that that is when it locates its patterns" (127). The ocean-brain actualizes dream thoughts by personifying them. Hence it is capable of a uniquely performative prosopopoeia. It surveys Kelvin's unconscious ideas as he sleeps and, laying bare his "most vulnerable" memory, endows it with life, face, and voice (156). The Rheya who waits for him in the morning is the living image of the Rheya who died in their apartment a decade before. She is the ocean-brain's realization of his human brain's contents. Yet she is not a ghost. For she has a material presence. Indeed she has superpowers. At the longed-for moment of contact with another world, another intelligence, all that Kelvin finds is a reproduction of his own thought patterns. "We have no need of other worlds," Snow warns him. "We need mirrors. We don't know what to do with other worlds" (72). Rheya is the speaking portrait of Kelvin's discourse with himself. She is fashioned in the image of his melancholy and his guilt, as if in a mirror, and he doesn't know what to do with her.

In Soderbergh's film, Rheya reminds Kelvin that they used to live in an apartment without pictures: no paintings on the walls, no snapshots on the refrigerator.[7] Soderbergh's Kelvin is, at first, an image hater. This aspect of his character is already available in Lem's novel. When he finally accepts that he is not asleep, that what he sees is not a dream image but "the real Rheya," "terror" overwhelms him.[8] The iconoclast adopts a paranoid relation to the copy. "I no longer told myself: 'It's a dream.' I had ceased to believe that," he confesses. "Now I was thinking: 'I must be ready to defend myself'" (57). So he lures "Rheya" into a shuttle craft and, in a moment of panic, launches it into space. Afterward he interprets his act of deception as a victory of reality over ideality. Sending the copy away, he assures himself, only brings him closer to the missing original: "I felt I was justified in thinking that I had defeated the 'simulacra,' and that behind the illusion, contrary to all expectation, I had found the real Rheya again—the Rheya of my memories" (65). In the force field of Solaris, a whole system of binary oppositions turns upside down. A memory is more real than the living reality, and the reality more illusory than the memory. The abstract is concrete; the concrete, abstract. There is at once a personification of ideas and an idealization of persons.

Kelvin soon finds himself caught up in the play of inversions. After he reads Messenger's explanation of "Berton's" visions, he loses his sense of the difference between the copy and the original, illusion and reality. The reaction formation that is supposed to make him feel ashamed before the simulacrum collapses: "Soon, I told myself, we would cease to be ashamed, to keep ourselves apart. If we could not get rid of our visitors, we would accustom ourselves to their presence, learn to live with them" (88). The reformed iconoclast is now ready to romance his moving, breathing dream image.

The visitors, like survivals generally, are governed by a powerful repetition compulsion, as if "plugged into a contrivance which goes round and round, endlessly repeating itself, like a gramophone record" (104). Hence Rheya returns to him almost as soon as he sends her away. When she appears at his door, he invites her in, saying, more to himself than to her, "Don't be frightened" (89). His transformation from image hater to image lover is abrupt. In the morning he battles the simulacrum and in the evening he embraces it. The next day, as Rheya looks on, he taunts Sartorius by repeating Breton's hypothesis that sometimes the idea is more real than the thing itself: "In a way, it's a super-copy, a reproduction which is superior to the original" (101). The melancholy Solarist "works through" the "trauma" of losing "the real Rheya" and replaces her with an actual idea. "Now all I see," he tells her, "is you" (146). The image in the mirror has taken the world's place.

In Soderbergh's film, when Kelvin announces his intention to return to Earth with his latest Rheya, Gordon accuses him of breaking a fundamental "taboo" against the mixing of kinds. "She is not human. Try to understand that if you can understand anything," she urges him. "She's a copy, a facsimile, and she's seducing you all over again." Then, before rising to leave, she spits, "You're sick."[9] It is as if he had committed incest. Not only does he let himself be "seduced" by an appearance, but, worse, he affirms that the appearance is worth more than the woman. Gordon cannot tolerate the possibility that the potentiality to be is balanced by the potentiality to not-be. How then would she respond to Peirce's assertion, published in 1868, that the human subject is "identical" to the sign? Says Peirce, "that every thought is an *external* sign, proves that man is an external sign. That is to say, the man and the external sign are identical."[10] There is no absolute boundary between the signs that we think, our "ideas" and "memories," and the signs that we are—between what can not-be and what is. Could it be that we humans are copies too? Ironically, the film is shot with a consistently shallow depth of field, which blurs backgrounds and encourages the viewer to stop at the surface, to adore appearance.

The tension between potentiality and impotentiality persists throughout the novel as a contradiction between two levels of discourse. The first limits the range of what is to what can be, as if actuality emerges exclusively from potentiality. It finds its voice in Sartorius, who insists on finding a scientific explanation for the external sign. "I put it to you as follows," he declares in a teleconference, "what are the Phi-creatures [that is, the "visitors"]? They are not autonomous individuals, nor copies of actual persons. They are merely projections materializing from our brains, based on a given individual."[11] He proposes (lamely) that they are neutrino structures stabilized by a magnetic field. "While our structure is made of atoms," he asserts in Tarkovsky's film, "theirs consists of neutrinos."[12] So he sets about building an "annihilator," as if the extermination of an entire species were a self-evidently legitimate project.

The second level opens the range of what is to include what can not-be, for actuality emerges also from impotentiality. Kelvin encounters it in the library. After almost eight decades of observation, scientists have compiled a vast archive of hypotheses about Solaris but have failed to verify a single one: "our scholarship, all the information accumulated in the libraries," he laments, "amounted to a useless jumble of words, a sludge of statements and suppositions" (22–23). The discourse about Solaris precipitates a crisis of discourse in general. Scientists have learned nothing from Solaris except their own incapacity to describe things and state facts. Solaristics is a failure of constative language. The ocean-brain, in contrast, prefers immediation to communication. It makes hypotheses into phenomena instead of pointing out correspondences between them. Solaris is a triumph of performative language.

The tension between levels affirms the impotentiality of theory even as it calls for a theory of impotentiality. Rheya is tangled up in a similar contradiction. She is a being who exists in the mode of nonbeing. Kelvin takes her to the laboratory and, obeying the methodology for producing verifiable observations of subcellular structures, makes a slide of her blood. Then he puts it under a microscope. "There should have been the ferment of a quivering cloud of atoms," he says, "but I saw nothing" (98). The experiment gives him a firsthand encounter with the potentiality of impotentiality: "Was this body, frail and weak in appearance but indestructible in reality, actually made of nothing" (99)? Not even the newly born image lover can free himself from the prejudice that determines force as the actuality of potentiality. He neglects Aristotle's warning that every potentiality is simultaneously the potentiality of the negation of what it is the potentiality of. "This *potential not to*," Agamben stresses, "is the cardinal secret of the Aristotelian doctrine of potentiality, which transforms every potentiality in itself into an impotentiality."[13] The "secret" to understanding Agamben's interpretation, though, is to remember that he combines Aristotle's doctrine with Sartre's. "Man is the being through whom nothingness comes to the world," Sartre affirms. "But this question provokes another: What must man be in his being in order that through him nothingness may come to being?"[14] Lem's novel takes Sartre a little too literally. Rheya is a being who consists entirely of her own nothingness. She is what results when the ocean-brain, as if in answer to Sartre's question, brings nothingness into being. In the end she chooses to face Sartorius's annihilator rather than face up to her intolerable potentiality to exist in the mode of impotentiality. But Kelvin's idea of her always included the potential for suicide.

What both Rheya and Kelvin fail to understand is that there is nothing unusual about her condition. Beings like her come into being all the time. Indeed nothing could be more common. For she is an effect of reading. Solaris, moreover, is a reader. "It succeeded in recreating a human being who exists only in my memory," Kelvin admits to Snow, "because it is able to read us like a book" (193). Reading, especially the reading of fiction, is an event of animation, a generative prosopopoetic act.[15] When the ocean-brain brings its "Phi-creatures" into being, it does what human readers do every day. It breathes life into signs and sets them in motion. Solaris, however, cannot say what it reads. It can only make what it reads real. But every reader does the same, though in a more limited way. Solaris simply takes reading to its limit, conducting the kind of performative interpretation that is conventionally reserved for the gods. Kelvin is aware that he is being read. After all, like the rest of the station's occupants, he is a character in a novel. But he neglects to read the act of reading. He takes refuge in theology instead, asking Snow whether, in the history of religions, "there was ever a belief in an . . . imperfect god."[16] The "essential characteristic" of such a god, if it existed, would be its potential for impotentiality (197). It would be defined not by what it can do but by what it cannot: "a god limited in his omniscience and power, fallible, incapable of foreseeing the consequences of his acts, and creating things that lead to horror" (197). Snow concedes that "Solaris" may well be "the first phase" in the growth of a god that is simultaneously the negation of what it is the potentiality of. Is this the solution to the novel's riddle? Is Solaris the god of impotentiality? Snow congratulates Kelvin for coming up with "a completely new hypothesis about Solaris" (199), but Kelvin has already lost faith in hypothetical reason, perhaps because the Solarist literature leaves him stranded in "an increasingly tangled maze where every apparent exit [leads] to a dead end" (169). His problem is that he fails to practice magical criticism.

For there is another possibility. What if the ocean that reads its own read-ers is a force of interpretation in Peirce's depersonified sense? The "Solar-ists" interpret the ocean-brain's discourse as a means to interpret their own, as if playing with mirrors. But they miss the opportunity to interpret what this alien intelligence tells them about interpretation itself. Solaris traffics in signs that grow. It develops external signs out of the signs that humans repress. As it reads its readers, who cannot read it in turn, it enriches their inner discourse with a principle of change that cannot be explained in terms of physical causality because it proceeds on the hypothesis of semiosis: "an action, or influence, which is, or involves, a cooperation of *three* subjects, such as a sign, its object, and its interpretant."[17] The search for an effec-tivity beyond causality remains an unfinished project. Yet it keeps finding the means to repeat itself as if it had never begun. "That human existence should repeat itself, well and good," Kelvin complains, "but that it should repeat itself like a hackneyed tune, or a record a drunkard keeps playing as he feeds coins into the jukebox . . ." (204). His frustration is not unjustified. The prohibition of general mimesis feeds on the desire it forbids. What en-sues is an open series of displacements. The event of displacement occurs, naturally, in now-time. Hence there is no danger the drunkard will run out of coins any time soon.

NOTES

INTRODUCTION: WHAT ARE SAVAGES FOR?

1. Sigmund Freud, *Totem and Taboo*, in *The Standard Edition of the Complete Psychological Works of Sigmund Freud*, trans. James Strachey and others (London: Hogarth Press, 1955), 13:18.

2. Charles Sanders Peirce, "On the Nature of Signs," in *Peirce on Signs*, ed. James Hoopes (Chapel Hill: University of North Carolina Press, 1991), 141.

3. James G. Frazer, *The Golden Bough*, abridged ed. (New York: Macmillan, 1951), 284.

4. Freud, *Totem and Taboo*, 30.

5. Sigmund Freud, *Totem und Tabu*, in *Studienausgabe* (Frankfurt: Fischer Taschenbuch Verlag, 1982), 9:367.

6. Roman Jakobson, "Two Aspects of Language and Two Types of Aphasic Disturbances," in *Language in Literature*, ed. Krystyna Pomorska and Stephen Rudy (Cambridge, MA: Harvard University Press, 1987), 113.

7. Edward Burnett Tylor, *Primitive Culture* (New York: Henry Holt, 1874), 1:116; Freud, *Totem and Taboo*, 79.

8. Frazer, *Golden Bough*, 825.

9. Freud, *Totem and Taboo*, 64.

10. John Lubbock, *The Origin of Civilisation and the Primitive Condition of Man*, ed. Peter Rivière (Chicago: University of Chicago Press, 1978), lxv.

11. Jacques Derrida, "Différance," in *Margins of Philosophy*, trans. Alan Bass (Chicago: University of Chicago Press, 1982), 9.

12. Freud, *Totem and Taboo*, 1.

13. Tylor, *Primitive Culture*, 1:21.

14. Karl Bücher, *Industrial Evolution*, trans. S. Morley Wickett (New York: Henry Holt, 1901), 3.

15. W. J. T. Mitchell, *Picture Theory* (Chicago: University of Chicago Press, 1994), 152.

16. Ludwig Wittgenstein, *Philosophical Investigations*, 2nd ed., trans. G. E. M. Anscombe (Oxford: Blackwell, 1953), 79.

17. Friedrich Nietzsche, *On the Genealogy of Morality*, trans. Carol Diethe (Cambridge: Cambridge University Press, 1994), 49.

18. Samuel de Champlain, *The Voyages and Explorations of Samuel de Champlain*, 2 vols., trans. Annie Nettleton Bourne (Toronto: Courier Press, 1911), 1:178, 2:172.

19. Friedrich Nietzsche, *Beyond Good and Evil*, trans. Walter Kaufmann (New York: Vintage, 1966), §34.

20. Friedrich Nietzsche, *The Will to Power*, trans. Walter Kaufman and R. J. Hollingdale (New York: Vintage Books, 1967), §461.

21. Friedrich Nietzsche, *Twilight of the Idols*, in *The Portable Nietzsche*, ed. and trans. Walter Kaufman (New York: Penguin Books, 1954), 482.

22. Herbert Spencer, *The Principles of Sociology*, 3rd ed. (New York: D. Appleton, 1893), 2:681.

23. Nietzsche, *Beyond Good and Evil*, §24.

24. Salman Rushdie, *Fury* (Toronto: Vintage Canada, 2002), 7.

25. Nietzsche, *Beyond Good and Evil*, §34.

26. Jean Baudrillard, "The Precession of Simulacra," in *Simulations*, trans. Paul Foss, Paul Patton, and Philip Beitchman (New York: Semiotext(e), 1983), 4.

27. Rushdie, *Fury*, 143.

28. Frazer, *Golden Bough*, 826.

29. Charles Sanders Peirce, "The Seven Systems of Metaphysics," in *The Essential Peirce: Volume 2 (1893–1913)*, ed. Peirce Edition Project (Bloomington: Indiana University Press, 1998), 183.

30. Theodor W. Adorno and Max Horkheimer, "The Concept of Enlightenment," in *Dialectic of Enlightenment*, trans. John Cumming (New York: Continuum, 1990), 6.

31. Charles Sanders Peirce, "New Elements," in *Essential Peirce*, 2:322.

32. Peirce, "Seven Systems of Metaphysics," 184.

33. Aristotle, *Physics*, trans. Robin Waterfield (Oxford: Oxford University Press, 1996), 33/192b.

34. Peirce, "Seven Systems of Metaphysics," 193.

35. Johann Gottfried von Herder, "Treatise on the Origin of Language," in *Philosophical Writings*, trans. and ed. Michael N. Forster (Cambridge: Cambridge University Press, 2002), 100.

36. Giambattista Vico, *The New Science of Giambattista Vico*, trans. Thomas Goddard Bergin and Max Harold Fisch (Ithaca, NY: Cornell University Press, 1968), §349; Hayden White, "The Tropics of History: The Deep Structure of the *New Science*," in *Tropics of Discourse* (Baltimore: Johns Hopkins University Press, 1978), 201.

37. Hayden White agrees that Vico regards savage-poetic language as a force of invention rather than a mode of imitation: "Men's relationships with their worlds, social and natural, was mediated by consciousness in a crucial way, and especially by speech, which was not, for Vico, merely a verbal representation of the world of *praxis*, a reproduction in a consciousness of the world of things and the actual relations between them, but a reproductive and creative, active and inventive power." White, "Tropics of History," 199. White attributes to Vico a theory of language that Vico attributes to "first people," overlooking Vico's racialization of poetic logic.

38. Paul Ricoeur, *The Rule of Metaphor*, trans. Robert Czerny, with Kathleen McLaughlin and John Costello (Toronto: University of Toronto Press, 1977), 197. This paragraph also alludes to passages from pages 145, 224, and 230.

39. Theodor W. Adorno and Walter Benjamin, *The Complete Correspondence, 1928–1940*, ed. Henri Lonitz, trans. Nicolas Walker (Cambridge, MA: Harvard University Press, 1999), 38.

40. Adorno and Horkheimer, "Concept of Enlightenment," 8.

41. Walter Benjamin, "Criticism as the Fundamental Discipline of History," in *Selected Writings: Volume 2, 1927–1934*, trans. Rodney Livingstone and others, ed. Michael W. Jennings, Howard Eiland, and Gary Smith (Cambridge, MA: Harvard University Press, 1999), 415; Benjamin, "Kritik als Grundwissenschaft der Literaturgeschichte," in *Gesammelte Schriften*, vol. 6, ed. Rolf Tiedemann and Hermann Schweppenhäuser (Frankfurt: Suhrkamp Verlag, 1985), 173.

42. Wilhelm Dilthey, "The Development of Hermeneutics," in *Selected Writings*, ed. H. P. Rickman (Cambridge: Cambridge University Press, 1976), 256.

43. Walter Benjamin, *The Concept of Criticism in German Romanticism*, in *Selected Writings: Volume 1, 1913–1926*, ed. Marcus Bullock and Michael W. Jennings (Cambridge, MA: Harvard University Press, 1996), 142 (emphasis added); Benjamin, *Der Begriff der Kunstkritik in der deutschen Romantik*, in *Gesammelte Schriften*, vol. 1, bk. 1, ed. Rolf Tiedemann and Hermann Schweppenhäuser (Frankfurt: Suhrkamp Verlag, 1974), 51.

44. Novalis, "General Draft," in *Philosophical Writings*, trans. and ed. Margaret Mahony Stoljar (Albany: State University of New York Press, 1997), §12.

45. Novalis, "Miscellaneous Observations," in *Philosophical Writings*, §20. Schlegel locates this fold in between idealization and realization: "A perfect project should be at once completely subjective and completely objective, should be an indivisible and living individual. . . . What is essential is to be able to idealize and realize objects immediately and simultaneously: to complete them and in part carry them out within oneself." The "transcendental" is "precisely whatever relates to the joining or separating of the ideal and the real." Friedrich Schlegel, "Athenaeum Fragments," in *Friedrich Schlegel's "Lucinde" and the Fragments*, trans. Peter Firchow (Minneapolis: University of Minnesota Press, 1971), §22.

46. Novalis, "Logological Fragments II," in *Philosophical Writings*, §43; Novalis, "Logological Fragments I," §6.

47. Benjamin, *Concept of Criticism in German Romanticism*, 151/65. (Throughout the volume, page numbers separated by a solidus indicate first those of the English edition and then those of the original-language edition.)

48. Adorno and Horkheimer, "Concept of Enlightenment," 19.

49. F. W. J. Schelling, *Ideas for a Philosophy of Nature*, trans. Errol E. Harris and Peter Heath (Cambridge: Cambridge University Press, 1988), 35.

50. Martin Heidegger, "On the Essence and Concept of Φύσις in Aristotle's *Physics* B, I," trans. Thomas Sheehan, in *Pathmarks*, ed. William McNeill (Cambridge: Cambridge University Press, 1998), 186.

51. Aristotle, *Physics*, 34–35/193b.

52. Philippe Lacoue-Labarthe, "Diderot: Paradox and Mimesis," in *Typography*, ed. Christopher Fynsk (Stanford: Stanford University Press, 1998), 255.

53. Charles Sanders Peirce, "What Is a Sign?" in *Essential Peirce*, 2:10.

54. Martin Heidegger, "The Nature of Language," in *On the Way to Language,* trans. Peter D. Hertz (San Francisco: HarperCollins, 1971), 100. This way of reading Heidegger reading Hölderlin is suggested by Ricoeur, *Rule of Metaphor,* 284.

55. Heidegger, "Nature of Language," 99.

56. Antonin Artaud, "The Theater and Cruelty," in *The Theater and Its Double,* trans. Mary Caroline Richards (New York: Grove Press, 1958), 10.

57. Artaud, "Man against Destiny," in *Selected Writings,* ed. Susan Sontag (Berkeley: University of California Press, 1988), 362.

58. Artaud, "Theater and Culture," in *The Theater and Its Double,* 11; Artaud, "What I Came to Mexico to Do," in *Selected Writings,* 373.

59. Artaud, "What I Came to Mexico to Do," 374.

60. Martin Heidegger, "What Are Poets For?" in *Poetry, Language, Thought,* trans. Albert Hofstadter (New York: Harper and Row, 1971), 132; Heidegger, "Why Poets?" in *Off the Beaten Track,* ed. and trans. Julian Young and Kenneth Haynes (Cambridge: Cambridge University Press, 2002), 232–33.

61. Heidegger, "Why Poets?" 232.

CHAPTER 1. DISCOURSE IS NOW

1. Charles Alexander Eastman (Ohiyesa), *From the Deep Woods to Civilization* (Lincoln: University of Nebraska Press, 1977), 35.

2. Karl Marx, *Capital,* vol. 1, trans. Ben Fowkes (New York: Vintage Books, 1977), 875.

3. Ibid., 1:873; Marx, *Das Kapital, Erster Band,* Karl Marx Friedrich Engels Werke, vol. 23 (Berlin: Dietz Verlag, 1969), 741.

4. Jacques Derrida, "Signature, Event, Context," in *Margins of Philosophy,* trans. Alan Bass (Chicago: University of Chicago Press, 1982), 320; Derrida, "Signature événément contexte," in *Marges de la philosophie* (Paris: Éditions de Minuit, 1972), 379.

5. I borrow the notion of a decline of context from Gil Anidjar, *"Our Place in al-Andalus"* (Stanford: Stanford University Press, 2002). The problem amounts to this: What is the context of "context"? What container can hold the container of events? Or, simply, what is the history of "history"?

6. Adam Smith, *An Inquiry into the Nature and Causes of the Wealth of Nations,* ed. Edwin Cannan (New York: Modern Library, 1994), lix.

7. Martin Heidegger, *Being and Time,* trans. John Macquarrie and Edward Robinson (San Francisco: HarperSanFrancisco, 1962), 235–41.

8. Herder, for example, describes savage language itself as a balance of prodigality and parsimony: "The language of the savage *Caribs* is almost divided into two languages belonging to the women and the men, and the most common things— bed, moon, sun, bow—the two sexes name differently. What an excess of synonyms! And yet precisely these Caribs have only four words for the colors, to which they must refer all others. What poverty!" Johann Gottfried von Herder, "Treatise on the Origin of Language," in *Philosophical Writings,* trans. and ed. Michael N. Forster (Cambridge: Cambridge University Press, 2002), 117–18.

9. Georges Bataille, *Erotism: Death and Sensuality,* trans. Mary Dalwood (San Francisco: City Lights Books, 1986), 186.

10. Bataille is alluding to Freud's claim, in *Beyond the Pleasure Principle*, that the life drive is clamorous while the death drive is silent. Bataille superimposes the parsimony principle onto the life drive, which binds energy, and the prodigality principle onto the death drive, which unbinds it.

11. Arthur Schopenhauer, *The World as Will and Representation*, trans. E. F. J. Payne (New York: Dover, 1958), 1:36.

12. Friedrich Nietzsche, "On the Uses and Disadvantages of History for Life," in *Untimely Meditations*, trans. R. J. Hollingdale (Cambridge: Cambridge University Press, 1997), 60.

13. See Anidjar, *"Our Place in al-Andalus,"* 64.

14. J. Hugonard, Indian Industrial School, Fort Qu'Appelle, N.W.T., to David Laird, Indian Commissioner, Winnipeg, Manitoba, National Archives of Canada, Department of Indian Affairs, Record Group 10, "Black Series," vol. 3825, file 60 511-1, November 23, 1903.

15. Ibid.

16. Michel Foucault, *The Archaeology of Knowledge and the Discourse on Language*, trans. A. M. Sheridan Smith (New York: Pantheon Books, 1972), 119.

17. W. R. Tucker, Moosewood Sioux Reserve, to the Department of Indian Affairs, Ottawa, Ontario, National Archives of Canada, Department of Indian Affairs, Record Group 10, "Black Series," vol. 3825, file 60 511-2, January 5, 1904.

18. Deputy Superintendent General of Indian Affairs, Ottawa, Ontario, to T. Cory, Indian Agent, Carlyle, Saskatchewan, National Archives of Canada, Department of Indian Affairs, Record Group 10, "Black Series," vol. 3825, file 60 511-2, March 9, 1909.

19. R. Logan, Indian Agent, Portage la Prairie, Manitoba, to the Secretary of the Department of Indian Affairs, Ottawa, Ontario, National Archives of Canada, Department of Indian Affairs, Record Group 10, "Black Series," vol. 3825, file 60 511-2, October 24, 1910.

20. [E. H.] Yeomans, Brocket, Alberta, to D. C. Scott, the Acting Deputy Superintendent General of Indian Affairs, Ottawa, Ontario, National Archives of Canada, Department of Indian Affairs, Record Group 10, "Black Series," vol. 3825, file 60 511-2, October 27, 1910.

21. Smith, *Wealth of Nations,* 379.

22. D. C. Scott, Circular Memorandum [draft], National Archives of Canada, Department of Indian Affairs, Record Group 10, "Black Series," vol. 3826, file 60 511-3, stamped February 23, 1915; Scott, Circular Memorandum, vol. 3826, file 60 511-4, part 1, August 19, 1915; E. Brian Titley, *A Narrow Vision* (Vancouver: UBC Press, 1986), 174–75.

23. Canada, *Statutes of Canada, 1914,* 4–5 George V (Ottawa: King's Printer, 1914), 227.

24. The condemnation of dancing is not unique to Indian affairs administrators. Elias Boudinot, writing in the *Cherokee Phoenix*, similarly compares the prodigality of dancing with the parsimony of industry:

> when the day appeared, instead of going to their farms, and labouring for
> the support of their families, the young and middle aged of the males were
> seen to leave their houses, their faces fantastically painted, and their heads
> decorated with feathers, and step off with a merry whoop, which indicated

that they were *real men,* to a ball play, or a meeting of a similar nature. Such
in a word was the life of a Cherokee in those days during spring and summer
seasons. In the fall and winter seasons they were gone to follow the chase,
which occupation enabled them to purchase of the traders a few items of
clothing, sufficient to last perhaps until the next hunting time. From the soil
they derived a scanty supply of corn, barely enough to furnish them with gah-
no-ha-nah and this was obtained by the labor of women and grey headed men,
for custom would have it that it was disgraceful for a young man to be seen
with a hoe in his hand, except on particular occasions.

Elias Boudinot, *Cherokee Editor: The Writings of Elias Boudinot,* ed. Theda Purdue
(Knoxville: University of Tennessee Press, 1983), 103.

25. Austin Clarke, *The Origin of Waves* (Toronto: McClelland and Stewart,
1997), 19.

26. Foucault, *Archaeology of Knowledge,* 101.

27. Hayden White, *Metahistory* (Baltimore: Johns Hopkins University Press,
1973), 18.

28. Foucault, *Archaeology of Knowledge,* 27; Foucault, *L'archéologie du savoir*
(Paris: Éditions Gallimard, 1969), 38.

29. Jean Jacques Rousseau, "Discourse on the Origin and Foundations of
Inequality among Men or Second Discourse," in *The "Discourses" and Other Early
Political Writings,* trans. Victor Gourevitch (Cambridge: Cambridge University
Press, 1997), 143.

30. Rousseau repeats his statement about savage inertia in "Essay on the Origin
of Languages," in *"Discourses" and Other Early Political Writings,* 272–73n:

The extent to which man is naturally lazy is inconceivable. It would seem
that he lives solely in order to sleep, to vegetate, to remain motionless; he
can scarcely decide to go through the motions required to keep from dying
of hunger. Nothing keeps the savages loving their state as much as this
delicious indolence. The passions that cause man to be restless, provident,
active, are born only in society. To do nothing is man's primary and strongest
passion after that of self-preservation. If one looked at it more closely, one
would find that even among us people work only in order to get to rest: it is
still laziness that makes us industrious.

31. Baldwin Spencer and F. J. Gillen, *The Native Tribes of Central Australia*
(New York: Dover, 1968), 18–19.

32. Rousseau, "Discourse on the Origin and Foundations of Inequality among
Men," 169.

33. Karl Bücher, *Industrial Evolution,* trans. S. Morley Wickett (New York:
Henry Holt, 1901), 7.

34. Henri Bergson distinguishes between two sorts of present moment: an ideal
and a real present. The ideal present marks the "indivisible limit" between past and
future. It is time reduced to a mathematical point. The real, "living" present, in
contrast, possesses duration. It is a minimal slice of future-oriented time. The living
present orients the immediate past toward the immediate future for the realization
of some purpose. It is a unit for measuring productive labor. After he defines these

two sorts of present, though, Bergson goes on to mention a third that exceeds the notion of the present altogether. It is the spontaneous present in which children and savages repeat past actions. Children, he says, "follow the impression of the moment." Their memory is purely spontaneous. They do not mobilize the past for the realization of future ends. Nor, he adds, do "savages": "Indeed we observe this same exaggeration of spontaneous memory in men whose intellectual development hardly goes beyond that of childhood. A missionary, after preaching a long sermon to some African savages, heard one of them repeat it textually, with the same gestures, from beginning to end." Spontaneous, repetitive memory irrupts in now-time. What it repeats, moreover, is a text. It is a peculiarly textual memory. Henri Bergson, *Matter and Memory*, trans. Nancy Margaret Paul and W. Scott Palmer (New York: Zone Books, 1991), 137–38, 154.

35. Sigmund Freud, *Beyond the Pleasure Principle*, in *The Standard Edition of the Complete Psychological Works of Sigmund Freud*, trans. James Strachey and others (London: Hogarth Press, 1955), 18:38.

36. Sigmund Freud, "Project for a Scientific Psychology," in *Standard Edition*, 1:295.

37. What always returns to the same place—this is Lacan's definition of the real: "The real, I have told you, is that which is always in the same place" and consequently can "always" be "found again." What about what always returns in the same particle of time? Jacques Lacan, *The Ethics of Psychoanalysis, 1959–1960*, trans. Dennis Porter and ed. Jacques-Alain Miller (New York: W. W. Norton, 1992), 70.

38. Freud, *Beyond the Pleasure Principle*, 36.

39. Walter Benjamin, "On the Concept of History," in *Selected Writings: Volume 4, 1938–1940*, trans. Edmund Jephcott and others, ed. Howard Eiland and Michael W. Jennings (Cambridge, MA: Harvard University Press, 2003), 395; Benjamin, "Über den Begriff der Geschichte," in *Gesammelte Schriften*, vol. 1, bk. 2, ed. Rolf Tiedemann and Hermann Schweppenhäuser (Frankfurt: Suhrkamp Verlag, 1974), 701.

40. Walter Benjamin, *The Arcades Project*, trans. Howard Eiland and Kevin McLaughlin (Cambridge, MA: Harvard University Press, 1999), 474.

41. Benjamin, "On the Concept of History," 390.

42. Benjamin, *Arcades Project*, 463.

43. Benjamin, "On the Concept of History," 392.

44. Spencer and Gillen, *Native Tribes of Central Australia*, vii.

CHAPTER 2. THE NEW BARBARISM

1. Friedrich Nietzsche, *The Will to Power*, trans. Walter Kaufman and R. J. Hollingdale (New York: Vintage Books, 1967), §868; Nietzsche, *Der Wille zur Macht*, in *Gesammelte Werke*, vol. 19 (Munich: Musarion Verlag, 1926), §868.

2. Friedrich Nietzsche, *On the Genealogy of Morality*, ed. Keith Ansell-Pearson and trans. Carol Diethe (Cambridge: Cambridge University Press, 1994), 25; Nietzsche, *Zur Genealogie der Moral*, in *Werke in Drei Bänden*, ed. Karl Schlechta, vol. 2. (Munich: Carl Hanser Verlag, 1955), 786.

3. Joseph Conrad, *Heart of Darkness*, 3rd ed., ed. Robert Kimbrough (New York: W. W. Norton, 1963), 25.

4. Nietzsche, *Will to Power*, §900.

5. Ovid, *Metamorphoses*, trans. Charles Martin (New York: W. W. Norton, 2004), lines 105–25.

6. Aeschylus, *Prometheus Bound*, trans. David Grene, in *The Complete Greek Tragedies: Aeschylus I*, ed. David Grene and Richard Lattimore (New York: Modern Library, 1942), lines 437–506.

7. Friedrich Nietzsche, *The Birth of Tragedy*, in *The Birth of Tragedy and The Case of Wagner*, trans. Walter Kaufmann (New York: Vintage, 1967), 72; Nietzsche, *Die Geburt der Tragödie*, in *Werke in Drei Bänden*, ed. Karl Schlechta, vol. 1 (Munich: Carl Hanser Verlag, 1954), 60.

8. Aristotle, *Physics*, trans. Robin Waterfield (Oxford: Oxford University Press, 1996), 35/193b, 56–57/200b–201a.

9. Johann Wolfgang von Goethe, "Prometheus," in *Twenty-Five German Poets: A Bilingual Collection*, trans. and ed. Walter Kaufmann (New York: W. W. Norton, 1962), 24–27.

10. Friedrich Nietzsche, *Twilight of the Idols*, in *The Portable Nietzsche*, ed. and trans. Walter Kaufman (New York: Penguin Books, 1954), 560; Nietzsche, *Götzen-Dämmerung*, in *Werke in Drei Bänden*, 2:1030.

11. Nietzsche, *Will to Power*, §899 (translation slightly modified).

12. Cf. Nietzsche, *Birth of Tragedy*, 68.

13. Nietzsche, *Twilight of the Idols*, 547–48/1019–20 (translation slightly modified).

14. Walter Benjamin, "On the Concept of History," in *Selected Writings: Volume 4, 1938–1940*, ed. Howard Eiland and Michael W. Jennings, and trans. Edmund Jephcott and others (Cambridge, MA: Harvard University Press, 2003), 396. Benjamin conceives of the explosion as a world-historical ejaculation and warns the historical materialist not to let his manly forces "be drained by the whore called 'Once upon a time' in historicism's bordello" (396). The gendering of the event is already going on in Nietzsche's Dionysian pessimism.

15. Friedrich Nietzsche, *Thus Spoke Zarathustra*, in *Portable Nietzsche*, 127.

16. Nietzsche, *Will to Power*, §1067.

17. Jean-Luc Nancy, "Myth Interrupted," in *The Inoperative Community*, ed. Peter Connor and trans. Peter Connor, Lisa Garbus, Michael Holland, and Simona Sawhney (Minneapolis: University of Minnesota Press, 1991), 45, 161n21.

18. Philippe Lacoue-Labarthe and Jean-Luc Nancy, "The Nazi Myth," *Critical Inquiry* 16.2 (1990): 297.

19. Lévy-Bruhl's account of participation receives a fuller treatment in chapter 4.

20. Nancy, "Myth Interrupted," 46.

21. Theodor W. Adorno and Max Horkheimer, "The Concept of Enlightenment," in *Dialectic of Enlightenment*, trans. John Cumming (New York: Continuum, 1990), 8.

22. Aristotle, *Physics*, 118–21/224b–25b.

23. Friedrich Nietzsche, *Human, All Too Human: A Book for Free Spirits*, trans. R. J. Hollingdale (Cambridge: Cambridge University Press, 1986), §285;

Nietzsche, *Menschliches, Allzumenschliches, Erster Band,* in *Werke in Drei Bänden,* 1:§285.

24. Friedrich Nietzsche, *The Gay Science,* trans. Walter Kaufmann (New York: Vintage, 1974), §329 (translation slightly modified).

25. Nietzsche, *Human, All Too Human,* §236.

26. Nietzsche, *Twilight of the Idols,* 485.

27. Martin Heidegger, *The Will to Power as Art,* in *Nietzsche,* trans. David Farrell Krell (San Francisco: HarperCollins, 1979), 1:154.

28. Nietzsche, *Human, All Too Human,* §§236, 251.

29. Nietzsche echoes the advice of John Lubbock, who warns ethnographers not to trust the testimony of the stereotypically shifty native informant: "the mind of the savage, like that of the child, is easily fatigued, and he will then give random answers to spare himself the trouble of thought." John Lubbock, *The Origin of Civilisation and the Primitive Condition of Man,* ed. Peter Rivière (Chicago: University of Chicago Press, 1978), 4–5.

30. Claude Lévi-Strauss, *The Savage Mind* (Chicago: University of Chicago Press, 1966), 164.

31. Gadamer affirms the living metaphoricity of language—he calls it "verbal energeia"—in *Truth and Method,* which doubtless qualifies him for admission to the ranks of the savage philosophers. Hans-Georg Gadamer, *Truth and Method,* 2nd ed., trans. Joel Weinsheimer and Donald G. Marshall (New York: Continuum, 1988), 431–32, 442.

32. Edward Burnett Tylor, *Primitive Culture,* 2nd ed. (New York: Henry Holt, 1874), 1:425–26.

33. Nietzsche, *Human, All Too Human,* §5.

34. Tylor, *Primitive Culture,* 1:477.

35. David Hume, *The Natural History of Religion,* in *Principal Writings on Religion,* ed. J. C. A. Gaskin (Oxford: Oxford University Press, 1993), 141.

36. For the concept of theoretical optimism, see Nietzsche, *Birth of Tragedy,* 95.

37. Tylor, *Primitive Culture,* 2:108–9.

38. Nietzsche, *Human, All Too Human,* §111; Lubbock, *Origin of Civilisation,* 191.

39. Lubbock, *Origin of Civilisation,* 189.

40. Tylor, *Primitive Culture,* 2:144.

41. Lubbock argues instead that the fetishist aims to control a god by embodying it in a manipulable object; the worshipers of a fetish can, he explains, "beat" it when it fails to answer their prayers. Lubbock, *Origin of Civilisation,* 165.

42. Tylor, *Primitive Culture,* 1:16.

43. Nietzsche, *Human, All Too Human,* §13.

44. Nietzsche, *Gay Science,* §59.

45. Friedrich Nietzsche, *Ecce Homo,* trans. R. J. Hollingdale (London: Penguin Books, 1979), 61; Nietzsche, *Ecce homo,* in *Werke in Drei Bänden,* 2:1120.

46. Friedrich Nietzsche, *Daybreak,* ed. Maudemarie Clark and Brian Leiter, trans. R. J. Hollingdale (Cambridge: Cambridge University Press, 1997), §31; Nietzsche, *Morgenröthe,* in *Werke in Drei Bänden,* 1:§31.

47. Nietzsche, *Will to Power,* §1067.

48. Nietzsche, *Twilight of the Idols*, 482–83.

49. Tylor, *Primitive Culture*, 1:160.

50. As noted in the introduction, this analysis is commonly attributed to Roman Jakobson, who in turn attributes it to Frazer and to Freud. Roman Jakobson, "Two Aspects of Language and Two Types of Aphasic Disturbances," in *Language in Literature*, ed. Krystyna Pomorska and Stephen Rudy (Cambridge, MA: Harvard University Press, 1987), 113.

51. Aristotle, *Poetics*, trans. Richard Janko (Indianapolis: Hackett Publishing, 1987), 28–29/57b.

52. Jacques Derrida, "White Mythology: Metaphor in the Text of Philosophy," in *Margins of Philosophy*, trans. Alan Bass (Chicago: University of Chicago Press, 1982), 215; Paul de Man, "Metaphor (*Second Discourse*)," in *Allegories of Reading* (New Haven: Yale University Press, 1979), 146.

53. Aristotle, *The Art of Rhetoric*, trans. H. C. Lawson-Tancred (London: Penguin Books, 1991), 235/1410b (emphasis added); Aristotle, *Poetics*, 4–5/48b; the ensuing discussion is indebted to Paul Ricoeur, *The Rule of Metaphor*, trans. Robert Czerny, with Kathleen McLaughlin and John Costello (Toronto: University of Toronto Press, 1977), 32–35.

54. Aristotle, *Physics*, 57–58/201a.

55. Aristotle, *Metaphysics*, trans. Hugh Lawson-Tancred (London: Penguin Books, 1998), 263–65/1048a.

56. Ricoeur cites and partly translates this sentence in *Rule of Metaphor*, 34.

57. Aristotle, *On The Soul*, trans. J. A. Smith, in *Introduction to Aristotle*, ed. Richard McKeon (New York: Modern Library, 1947), 170–71/411b–12a.

58. Paul Ricoeur, *Rule of Metaphor*, 21; Ricoeur, "Creativity in Language," in *The Philosophy of Paul Ricoeur: An Anthology of His Work*, ed. Charles E. Regan and David Stewart (Boston: Beacon Press, 1978), 130. The verse literally means, "The earth is blue like an orange."

59. Ricoeur, *Rule of Metaphor*, 7, 21.

60. Ricoeur, "Creativity in Language," 123.

61. Ricoeur, *Rule of Metaphor*, 23. Cf. Nietzsche: "We can destroy only as creators," *Gay Science*, §58.

62. Tylor, *Primitive Culture*, 1:285.

63. Ricoeur, *Rule of Metaphor*, 43.

64. Ricoeur, "Creativity in Discourse," 130.

65. Nietzsche, *Human, All Too Human*, §265.

66. Tylor, *Primitive Culture*, 1:407.

67. Tylor concedes that pockets of energeia survive in the most everyday acts of communication: "To this day there go about the world endless stories told as matter of known reality, but which a critical examination shows to be mere inferences, often utterly illusory ones, from facts which have stimulated the invention of some curious enquirer." Tylor, *Primitive Culture*, 1:369.

68. Nietzsche, *Birth of Tragedy*, 63.

69. Nietzsche, *Twilight of the Idols*, 518/995.

70. Nietzsche, *Will to Power*, §853.

71. Nietzsche's account of frenzy, or intoxication (*der Rausch*), which is allegedly premodern, recurs in Rushdie's recent account of fury, which is allegedly post-

modern. Frenzy, for Nietzsche, is at once savage and Dionysian; fury, for Rushdie, is, well, American. Salman Rushdie, *Fury* (Toronto: Vintage Canada, 2001), 54, 178.

72. Nietzsche, *Twilight of the Idols*, 495.

73. Nietzsche, *Will to Power*, §485.

74. Nietzsche, *Gay Science*, §58.

CHAPTER 3. THE MANA TYPE

1. Edward Burnett Tylor, *Primitive Culture* (New York: Henry Holt, 1874), 1:443–44; J. Leighton Wilson, *Western Africa* (New York: Harper and Brothers, 1856), 395 (emphasis added).

2. Max Müller, *Comparative Mythology*, ed. A. Smythe Palmer (London: G. Routledge, [1909]), 72–73.

3. Tylor, *Primitive Culture*, 1:284.

4. Theodor Adorno and Max Horkheimer, "The Concept of Enlightenment," in *Dialectic of Enlightenment*, trans. John Cumming (New York: Continuum, 1990), 5.

5. Marcel Proust, *Swann's Way*, in *Remembrance of Things Past*, trans. C. K. Scott Moncrieff and Terence Kilmartin (New York: Vintage Books, 1981), 1:3; Proust, *Du côté de chez Swann*, in *À la recherche du temps perdu*, ed. Pierre Clarac and André Ferré (Paris: Éditions Gallimard, 1954), 1:3.

6. J. Hillis Miller, *Versions of Pygmalion* (Cambridge, MA: Harvard University Press, 1990), 13.

7. Gérard Genette, "Proust and Indirect Language," in *Figures of Literary Discourse*, trans. Alan Sheridan (New York: Columbia University Press, 1982), 243, 249; Genette, "Proust et le langage indirect," in *Figures II* (Paris: Éditions du Seuil, 1969), 240, 248.

8. Marcel Proust, *Cities of the Plain*, in *Remembrance of Things Past*, 2:968–69; Proust, *Sodome et Gomorrhe*, in *À la recherche du temps perdu*, 2:936–38; Genette, "Proust and Indirect Language," 247.

9. Genette, "Proust and Indirect Language," 243.

10. Proust, *Swann's Way*, 416/383.

11. Genette, "Proust and Indirect Language," 237/233. "The 'name' is not," he later adds, "the cause of the illusion, but it is very precisely its locus, in which it is concentrated and *crystallized* [*c'est en lui qu'elle se concentre et se cristallise*]" (244/242, emphasis added).

12. Tylor, *Primitive Culture*, 1:305 (emphasis added).

13. Genette, "Proust and Indirect Language," 237/233.

14. Aristotle, *On the Soul*, trans. J. A. Smith, in *Introduction to Aristotle*, ed. Richard McKeon (New York: Modern Library, 1947), 177/414a.

15. Giorgio Agamben, "On Potentiality," in *Potentialities*, trans. Daniel Heller-Roazen (Stanford: Stanford University Press, 1999), 183. The passage is italicized in the original.

16. See also Giorgio Agamben, *Homo Sacer*, trans. Daniel Heller-Roazen (Stanford: Stanford University Press, 1998), 44–48.

17. Gérard Genette, "Proust Palimpsest," in *Figures of Literary Discourse*, trans. Alan Sheridan (New York: Columbia University Press, 1982), 204–5.

18. Proust, *Swann's Way*, 423/390.

19. Genette, "Proust Palimpsest," 205.

20. Genette, "Proust and Indirect Language," 248/247.

21. Aristotle, *Metaphysics*, trans. Hugh Lawson-Tancred (London: Penguin Books, 1998), 275/1050b.

22. Proust, *Swann's Way*, 420/387.

23. Agamben, "On Potentiality," 182.

24. Ferdinand de Saussure, *Course in General Linguistics*, trans. Roy Harris, ed. Charles Bally and Albert Sechehaye with Albert Riedlinger (La Salle, IL: Open Court, 1983), 67–68.

25. Émile Benveniste, "The Nature of the Linguistic Sign," in *Problems in General Linguistics*, trans. Mary Elizabeth Meek (Coral Gables, FL: University of Miami Press, 1971), 46.

26. For Saussure, the signified has no positive content but is defined negatively by its contrast with other patterns on the plane of thought. So too the signifier is distinguished by its difference from other patterns on the plane of sound. The signified is thus a signifier, but a mental rather than a spoken or written one. Saussure, *Course in General Linguistics*, 115–16.

27. Charles Sanders Peirce, "Sign," in *Peirce on Signs*, ed. James Hoopes (Chapel Hill: University of North Carolina Press, 1991), 239.

28. Charles Sanders Peirce, "New Elements," in *The Essential Peirce: Volume 2 (1893–1913)*, ed. Peirce Edition Project (Bloomington: Indiana University Press, 1998), 323.

29. Charles Sanders Peirce, "Some Consequences of Four Incapacities," in *The Essential Peirce: Volume 1 (1867–1893)*, ed. Nathan Houser and Christian Kloesel (Bloomington: Indiana University Press, 1992), 52.

30. Charles Sanders Peirce, "What Makes a Reasoning Sound?" in *Essential Peirce*, 2:255.

31. Proust, *Within A Budding Grove*, in *Remembrance of Things Past*, I: 708/658.

32. Peirce, "New Elements," 317.

33. Aristotle, *Metaphysics*, 275/1050b; Agamben, "On Potentiality," 182.

34. Aristotle, *Metaphysics*, 260/1047a–47b.

35. Proust, *Swann's Way*, 420–21/387.

36. Jacques Derrida, *Glas*, trans. John P. Leavey, Jr., and Richard Rand (Lincoln: University of Nebraska Press, 1986), 31b.

37. Proust, *Swann's Way*, 427/394.

38. Peirce, "New Elements," 324, 304 (emphasis added).

39. Proust, *Swann's Way*, 423–24/390.

40. Bronislaw Malinowski, "Myth in Primitive Psychology," in *Magic, Science and Religion, and Other Essays* (Garden City, NJ: Doubleday, 1954), 140.

41. J. L. Austin, *How to Do Things with Words*, 2nd ed., ed. J. O. Urmson and Marina Sbisà (Cambridge, MA: Harvard University Press, 1962), 99–101.

42. Austin's example of things *in pari materia* is worth noting. He cites the difference between the movement of a trigger finger and the movement of a trigger, as if to suggest that violence is always at issue in the doctrine of illocutionary forces. Austin, *How to Do Things with Words*, 113n1.

43. Peirce, "New Elements," 323.

44. Austin, *How to Do Things with Words*, 114.

45. Gottlob Frege, "Sense and Reference," in *Translations from the Philosophical Writings of Gottlob Frege*, ed. Peter Geach and Max Black (Oxford: Basil Blackwell, 1977), 62–63.

46. Andrew Lang, *The Secret of the Totem* (London: Longmans, Green, 1905), 117.

47. Sigmund Freud, *Totem and Taboo*, in *The Standard Edition of the Complete Psychological Works of Sigmund Freud*, trans. James Strachey and others (London: Hogarth Press, 1955), 13:112.

48. Proust, *Swann's Way*, 153/140.

49. The narrator mistakes the gesture for an insult. Only long afterward does he learn that she was inviting him to join her in a "naughty" game. Marcel Proust, *Time Regained*, in *Remembrance of Things Past*, 3:711–12.

50. Austin, *How to Do Things with Words*, 118.

51. In *The Captive* the narrator intimates that it is possible to call him "Marcel," but he does not therefore say that he *is* Marcel: "Then [Albertine] would find her tongue and say: 'My —' or 'My darling —' followed by my Christian name, which *if we give* the narrator the same name as the author of this book, would be 'My Marcel,' or 'My darling Marcel.'" Later, while he is waiting, and hoping, for Albertine to come to him, he receives a note from a nameless stranger: "a cyclist brought me a note from her bidding me be patient, and full of the charming expressions that she was in the habit of using. 'My darling dear Marcel, I return less quickly than this cyclist, whose bike I should like to borrow in order to be with you sooner.'" Albertine calls him "Marcel," but does he call himself "Marcel"? The note, after all, is sent in compensation for a failure of self-presence. Marcel Proust, *The Captive*, in *Remembrance of Things Past*, 3:69 (emphasis added), 153.

52. James G. Frazer, *The Golden Bough*, abridged ed. (New York: Macmillan, 1951), 53.

53. Freud, *Totem and Taboo*, 159.

54. Austin, *How to Do Things with Words*, 100.

55. Marcel Mauss [and Henri Hubert], *A General Theory of Magic*, trans. Robert Brain (London: Routledge and Kegan Paul, 1972), 107.

56. Austin, *How to Do Things with Words*, 14–15.

57. Giorgio Agamben, "*Pardes*: The Writing of Potentiality," in *Potentialities*, 218.

58. R. H. Codrington, *The Melanesians* (Oxford: Clarendon Press, 1891), 118n1.

59. Not every name confers power but only the names of those who had power while alive, for only they return as "spirits" after death. The rest are souls without capacities: "The ghost who is to be worshiped is the spirit of a man who in his lifetime had *mana* in him," says Codrington, while "the souls of common men"—those without mana—"are the common herd of ghosts, mere nobodies" (ibid., 125). Codrington says a spirit whose name carries force is called a *tindalo* and appears to the living in a visible, "bodily form" that is "not fleshly like the bodies of men," but physical and spiritual, real and ideal, at once (120).

60. Saussure, *Course in General Linguistics*, 105. Lévi-Strauss uses the terms "signifier" and "signified" in a different way from Saussure. Lévi-Strauss's

228 NOTES TO PAGES 123–125

"signifier" includes both the symbol and its interpretant and therefore corresponds to Saussure's notion of the sign. The "signified" is the object to which "the signifier" refers and therefore corresponds to Saussure's notion of the referent or thing.

61. Claude Lévi-Strauss, *Introduction to the Work of Marcel Mauss*, trans. Felicity Baker (London: Routledge and Kegan Paul, 1987), 60; Lévi-Strauss, "Introduction à l'oeuvre de Marcel Mauss," in *Sociologie et anthropologie* (Paris: Presses Universitaires de France, 1950), xlvii.

62. Mauss and Hubert, *General Theory of Magic*, 114–15.

63. Durkheim's account of "totemism" projects a comprehensive doctrine of discursive forces onto the aboriginal societies of central and northern Australia—and then disavows it. Metaphor is a substitution that animates on the basis of a resemblance; the totemic emblem is a substitution that electrifies on the basis of a nonresemblance. Metaphor proceeds on the premise that one thing is like another; totemism discharges its forces wherever there emerges a thing unlike any other. Metaphor finds identity in difference; totemism transmits energy via differences. Durkheim's name for totemic energy is "mana," but he can only approach it by naming something else. In North America, he says, among the nations "belonging to the great Sioux family" (as if each of these societies were the child of some great parent), "there is a pre-eminent power" from which "all the others" are derived, "and which is called *wakan*" (220–21). Wakan, like the totemic emblem, has power only insofar as it exceeds the limits of mimesis: "the natives do not represent it in a determined form" (221). Signs do not stand in for it; they put it to work. Hence Durkheim cannot say what "wakan" means but can only mention the acts that it performs: "Sometimes it is represented in the form of a wind, as a breath having its seat in the four cardinal points and moving everything; sometimes it is a voice heard in the crashing of the thunder; the sun, moon and stars are wakan" (221). Reasoning metaphorically, he discovers analogous forces at work across North America—or at least in books about it. The "same idea" is "found again" among "the Iroquois," and "the word *orenda* which expresses it is the exact equivalent of the wakan of the Sioux" (222). In the economy of Durkheim's text, every signifier of the mana type can be traded for every other without losing anything in the exchange. In "the islands of Melanesia," for example, "we find, under the name of *mana*, an idea which is the exact equivalent of the wakan of the Sioux and the orenda of the Iroquois" (223). Every name for this nonmetaphorical force is a metaphor for every other.

The postfigurative figure conducts energy between modes of substance that are not *in pari materia*. Durkheim defines it as "the original matter" out of which a whole universe of *im*material beings has been constructed (228). What he names mana is the substance of everything *in*substantial, an "ideal" force actualizing itself in "real" effects: "The spirits, demons, genii and gods of every sort are only the concrete forms taken by this energy, or 'potentiality,' as Hewitt calls it, in individualizing itself, in fixing itself upon a certain determined object or point in space, or in centering around an ideal and legendary being, though one conceived as real by the popular imagination" (228). Under the heading of totemism, Durkheim elaborates a class of signs that neither mean nor refer but rather cross the line that divides illocutionary acts from their nondiscursive consequences. Words act with the force of living bodies: "this force may be attached to words that are pronounced or movements that are made just as well as to corporal substances; the voice or the movements may serve as its vehicle, and it may produce its effect through their intermediacy, without the aid of any god or spirit" (229). Émile Durkheim, *The Elementary Forms of the Religious Life,* trans. Joseph Ward Swain (New York: Free Press, 1965), 211–31.

64. Codrington, *Melanesians,* 117.

65. Bronislaw Malinowski, "Magic, Science and Religion," in *Magic, Science and Religion, and Other Essays,* 77.

66. Malinowski, "Myth in Primitive Psychology," 94; Malinowski, "Magic, Science, and Religion," 70.

67. Malinowski, "Magic, Science, and Religion," 83.

68. Malinowski, "Myth in Primitive Psychology," 100–101.

69. J. M. R. Owens, "New Zealand before Annexation," in *The Oxford History of New Zealand,* 2nd ed., ed. Geoffrey W. Rice (Auckland: Oxford University Press, 1992), 29; Ranginui Walker, *Ka Whawhai Tonu Matou/Struggle without End* (Auckland: Penguin Books, 1990), 78–82.

70. Claudia Orange, *The Treaty of Waitangi* (Wellington: Allen and Unwin, 1987), 11.

71. Ibid., 12; Owens, "New Zealand before Annexation," 42.

72. Orange, *Treaty of Waitangi* 21; Owens, "New Zealand before Annexation," 42.

73. Ruth Ross, "The Treaty on the Ground," in *The Treaty of Waitangi* (Wellington: Department of University Extension, Victoria University, 1972), 21; Orange, *Treaty of Waitangi,* 21–22.

74. Orange, *Treaty of Waitangi,* 33–34; Owens, "New Zealand before Annexation," 51.

75. Orange, *Treaty of Waitangi,* 36–37.

76. Ibid., 41; Ross, "Treaty on the Ground," 20.

77. Ruth Ross, "Te Tiriti O Waitangi: Texts and Translations," *New Zealand Journal of History* 6.2 (1972): 136.

78. William Colenso, *The Authentic and Genuine History of the Signing of the Treaty of Waitangi* (Wellington: George Didsbury, 1890), 17.

79. The English text of the treaty is reprinted in Orange, *Treaty of Waitangi,* 258–59.

80. Colenso, *History of the Signing,* 17.

81. Ibid., 32; Orange, *Treaty of Waitangi,* 53–55.

82. The Crown claimed the North Island on the basis of the treaty and the South Island on the grounds that it was *terra nullius* at the time of "discovery." Walker, *Ka Whawhai Tonu Matou/Struggle without End,* 97; Owens, "New Zealand before Annexation," 52.

83. Mauss and Hubert, *General Theory of Magic,* 112–13.

84. Orange, *Treaty of Waitangi,* 77.

85. Orange, however, is skeptical of this argument (ibid., 42).

86. Ross, "Te Tiriti O Waitangi," 133.

87. Bruce Biggs, "Humpty-Dumpty and the Treaty of Waitangi," in *Waitangi: Māori and Pākehā Perspectives of the Treaty of Waitangi,* ed. I. W. Kawharu (Auckland: Oxford University Press, 1989), 305.

88. Ross, "Treaty on the Ground," 20, and "Te Tiriti O Waitangi," 140–41;
Walker, *Ka Whawhai Tonu Matou/Struggle without End*, 91–92.

89. Biggs, "Humpty-Dumpty and the Treaty of Waitangi," 305.

90. Ross, "Treaty on the Ground," 20.

91. Colenso, *History of the Signing*, 22, 24–25.

92. R. J. Walker, "The Treaty of Waitangi as the Focus of Māori Protest," in
Kawharu, *Waitangi: Māori and Pākehā Perspectives*, 264. Claudia Orange points
out that Nopera reversed this statement a year later. See Orange, *Treaty of Wait-*
angi, 83.

93. Ross, "Treaty on the Ground," 20–21; Walker "Treaty of Waitangi," 264.

94. Walker, "Treaty of Waitangi," 264; Ross, "Treaty on the Ground," 21–22,
and "Te Tiriti O Waitangi," 142–43.

95. Walker, "Treaty of Waitangi," 265.

96. I. W. Kawharu, introduction to *Waitangi: Māori and Pākehā Perspec-*
tives, xix.

97. Walker, "Treaty of Waitangi," 265.

98. Walker, *Ka Whawhai Tonu Matou/Struggle without End*, 93.

99. Kawharu, introduction to *Waitangi: Māori and Pākehā Perspectives*, xvii.

100. The displacement obeys Lacan's formula for hallucination: what is fore-
closed in the symbolic returns in the real. And yet it is savage thought, not "rational discourse," that is conventionally said to be hallucinatory.

101. Proust, *Swann's Way*, 379.

102. Charles Sanders Peirce, "Sundry Logical Conceptions," in *Essential Peirce*,
2:269, 287.

103. Charles Sanders Peirce, "Pragmatism," in *Essential Peirce*, 2:419.

104. Proust, *Swann's Way*, 381.

105. André Marie Ampère (1775–1836) is credited with developing a mathematical theory of electromagnetic phenomena; Antoine Laurent Lavoisier (1743–1794)
overthrew the doctrine of phlogistics and laid the groundwork of modern chemistry.
A Dictionary of Scientists, Oxford Reference Online, s.v. "André Marie Ampère"
and "Antoine Laurent Lavoisier," http://www.oxfordreference.com.

CHAPTER 4. COMMODITY TOTEMISM

1. Walter Benjamin, "On Language as Such and on the Language of Man," in *Se-*
lected Writings: Volume 1, 1913–1926, ed. Marcus Bullock and Michael W. Jennings
(Cambridge, MA: Harvard University Press, 1996), 62; Benjamin, "Über Sprache
überhaupt und über die Sprache des Menschen," in *Gesammelte Schriften*, vol. 2,
bk. 1, ed. Rolf Tiedemann and Hermann Schweppenhäuser (Frankfurt: Suhrkamp
Verlag, 1977), 141.

2. Immanuel Kant, *Critique of Judgement*, trans. Werner S. Pluhar (Indianapolis: Hackett Publishing, 1987), 181–2.

3. Aristotle, *On the Soul*, trans. J. A. Smith, in *Introduction to Aristotle*, ed.
Richard McKeon (New York: Modern Library, 1947), 169/411a.

4. Jacques Derrida, "Différance," in *Margins of Philosophy*, trans. Alan Bass
(Chicago: University of Chicago Press, 1982), 9.

5. James G. Frazer, *The Golden Bough*, abridged ed. (New York: Macmillan, 1951), 298.

6. Benjamin, "On Language as Such and on the Language of Man," 65.

7. Frazer, *Golden Bough*, 14.

8. Charles Sanders Peirce, "What Is a Sign?" in *The Essential Peirce: Volume 2 (1893–1913)*, ed. Peirce Edition Project (Bloomington: Indiana University Press, 1998), 5.

9. Walter Benjamin, "Antitheses concerning Word and Name," in *Selected Writings: Volume 2, 1927–1934*, trans. Rodney Livingstone and others, ed. Michael W. Jennings, Howard Eiland, and Gary Smith (Cambridge, MA: Harvard University Press, 1999), 717. The fragment is a note toward his essay "On the Mimetic Faculty." That he pursued these speculations into the mid-1930s suggests he never lost interest in the problem of immediation.

10. Andrew Lang, *The Secret of the Totem* (London: Longmans, Green, 1905), 117.

11. Benjamin, "On Language as Such and on the Language of Man," 68.

12. Walter Benjamin, "On the Mimetic Faculty," in *Selected Writings*, 2:721,; Benjamin, "Über das Mimetische Vermögen," in *Gesammelte Schriften*, vol. 2, bk. 1, 213.

13. Plato, *Cratylus*, in *Complete Works*, ed. John M. Cooper and D. S. Hutchinson (Indianapolis: Hackett Publishing, 1997), 102–3/384c–d, 142–43/426c, and 143/427c.

14. Giambattista Vico, *The New Science of Giambattista Vico*, trans. Thomas Goddard Bergin and Max Harold Fisch (Ithaca, NY: Cornell University Press, 1968), §447.

15. Frazer, *Golden Bough*, 284.

16. Ferdinand de Saussure, *Course in General Linguistics*, trans. Roy Harris, ed. Charles Bally and Albert Sechehaye with Albert Riedlinger (La Salle, IL: Open Court, 1983), 68–69. Saussure concedes later that some signs are absolutely arbitrary, whereas others are only relatively so. His examples of "relative motivation," however, are not cases of onomatopoeia. The French *vingt* (twenty) is absolutely arbitrary, whereas *dix-neuf* (nineteen) is relatively arbitrary (1) because it evokes the words of which it is composed, *dix* and *neuf*, and (2) because it shares the rule of its formation with the members of a series, *dix-huit* and *vingt-neuf*, etc. Similarly the English plural "men" is absolutely arbitrary because it is irregular, whereas "ships" is relatively arbitrary because it belongs to the series of regular plurals, such as "flags," "birds," and "books" (130–31).

17. Benjamin, "On the Mimetic Faculty," 721.

18. Benjamin did not live to see Hjelmslev's argument, published in 1943, that signifiers in different languages do not have the same signified at their core. Hjelmslev observes, for example, that the semantic field of the Welsh word *glas* overlaps the fields of three English words: "green," "blue," and "gray." Louis Hjelmslev, *Prolegomena to a Theory of Language*, trans. Francis J. Whitfield (Madison: University of Wisconsin Press, 1969), 53.

19. Lucien Lévy-Bruhl, *How Natives Think*, trans. Lilian A. Clare (Princeton: Princeton University Press, 1985), 16–17.

20. Roland Barthes, *Camera Lucida*, trans. Richard Howard (New York: Hill and Wang, 1981), 109.

21. Lévy-Bruhl, *How Natives Think*, 38.

22. Walter Benjamin, *The Concept of Criticism in German Romanticism*, in *Selected Writings*, 1:141, 148; Benjamin, *Der Begriff der Kunstkritik in der deutschen Romantik*, in *Gesammelte Schriften*, vol. 1, bk. 1, ed. Rolf Tiedemann and Hermann Schweppenhäuser (Frankfurt: Suhrkamp Verlag, 1974), 50, 60.

23. Walter Benjamin, "Capitalism as Religion," in *Selected Writings*, 1:290; Benjamin, "Kapitalismus als Religion," in *Gesammelte Schriften*, vol. 6, ed. Rolf Tiedemann and Hermann Schweppenhäuser (Frankfurt: Suhrkamp Verlag, 1985), 102.

24. Karl Marx, *Capital*, vol. 1, trans. Ben Fowkes (New York: Vintage Books, 1977), 165.

25. Karl Marx, *Capital*, vol. 3, trans. David Fernbach (Harmondsworth: Penguin Books, 1981), 515.

26. Karl Marx, "Economic and Philosophical Manuscripts," in *Early Writings*, trans. Rodney Livingstone and Gregor Benton (London: Penguin Books, 1975), 375; Marx, "Ökonomisch-philosophische Manuskripte aus dem Jahre 1844," in *Ergänzungsband*, Karl Marx Friedrich Engels Werke, vol. 1 (Berlin: Dietz Verlag, 1968), 563.

27. Frazer, *Golden Bough*, 215.

28. As quoted from William Shakespeare, *The Life of Timon of Athens*, ed. Stanley T. Williams (New Haven: Yale University Press, 1919), IV.iii.389–92. I enclose "Shakespeare's" in quotation marks because the play was evidently written by more than one author.

29. Marx, *Capital*, 1:284.

30. "Labour is, first of all, a process between man and nature, a process by which man, through his own actions, mediates, regulates and controls the metabolism between himself and nature. He confronts the materials of nature as a force of nature. He sets in motion the natural forces which belong to his own body, his arms, legs, head and hands, in order to appropriate the materials of nature in a form adapted to his own needs. Through this movement he acts upon external nature and changes it, and in this way he simultaneously changes his own nature. He develops the potentialities slumbering within nature, and subjects the play of its forces to his own sovereign power." Marx, *Capital*, 1:283.

31. The terms "personification" (*Personifizierung*) and "reification" (*Versachlichung*) are Marx's. Ibid., 3:969; Marx, *Das Kapital, Dritter Band*, Karl Marx Friedrich Engels Werke, vol. 25 (Berlin: Dietz Verlag, 1969), 838.

32. Karl Marx, "Excerpts from James Mill's *Elements of Political Economy*," in *Early Writings*, 260; Marx, "Auszüge aus James Mills Buch *Élemens d'économie politique*," in *Ergänzungsband*, 445.

33. Marx, "Economic and Philosophical Manuscripts," 327/515.

34. He will repeat the point in *Capital*: "Modern society, which already in its infancy had pulled Pluto by the hair of his head from the bowels of the earth, greets gold as its Holy Grail, as the glittering incarnation of its innermost principle of life." Marx, *Capital*, 1:230.

35. Ibid., 1:314; Marx, *Das Kapital, Erster Band*, vol. 23 of Karl Marx Friedrich Engels Werke (Berlin: Dietz Verlag, 1969), 221.

36. The premise that the sign is the union of a body and a soul is not unique to Marx. Derrida finds an analogous notion in Hegel, Saussure, and Husserl: "Hegel accords to the content of this meaning, this *Bedeutung*, the name and rank of soul (*Seele*). Of course it is a soul deposited in a body, in the body of the signifier, in the sensory flesh of intuition. The sign, as the unity of the signifying body and the signified ideality, becomes a kind of incarnation. Therefore the opposition of soul and body, and analogically the opposition of the intelligible and the sensory, condition the difference between the signified and the signifier, between the signifying intention (*bedeuten*), which is an animating activity, and the inert body of the signifier. This will remain true for Saussure; and also for Husserl, who sees the body of the sign as animated by the intention of signification, just as a body (*Körper*) when inhabited by *Geist* becomes a proper body (*Leib*). Husserl says of the living word that it is a *geistige Leiblichkeit*, a spiritual flesh." Jacques Derrida, "The Pit and the Pyramid: Introduction to Hegel's Semiology," in *Margins of Philosophy*, 82.

37. Karl Marx, *A Contribution to the Critique of Political Economy*, ed. Maurice Dobb, trans. S. W. Ryazanskaya (New York: International Publishers, 1970), 153–54.

38. Marx, "Economic and Philosophical Manuscripts," 378/566.

39. Karl Marx, *Capital*, vol. 2, trans. David Fernbach (Harmondsworth: Penguin Books, 1978), 299; Marx, *Das Kapital, Zweiter Band*, Karl Marx Friedrich Engels Werke, vol. 24 (Berlin: Dietz Verlag, 1970), 223; Marx, *Capital*, 1:283/192.

40. Karl Marx, *Grundrisse*, trans. Martin Nicolaus (Harmondsworth: Penguin Books, 1973), 361; Marx, *Ökonomische Manuskripte, 1857–58*, in *Karl Marx Friedrich Engels Gesamtausgabe, Zweite Abteilung*, vol. 1 (Berlin: Dietz Verlag, 1976), 272.

41. Marx, *Capital*, 2:299/223.

42. Marx, *Grundrisse*, 461; Marx, *Ökonomische Manuskripte, 1857–58*, in *Karl Marx Friedrich Engels Gesamtausgabe, Zweite Abteilung*, vol. 2 (Berlin: Dietz Verlag, 1981), 369.

43. Marx, *Capital*, 1:302/209.

44. Ibid., 2:185.

45. Ibid., 1:289–90/198.

46. Marx, *Grundrisse*, 298/1:218, and *Capital*, 1:315.

47. Marx, *Capital*, 1:342/247.

48. Ibid., 1:308/215. "Objectified labor ceases to exist in a dead state [*auf todt*] as an external, indifferent form on the substance, because it is itself again posited as a moment of living labor; as a relation of living labor to itself in an objective material, as the *objectivity* of living labor" (Marx, *Grundrisse*, 360/1:272).

49. Ben Fowkes translates *beseelt* by the phrase "filled with vitality." See Marx, *Capital*, 1:757/635.

50. Marx, *Grundrisse*, 364/1:275.

51. Marx, *Capital*, 1:258.

52. Ibid., 2:303/228.

53. Edward Burnett Tylor, *Primitive Culture*, 2nd ed. (New York: Henry Holt, 1874), 2:144.

54. James G. Frazer, "Totemism," in *Totemism and Exogamy* (London: Macmillan, 1910), 1:3–4, 52.

55. Lévy-Bruhl, *How Natives Think*, 91.

56. Frazer, "Totemism," 4.

57. Lang, *Secret of the Totem*, 117.

58. Marx, *Capital*, 3:1025.

59. Émile Durkheim, *The Elementary Forms of the Religious Life*, trans. Joseph Ward Swain (New York: Free Press, 1965), 37.

60. Walter Benjamin, "On the Concept of History," in *Selected Writings: Volume 4, 1938–1940*, trans. Edmund Jephcott and others, ed. Howard Eiland and Michael W. Jennings (Cambridge, MA: Harvard University Press, 2003), 389.

61. Walter Benjamin, *The Arcades Project*, trans. Howard Eiland and Kevin McLaughlin (Cambridge, MA: Harvard University Press, 1999), 209–10. The quotation within the quotation is cited by Benjamin as originating in N[orbert] Guterman and H[enri] Lefebvre, *La conscience mystifiée* (Paris: [Gallimard,]1936), 228.

62. Walter Benjamin, "The Fireside Saga," in *Selected Writings*, 2:152.

63. Walter Benjamin, "Surrealism: The Last Snapshot of the European Intelligentsia," in *Selected Writings*, 2:212.

64. "The historical materialist approaches a historical object only where it confronts him as a monad [a part that contains a whole universe of social relations]. In this structure he recognizes the sign of a messianic arrest of happening, or (to put it differently) a revolutionary chance in the fight for the oppressed past. He takes cognizance of it in order to blast a specific era out of the homogenous course of history; thus, he blasts a specific *life* out of the era, a specific work out of the *lifework*" (Benjamin, "On the Concept of History," 396, emphasis added).

CHAPTER 5. ALLEGORIES OF THE SUN, SPECTERS OF EXCESS

1. Eden Robinson, *Monkey Beach* (Toronto: Knopf Canada, 2000), 2.

2. "Repetition *and* first time: this is perhaps the question of the event as question of the ghost." Jacques Derrida, *Specters of Marx*, trans. Peggy Kamuf (New York: Routledge, 1994), 10.

3. Herbert Spencer, *Principles of Sociology* (New York: D. Appleton, 1893), 1:304–5 (emphasis added).

4. Friedrich Nietzsche, *Human, All Too Human*, trans. R. J. Hollingdale (Cambridge: Cambridge University Press, 1986), §5. I say "Spencer's" and "Nietzsche's," but the images are generic.

5. Spencer, *Principles of Sociology*, 1:134–35.

6. Robinson, *Monkey Beach*, 151.

7. Spencer, *Principles of Sociology*, 1:169.

8. Derrida, *Specters of Marx*, 11.

9. Spencer, *Principles of Sociology*, 1:242.

10. J. L. Austin, *How to Do Things with Words*, 2nd ed., ed. J. O. Urmson and Marina Sbisà (Cambridge, MA: Harvard University Press, 1962), 113.

11. Derrida, *Specters of Marx*, 41.

12. Austin, *How to Do Things with Words*, 113n1.

13. Derrida, *Specters of Marx*, 11.

14. Hegel's own definition of the verb "to sublate" (*Aufheben*) remains unsurpassed: "'*To sublate*' has a twofold meaning in [German]: on the one hand it means to preserve, to maintain, and equally it also means to cause to cease, to put an end to. . . . Thus what is sublated is at the same time preserved. . . . Something is sublated only in so far as it has entered into unity with its opposite." Georg Wilhelm Friedrich Hegel, *Science of Logic*, trans. A. V. Miller (1969; reprint, Atlantic Highlands, NJ: Humanities International Press, 1989), 107.

15. Marx points out that Hegel's allegory allows him to speak of historical change as if it were the product of natural forces. Hence his figure for history conjures history away: "the whole point of the exercise is to create an *allegory*, to confer on some empirically existent thing or other the *significance* of the realized Idea." Karl Marx, "Critique of Hegel's Doctrine of the State," in *Early Writings*, trans. Rodney Livingstone and Gregor Benton (London: Penguin Books, 1992), 99. Marx's notes could just as well be titled "Critique of Hegel's Doctrine of Magic."

16. Hegel is of course repeating a story that is repeated in both chapter 18 of the Gospel according to Luke and chapter 9 of the Gospel according to John.

17. G. W. F. Hegel, *The Philosophy of History*, trans. J. Sibree (New York: Dover, 1956), 103. This is a translation of the text edited by Eduard Gans and introduced by Karl Hegel, which is itself an interpretation of Hegel's lectures. I am less concerned with the particular author who signs the text than with the limited range of what it is possible for any author to say.

18. In *The Origin of Species*, Darwin strongly doubts that a variation within a species can be attributed to differences in conditions of life, such as climate, which, if they act at all, act only "indirectly." Spencer, however, in a remarkably un-Darwinian way, insists there is a direct relation between climate and variation within species. Charles Darwin, *On the Origin of Species* (Cambridge, MA: Harvard University Press, 1964), 132–34.

19. Compare Bataille's theory of general economy: "Solar energy is the source of life's exuberant development. The origin and essence of our wealth are given in the radiation of the sun, which dispenses energy—wealth—without any return." Georges Bataille, *Consumption*, vol. 1 of *The Accursed Share*, trans. Robert Hurley (New York: Zone Books, 1988), 28.

20. Spencer, *Principles of Sociology*, 1:6.

21. Franz Boas, *The Ethnography of Franz Boas*, ed. Ronald P. Rohner (Chicago: University of Chicago Press, 1969), 26.

22. Derrida, *Specters of Marx*, 51.

23. Lucien Lévy-Bruhl, *How Natives Think*, trans. Lilian A. Clare (Princeton: Princeton University Press, 1985), 48; Spencer, *Principles of Sociology*, 2:828.

24. Nietzsche calls these savages "Greeks": "Oh, those Greeks! They knew how to live. What is required for that is to stop courageously at the surface, the fold, the skin, to adore appearance, to believe in forms, tones, words, in the whole Olympus of appearance. Those Greeks were superficial—*out of profundity*." Friedrich Nietzsche, "Nietzsche contra Wagner," in *The Portable Nietzsche*, trans. Walter Kaufmann (Harmondsworth: Penguin Books, 1954), 683.

25. Robinson, *Monkey Beach*, 371.

26. Derrida, *Specters of Marx*, xvii.

27. "Young Liberals to Organize," *Sun* (Vancouver, B.C.), February 12, 1912, first section, p. 6.

28. "Nisga'a Offer Too Much, Reformers Say," *Vancouver Sun*, February 16, 1995, sec. A.

29. "Obtaining Nisga'a Deal Cost B.C. $3 Million," *Vancouver Sun*, March 26, 1996, sec. B.

30. Daniel Raunet, *Without Surrender, without Consent* (Vancouver: Douglas and McIntyre, 1996), 80.

31. Ibid., 79–80; Paul Tennant, *Aboriginal Peoples and Politics* (Vancouver: UBC Press, 1990), 55.

32. Raunet, *Without Surrender, without Consent*, 81.

33. Tennant, *Aboriginal Peoples and Politics*, 55.

34. British Columbia, *Sessional Papers*, 1887, 50 Vic., pp. 271–72.

35. British Columbia, *Sessional Papers*, 1888, 51 Vic., p. 414.

36. Ibid., 423–25; Tennant, *Aboriginal Peoples and Politics*, 59–64.

37. Tennant, *Aboriginal Peoples and Politics*, 86.

38. Raunet, *Without Surrender, without Consent*, 136; Tennant, *Aboriginal Peoples and Politics*, 89–91.

39. Raunet, *Without Surrender, without Consent*, 136–37.

40. Ibid., 141–42; Tennant, *Aboriginal Peoples and Politics*, 111–13.

41. Tennant, *Aboriginal Peoples and Politics*, 118.

42. *Calder et al. v. Attorney-General of British Columbia*, 8 DLR (3d), at 59 and 61.

43. *Calder et al. v. Attorney-General of British Columbia*, 13 DLR (3d), at 66–67.

44. *Calder et al. v. Attorney-General of British Columbia*, 34 DLR (3d), at 173–74.

45. Canada, House of Commons, *Debates*, February 1, 1973, 855; Canada, House of Commons, *Debates*, February 8, 1973, 1073; Tennant, *Aboriginal Peoples and Politics*, 171–72.

46. Tennant, *Aboriginal Peoples and Politics*, 172, 205.

47. Christopher McKee, *Treaty Talks in British Columbia* (Vancouver: UBC Press, 1996), 104.

48. Ibid., 30; Tennant, *Aboriginal Peoples and Politics*, 207–9. The crisis that erupted at Oka, Quebec, that summer was another factor.

49. McKee, *Treaty Talks in British Columbia*, 32–33.

50. "Fairness Can't Be Disproportionate," *Vancouver Sun*, September 19, 1995, sec. A.

51. Jacques Derrida, "Writing before the Letter," in *Of Grammatology*, trans. Gayatri Chakravorty Spivak (Baltimore: Johns Hopkins University Press, 1974), 26.

52. Hegel, *Science of Logic*, 318.

53. "Nisga'a Treaty Is Politic, if Not Necessarily Just," *Vancouver Sun*, February 20, 1996, sec. A.

54. "Erasmus Urges B.C. Indians to Back Commission Report," *Vancouver Sun*, December 13, 1996, sec. B.

55. "Nisga'a Deal to Cost Jobs, but Healthy in Long Term, Government Report Says," *Vancouver Sun*, December 16, 1996, sec. A.

56. British Columbia, *Sessional Papers*, 1887, 50 Vic., p. 253.

57. Tennant suggests that "Charles Burton" was probably the Kincolith chief Charles Barton. Tennant, *Aboriginal Peoples and Politics*, 248n16.

58. "Nisga'a Land Claim Settlement Forecast," *Vancouver Sun*, April 25, 1997, sec. B.

59. Bruce G. Miller, "Introduction," *BC Studies* 95 (1992): 3.

60. *Delgamuukw v. British Columbia*, 79 DLR (4th), at 200.

61. The pattern recurs later at 392: "the emptiness of the territory."

62. *Delgamuukw v. British Columbia*, 79 DLR (4th), at 186, 256–60; 153 DLR (4th), at 236–37.

63. *Delgamuukw v. British Columbia*, 153 DLR (4th), at 227.

64. *Delgamuukw v. British Columbia*, 104 DLR (4th), at 471–72, 542, 547; McKee, *Treaty Talks in British Columbia*, 31.

65. *Delgamuukw v. British Columbia*, 104 DLR (4th), at 471, 547, 601; McKee, *Treaty Talks in British Columbia*, 49.

66. *Delgamuukw v. British Columbia*, 153 DLR (4th), at 236, 241–42.

67. "Are B.C.'s Treasury, Economy in Peril of Going for a Song?" *Vancouver Sun*, December 19, 1997, sec. A.

68. "B.C. Indian Chiefs Lay Claim to Entire Province, Resources," *Vancouver Sun*, February 2, 1998, sec. A.

69. *Delgamuukw v. British Columbia*, 153 DLR (4th), at 263–64.

70. The next day the *Sun* published a letter from the First Nations Summit Task Group, which pointedly denies that treaty negotiations are an infinite struggle for control of finite resources. "First Nations Seek Economically Strong B.C.," *Vancouver Sun*, February 3, 1998, sec. A.

71. "Nisga'a Negotiators Are on Right Road," *Vancouver Sun*, February 2, 1998, sec. A.

72. "Despite Delgamuukw, Life in B.C. Must Go On," *Vancouver Sun*, April 16, 1998, sec. A.

73. "Delgamuukw Turned the World of B.C. and Lawyers Upside Down," *Vancouver Sun*, June 18, 1998, sec. A.

74. "Tribal Land Transfers Expected in Treaty Talks," *Vancouver Sun*, June 20, 1998, sec. A.

75. "Total Tab for the Nisga'a Deal Reaches $445 Million," *Vancouver Sun*, July 17, 1998, sec. A.

76. "Nisga'a Deal Welcome, but Give Us the Details," *Vancouver Sun*, July 17, 1998, sec. A.

77. "Total Tab for the Nisga'a Deal Reaches $445 Million," *Vancouver Sun*, July 17, 1998, sec. A.

78. Canada, Federal Treaty Negotiation Office; British Columbia, Ministry of Aboriginal Affairs; Nisga'a Nation, Nisga'a *Final Agreement*, n.p., n.d., 159.

79. "NDP Aims to Make Political Hay of the Nisga'a Treaty," *Vancouver Sun*, July 16, 1998, sec. A.

80. "Campbell Calls for Referendum," *Vancouver Sun*, August 11, 1998, sec. A.

81. "Liberals Were Right to Reveal Treaty Details," *Vancouver Sun*, July 23, 1998, sec. A.

82. "'No longer beggars in our own lands, we now go forward,'" *Vancouver Sun*, August 5, 1998, sec. A (emphasis added).

83. Philip Drucker, *Indians of the Northwest Coast* (Garden City, NJ: American Museum Service Books, 1955), 1.

84. Tennant, *Aboriginal Peoples and Politics*, 6–7.

85. "What You Get from Behind Closed Doors—A Rotten Deal," *Vancouver Sun*, November 10, 1998, sec. A.

86. "What We Don't Know Today Could Hurt Us Tomorrow," *Vancouver Sun*, November 25, 1998, sec. A.

87. Samuel Beckett, *The Unnamable*, in *Three Novels by Samuel Beckett* (New York: Grove Press, 1958), 299.

88. "Ceremony Opens Nisga'a Treaty Debate," *Vancouver Sun*, December 1, 1998, sec. A; "Royal Welcome Set for Nisga'a Visit to Victoria," *Vancouver Sun*, November 30, 1998, sec. A.

89. "Hoopla Unnecessary, but Treaty Debate Is Welcome," *Vancouver Sun*, December 1, 1998, sec. A.

90. "Liberals, NDP Prepare for Vote on Treaty," *Vancouver Sun*, April 22, 1999, sec. A.

91. "Debate Treaty Till Fears Are Put to Rest," *Vancouver Sun*, November 24, 1999, sec. A.

92. "Liberals Plan to Limit Debate on Nisga'a Deal," *Vancouver Sun*, December 2, 1999, sec. A.

93. "Reform Plans to Tie up House over Nisga'a," *Vancouver Sun*, December 7, 1999, sec. A.

94. "MPs Battle Fatigue as Reform Attacks Nisga'a," *Vancouver Sun*, December 9, 1999, sec. A.

95. "Nisga'a Treaty Is Passed, but Court Cases Go On," *Vancouver Sun*, April 15, 2000, sec. A.

CODA: THE *SOLARIS* HYPOTHESIS

1. Stanislaw Lem, *Solaris*, trans. Joanna Kilmartin and Steve Cox (San Diego: Harcourt, 1970).

2. This is one of the novel's many plays on names. Gustav Fechner (1801–1887) was the founder of psychophysics, the experimental study of relationships between mental events and brain processes. See Michael Heidelberger, *Nature from Within: Gustav Fechner and His Psychophysical Worldview*, trans. Cynthia Klohr (Pittsburgh: University of Pittsburgh Press, 2004). William Thomson, Baron Kelvin of Largs, introduced the term "energy" into scientific language. See Crosbie Smith, "Lord Kelvin: Scientist of Energy," in *Superconductor Science and Technology* 4 (1991): 502–6. Rhea, like Prometheus, was one of the Titans. In Homer's *Iliad* Hera credits her with giving birth to gods. Homer, *The Iliad*, trans. Robert Fagles (New York: Penguin Books, 1990), bk. 14, lines 241–53.

3. André Breton, *Manifestoes of Surrealism*, trans. Richard Seaver and Helen R. Lane (Ann Arbor: University of Michigan Press, 1969), 26.

4. Lem, *Solaris*, 71.

5. Joseph Conrad, *Heart of Darkness*, ed. Robert Kimbrough (New York: W. W. Norton, 1963), 60.

6. Lem, *Solaris*, 47–48.

7. Steven Soderbergh, dir., *Solaris* (Twentieth Century Fox, 2002), scene 10.

8. Lem, *Solaris*, 58.

9. Soderbergh, *Solaris*, scene 16.

10. Charles Sanders Peirce, "Some Consequences of Four Incapacities," in *The Essential Peirce: Volume 1 (1867–1893)*, ed. Nathan Houser and Christian Kloesel (Bloomington: Indiana University Press, 1992), 54.

11. Lem, *Solaris*, 102.

12. Andrei Tarkovsky, dir., *Solaris* (Mosfilm Studios, 1972), chap. 20.

13. Giorgio Agamben, "*Pardes:* The Writing of Potentiality," in *Potentialities*, trans. Daniel Heller-Roazen (Stanford: Stanford University Press, 1999), 215.

14. Jean-Paul Sartre, *Being and Nothingness*, trans. Hazel E. Barnes (New York: Washington Square Press, 1956), 59.

15. J. Hillis Miller, *Versions of Pygmalion* (Cambridge, MA: Harvard University Press, 1990), 13.

16. Lem, *Solaris*, 197.

17. Charles Sanders Peirce, "Pragmatism," in *The Essential Peirce: Volume 2 (1893–1913)*, ed. Peirce Edition Project (Bloomington: Indiana University Press, 1998), 411.

REFERENCES

Adorno, Theodor W., and Walter Benjamin. *The Complete Correspondence, 1928–1940.* Edited by Henri Lonitz. Translated by Nicolas Walker. Cambridge, MA: Harvard University Press, 1999.

Adorno, Theodor W., and Max Horkheimer. "The Concept of Enlightenment." In *Dialectic of Enlightenment,* translated by John Cumming, 3–42. New York: Continuum, 1990.

Aeschylus. *Prometheus Bound.* Translated by David Grene. In *The Complete Greek Tragedies: Aeschylus I,* edited by David Grene and Richard Lattimore, 1:91–245. New York: Modern Library, 1942.

Agamben, Giorgio. *Homo Sacer: Sovereign Power and Bare Life.* Translated by Daniel Heller-Roazen. Stanford: Stanford University Press, 1998.

———. *Idea of Prose.* Translated by Michael Sullivan and Sam Whitsitt. Albany: State University of New York Press, 1995.

———. *Potentialities: Collected Essays in Philosophy.* Edited and translated by Daniel Heller-Roazen. Stanford: Stanford University Press, 1999.

Anidjar, Gil. *"Our Place in al-Andalus": Kabbalah, Philosophy, Literature in Arab Jewish Letters.* Stanford: Stanford University Press, 2002.

Aristotle. *The Art of Rhetoric.* Translated by H. C. Lawson-Tancred. London: Penguin Books, 1991.

———. *Metaphysics.* Translated by Hugh Lawson-Tancred. London: Penguin Books, 1998.

———. *On the Soul.* Translated by J. A. Smith. In *Introduction to Aristotle,* edited by Richard McKeon, 143–235. New York: Modern Library, 1947.

———. *Physics.* Translated by Robin Waterfield. Oxford: Oxford University Press, 1996.

———. *Poetics.* Translated by Richard Janko. Indianapolis: Hackett Publishing, 1987.

Artaud, Antonin. *Selected Writings.* Edited by Susan Sontag. Translated by Helen Weaver. Berkeley: University of California Press, 1976.

———. *The Theater and Its Double.* Translated by Mary Caroline Richards. New York: Grove Press, 1958.

Austin, J. L. *How to Do Things with Words.* 2nd ed. Edited by J. O. Urmson and Marina Sbisà. Cambridge, MA: Harvard University Press, 1962.

Barthes, Roland. *Camera Lucida: Reflections on Photography.* Translated by Richard Howard. New York: Hill and Wang, 1981.

———. *Mythologies.* Translated by Annette Lavers. New York: Hill and Wang, 1972.

———. "Proust et les noms." In *To Honor Roman Jakobson: Essays on the Occasion of His Seventieth Birthday,* 1:150–58. The Hague: Mouton, 1967.

Bataille, Georges. *Consumption.* Vol. 1 of *The Accursed Share: An Essay on General Economy.* Translated by Robert Hurley. New York: Zone Books, 1991.

———. *Erotism: Death and Sensuality.* Translated by Mary Dalwood. San Francisco: City Lights Books, 1986.

———. *The History of Eroticism.* Vol. 2 of *The Accursed Share: An Essay on General Economy.* Translated by Robert Hurley. New York: Zone Books, 1991.

———. *Sovereignty.* Vol. 3 of *The Accursed Share: An Essay on General Economy.* Translated by Robert Hurley. New York: Zone Books, 1991.

———. *Visions of Excess: Selected Writings, 1927–1939.* Translated by Allan Stoekl, with Carl R. Lovitt and Donald M. Leslie, Jr. Minneapolis: University of Minnesota Press, 1985.

Baudrillard, Jean. *For a Critique of the Political Economy of the Sign.* Translated by Charles Levin. St. Louis: Telos Press, 1981.

———. *The Mirror of Production.* Translated by Mark Poster. St. Louis: Telos Press, 1975.

———. "The Precession of Simulacra." In *Simulations,* translated by Paul Foss, Paul Patton, and Philip Beitchman, 1–79. New York: Semiotext(e), 1983.

Beckett, Samuel. *The Unnamable.* In *Three Novels by Samuel Beckett.* New York: Grove Press, 1958.

Benjamin, Walter. *The Arcades Project.* Translated by Howard Eiland and Kevin McLaughlin. Cambridge, MA: Harvard University Press, 1999.

———. *Gesammelte Schriften.* Edited by Rolf Tiedemann and Hermann Schweppenhäuser. Frankfurt: Suhrkamp Verlag, 1974–85.

———. *Selected Writings: volume 1, 1913–1926.* Edited by Marcus Bullock and Michael W. Jennings. Cambridge, MA: Harvard University Press, 1996.

———. *Selected Writings: volume 2, 1927–1934.* Translated by Rodney Livingstone and others. Edited by Michael W. Jennings, Howard Eiland, and Gary Smith. Cambridge, MA: Harvard University Press, 1999.

———. *Selected Writings: volume 3, 1935–1938.* Translated by Edmund Jephcott, Howard Eiland, and others. Edited by Howard Eiland and Michael W. Jennings. Cambridge, MA: Harvard University Press, 2002.

———. *Selected Writings: volume 4, 1938–1940.* Translated by Edmund Jephcott and others. Edited by Howard Eiland and Michael W. Jennings. Cambridge, MA: Harvard University Press, 2003.

Benveniste, Émile. *Problems in General Linguistics*. Translated by Mary Elizabeth Meek. Coral Gables, FL: University of Miami Press, 1971.

Bergson, Henri. *Matter and Memory*. Translated by Nancy Margaret Paul and W. Scott Palmer. New York: Zone Books, 1991.

Best, Elsdon. *Spiritual and Mental Concepts of the Maori*. Wellington: W. A. G. Skinner, 1922.

Biggs, Bruce. "Humpty-Dumpty and the Treaty of Waitangi." In *Waitangi: Māori and Pākehā Perspectives of the Treaty of Waitangi*, edited by I. W. Kawharu. Auckland: Oxford University Press, 1989.

Boas, Franz. *The Ethnography of Franz Boas: Letters and Diaries of Franz Boas Written on the Northwest Coast from 1886 to 1931*. Edited by Ronald P. Rohner. Chicago: University of Chicago Press, 1969.

Borrows, John. "Re-Living the Present: Title, Treaties, and the Trickster in British Columbia." *BC Studies* 120 (1998–99): 99–108.

Boudinot, Elias. *Cherokee Editor: The Writings of Elias Boudinot*. Edited by Theda Purdue. Knoxville: University of Tennessee Press, 1983.

Brady, Ivan. "Anthropological Poetics." In *Handbook of Qualitative Research*, 2nd ed., edited by Norman K. Denzin and Yvonna S. Lincoln, 949–79. Thousand Oaks, CA: Sage Publications, 2000.

———. "In Defense of the Sensual: Meaning Construction in Ethnography and Poetics." *Qualitative Inquiry* 10.4 (2004): 622–44.

Breton, André. *Manifestoes of Surrealism*. Translated by Richard Seaver and Helen R. Lane. Ann Arbor: University of Michigan Press, 1969.

British Columbia. "Papers Relating to the Commission Appointed to Enquire into the State and Condition of the Indians of the North-West Coast of British Columbia." *Sessional Papers*, 1888, 51 Vic. 415–62.

———. "Report of Conferences between the Provincial Government and Indian Delegates from Fort Simpson and Nass River." *Sessional Papers*, 1887, 50 Vic. 251–72.

Brodersen, Momme. *Walter Benjamin: A Biography*. Translated by Malcolm R. Green and Ingrida Ligers. Edited by Martina Dervis. London: Verso, 1996.

Bücher, Karl. *Industrial Evolution*. Translated by S. Morley Wickett. New York: Henry Holt, 1901.

Calder et al. v. Attorney-General of British Columbia. 8 Dominion Law Reports (3d), 59 (Supreme Court of British Columbia, October 17, 1969); 13 DLR (3d), 64 (British Columbia Court of Appeal, May 7, 1970); 34 DLR (3d), 145 (Supreme Court of Canada, January 31, 1973).

Canada. House of Commons. *Debates*, January 4–February 9, 1973.

———. National Archives of Canada. Department of Indian Affairs. Record Group 10. "Black Series." Vol. 3825. Files 60 511-1, 60 511-2, 60 511-3, and 60 511-4, pt. 1.

———. *Statutes of Canada, 1914*. 4–5 George V. Ottawa: King's Printer, 1914.

Canada, British Columbia, and Nisg̱a'a Nation. *Nisg̱a'a Final Agreement and Appendices*. N.p., n.d.

Capell, A. "The Word 'Mana': A Linguistic Study." *Oceania* 9 (1938): 89–96.

Champlain, Samuel de. *The Voyages and Explorations of Samuel de Champlain.*
2 vols. Translated by Annie Nettleton Bourne. Edited by Edward Gaylord
Bourne. Toronto: Courier Press, 1911.

Clarke, Austin. *The Origin of Waves.* Toronto: McClelland and Stewart, 1997.

Clifford, James. *The Predicament of Culture: Twentieth-Century Ethnography,
Literature, and Art.* Cambridge, MA: Harvard University Press, 1988.

Codrington, R. H. *The Melanesians: Studies in Their Anthropology and Folk-Lore.*
Oxford: Clarendon Press, 1891.

Colenso, William. *The Authentic and Genuine History of the Signing of the Treaty
of Waitangi, New Zealand, February 5 and 6, 1840.* Wellington: George
Didsbury, 1890.

Comte, Auguste. *The Positive Philosophy of Auguste Comte.* 2 vols. 2nd ed. Translated by Harriet Martineau. London: Trubner and Co., 1875.

———. *Système de politique positive ou Traité de sociologie instituant la religion
de l'humanité. Tome troisième contenant la dynamique sociale ou la traité
générale du progrès humain (Philosophie de l'histoire).* Vol. 9 of *Oeuvres.* 1853.
Reprint; Paris: Éditions Anthropos, 1970.

Conrad, Joseph. *Heart of Darkness.* 3rd ed. Edited by Robert Kimbrough. New York:
W. W. Norton, 1963.

Crapanzano, Vincent. "The Moment of Prestidigitation: Magic, Illusion, and Mana
in the Thought of Emile Durkheim and Marcel Mauss." In *Prehistories of the
Future: The Primitivist Project and the Culture of Modernism,* 95–113. Stanford: Stanford University Press, 1995.

Culhane, Dara. *The Pleasure of the Crown: Anthropology, Law and First Nations.*
Vancouver: Talonbooks, 1998.

Darwin, Charles. *On the Origin of Species.* 1859. Reprint; Cambridge, MA: Harvard
University Press, 1964.

De Certeau, Michel. *The Writing of History.* Translated by Tom Conley. New York:
Columbia University Press, 1988.

Deleuze, Gilles. *Difference and Repetition.* 1968. Translated by Paul Patton. New
York: Columbia University Press, 1994.

———. *Proust and Signs.* New York: George Braziller, 1972.

Delgamuukw v. British Columbia. 79 Dominion Law Reports (4th), 185 (Supreme
Court of British Columbia, March 8, 1991); 104 DLR (4th), 470 (British Co-
lumbia Court of Appeal, June 25, 1993); 153 DLR (4th), 193 (Supreme Court of
Canada, December 11, 1997).

De Man, Paul. "Autobiography as Defacement." In *The Rhetoric of Romanticism,*
67–81. New York: Columbia University Press, 1984.

———. "Hypogram and Inscription." In *The Resistance to Theory,* 27–53. Minneapolis: University of Minnesota Press, 1986.

———. "Kant and Schiller." In *Aesthetic Ideology,* edited by Andrzej Warminski,
129–62. Minneapolis: University of Minnesota Press, 1996.

———. "Metaphor (*Second Discourse*)." In *Allegories of Reading: Figural Language in Rousseau, Nietzsche, Rilke, and Proust*, 135–59. New Haven: Yale University Press, 1979.

———. "The Rhetoric of Temporality." In *Blindness and Insight: Essays in the Rhetoric of Contemporary Criticism*. 2nd ed. Minneapolis: University of Minnesota Press, 1983.

Derrida, Jacques. "Différance." In *Margins of Philosophy*, translated by Alan Bass, 1–27. Chicago: University of Chicago Press, 1982.

———. *Glas*. Translated by John P. Leavey, Jr., and Richard Rand. Lincoln: University of Nebraska Press, 1986.

———. "The Pit and the Pyramid: Introduction to Hegel's Semiology." In *Margins of Philosophy*, translated by Alan Bass, 69–108. Chicago: University of Chicago Press, 1982.

———. "Signature, Event, Context." In *Margins of Philosophy*, translated by Alan Bass, 307–30. Chicago: University of Chicago Press, 1982. Translation of "Signature événément contexte." In *Marges de la philosophie*, 365–93. Paris: Éditions de Minuit, 1972.

———. *Specters of Marx: The State of the Debt, the Work of Mourning, and the New International*. Translated by Peggy Kamuf. New York: Routledge, 1994.

———. "White Mythology: Metaphor in the Text of Philosophy." In *Margins of Philosophy*, translated by Alan Bass, 207–71. Chicago: University of Chicago Press, 1982.

———. "Writing before the Letter." In *Of Grammatology*, translated by Gayatri Chakravorty Spivak, 1–93. Baltimore: Johns Hopkins University Press, 1974.

A Dictionary of Scientists: Oxford Reference Online. Oxford: Oxford University Press, 1999. http://www.oxfordreference.com.

Dilthey, Wilhelm. "The Development of Hermeneutics." In *Selected Writings*, edited by H. P. Rickman. Cambridge: Cambridge University Press, 1976.

Drucker, Philip. *Indians of the Northwest Coast*. Garden City, NJ: American Museum Service Books, 1955.

Duns Scotus, John. *Philosophical Writings*. Edited by Allan Wolter. Edinburgh: Thomas Nelson and Sons, 1962.

Durkheim, Émile. *The Elementary Forms of the Religious Life*. Translated by Joseph Ward Swain. 1915. Reprint; New York: Free Press, 1965.

Eastman, Charles Alexander (Ohiyesa). *From the Deep Woods to Civilization: Chapters in the Autobiography of an Indian*. Reprint, with an introduction by Raymond Wilson. Lincoln: University of Nebraska Press, 1977.

Fabian, Johannes. *Time and the Other: How Anthropology Makes Its Object*. New York: Columbia University Press, 1983.

Fechner, Gustav. *Elements of Psychophysics*. Vol. 1. Translated by Helmut E. Adler. Edited by David H. Howes and Edwin G. Boring. New York: Holt, Rinehart and Winston, 1966.

Fichte, J. G. *Science of Knowledge.* Edited and translated by Peter Heath and John Lachs. Cambridge: Cambridge University Press, 1982.

Firth, Raymond. "The Analysis of Mana: An Empirical Approach." In *Tikopia Ritual and Belief,* 174–94. London: Allen and Unwin 1967.

———. *Primitive Economics of the New Zealand Maori.* London: George Routledge and Sons, 1929.

———. *Primitive Polynesian Economy.* London: George Routledge and Sons, 1939.

Foster, Hamar. "Honoring the Queen: A Legal and Historical Perspective on the Nisga'a Treaty." *BC Studies* 120 (1998–99): 11–35.

Foucault, Michel. *The Archaeology of Knowledge and the Discourse on Language.* Translated by A. M. Sheridan Smith. New York: Pantheon Books, 1972. Translation of *L'archéologie du savoir.* Paris: Éditions Gallimard, 1969.

Frazer, James G. *The Golden Bough: A Study in Magic and Religion.* 3rd ed. 12 vols. London: Macmillan, 1911.

———. *The Golden Bough: A Study in Magic and Religion.* Abridged ed. New York: Macmillan, 1951.

———. "Totemism." In *Totemism and Exogamy: A Treatise on Certain Early Forms of Superstition and Society,* 1:1–87. London: Macmillan, 1910.

Frege, Gottlob. *Translations from the Philosophical Writings of Gottlob Frege.* Edited by Peter Geach and Max Black. Oxford: Basil Blackwell, 1977.

Freud, Sigmund. *Beyond the Pleasure Principle.* In *The Standard Edition of the Complete Psychological Works of Sigmund Freud,* translated by James Strachey and others, 18:1–64. London: Hogarth Press, 1955.

———. *Group Psychology and the Analysis of the Ego.* In *The Standard Edition of the Complete Psychological Works of Sigmund Freud,* translated by James Strachey and others, 18:65–143. London: Hogarth Press, 1955.

———. *The Interpretation of Dreams.* In *The Standard Edition of the Complete Psychological Works of Sigmund Freud,* translated by James Strachey and others, vols. 4 and 5. London: Hogarth Press, 1955.

———. "Project for a Scientific Psychology." In *The Standard Edition of the Complete Psychological Works of Sigmund Freud,* translated by James Strachey and others, 1:281–397. London: Hogarth Press, 1955.

———. *Totem and Taboo.* In *The Standard Edition of the Complete Psychological Works of Sigmund Freud,* translated by James Strachey and others, 13:1–162. London: Hogarth Press, 1955. Translation of *Totem und Tabu (Einige Übereinstimmungen im Seelenleben der Wilden und der Neurotiker).* In *Studienausgabe,* vol. 9: *Fragen der Gesellschaft Ursprünge der Religion,* 287–444. Frankfurt: Fischer Taschenbuch Verlag, 1982.

Gadamer, Hans-Georg. *Truth and Method.* 2nd rev. ed. Translated by Joel Weinsheimer and Donald G. Marshall. New York: Continuum, 1988.

Genette, Gérard. "Proust and Indirect Language." In *Figures of Literary Discourse,* translated by Alan Sheridan, 229–95. New York: Columbia University Press,

1982. Translation of "Proust et le langage indirect." In *Figures II: Essais*, 223–94. Paris: Éditions de Seuil, 1969.

———. "Proust Palimpsest." In *Figures of Literary Discourse*, translated by Alan Sheridan, 203–28. New York: Columbia University Press, 1982.

Goethe, Johann Wilhelm von. *Faust*. Translated by Walter Kaufmann. New York: Anchor Books, 1961.

———. "Prometheus." In *Twenty-Five German Poets: A Bilingual Collection*, translated and edited by Walter Kaufmann, 24–27. New York: W. W. Norton, 1962.

Gosnell, Joe. "Speech to the British Columbia Legislature, December 2, 1998." *BC Studies* 120 (1998–99): 5–10.

Greenblatt, Stephen. *Marvellous Possessions: The Wonder of the New World*. Chicago: University of Chicago Press, 1991.

Hegel, Georg Wilhelm Friedrich. *The Philosophy of History*. Translated by J. Sibree. New York: Dover, 1956. Translation of *Vorlesungen über die Philosophie der Geschichte*. Edited by Eduard Gans. Berlin: Verlag von Dunder und Humblot, 1840.

———. *Science of Logic*. Translated by A. V. Miller. 1969. Reprint; Atlantic Highlands, NJ: Humanities Press International, 1989.

Heidegger, Martin. *Being and Time*. Translated by John Macquarrie and Edward Robinson. San Francisco: HarperSanFrancisco, 1962.

———. "The Nature of Language." In *On the Way to Language*. Translated by Peter D. Hertz. San Francisco: HarperCollins, 1971.

———. "On the Essence and Concept of Φύσις in Aris totle's *Physics* B, I." Translated by Thomas Sheehan. In *Pathmarks*, edited by William McNeill, 183–230. Cambridge: Cambridge University Press, 1998.

———. "The Thing." In *Poetry, Language, Thought*, translated by Albert Hofstadter, 163–86. New York: Harper and Row, 1971.

———. "What Are Poets For?" In *Poetry, Language, Thought*, translated by Albert Hofstadter, 89–142. New York: Harper and Row, 1971.

———. "Why Poets?" In *Off the Beaten Track*, edited and translated by Julian Young and Kenneth Haynes, 200–241. Cambridge: Cambridge University Press, 2002.

———. *The Will to Power as Art*. Vol. 1 of *Nietzsche*. Translated by David Farrell Krell. San Francisco: HarperCollins, 1979.

Heidelberger, Michael. *Nature from Within: Gustav Fechner and His Psychophysical Worldview*. Translated by Cynthia Klohr. Pittsburgh: University of Pittsburgh Press, 2004.

Helmholtz, Hermann von. *Science and Culture: Popular and Philosophical Essays*. Edited by David Cahan. Chicago: University of Chicago Press, 1995.

Herder, Johann Gottfried von. "Treatise on the Origin of Language." In *Philosophical Writings*, translated and edited by Michael N. Forster, 65–164. Cambridge: Cambridge University Press, 2002.

Hjelmslev, Louis. *Prolegomena to a Theory of Language.* Translated by Francis J. Whitfield. Madison: University of Wisconsin Press, 1969.

Hocart, A. M. "Mana." *Man* 46 (1914): 97–101.

———. "Mana Again." *Man* 79 (1922): 139–41.

Hogbin, H. Ian. "Mana." *Oceania* 6.3 (1936): 241–74.

Homer. *The Iliad.* Translated by Robert Fagles. New York: Penguin Books, 1990.

Hugo, Victor. *Les misérables.* Translated by Charles E. Wilbour. New York: Knopf, 1997.

Hume, David. *The Natural History of Religion.* In *Principal Writings on Religion, including Dialogues concerning Natural Religion and the Natural History of Religion,* edited by J. C. A. Gaskin, 134–96. Oxford: Oxford University Press, 1993.

Jakobson, Roman. "Two Aspects of Language and Two Types of Aphasic Disturbances." In *Language in Literature,* edited by Krystyna Pomorska and Stephen Rudy, 95–114. Cambridge, MA: Harvard University Press, 1987.

Kant, Immanuel. *Critique of Judgement.* Translated by Werner S. Pluhar. Indianapolis: Hackett Publishing, 1987.

Kawharu, I. W. Introduction to *Waitangi: Māori and Pākehā Perspectives of the Treaty of Waitangi,* edited by I. W. Kawharu, x–xxii. Auckland: Oxford University Press, 1989.

Lacan, Jacques. *The Ethics of Psychoanalysis, 1959–1960.* Translated by Dennis Porter. Vol. 7 of *The Seminar of Jacques Lacan,* edited by Jacques-Alain Miller. New York: W. W. Norton, 1992.

Lacoue-Labarthe, Philippe. *Typography: Mimesis, Philosophy, Politics.* Edited by Christopher Fynsk. Stanford: Stanford University Press, 1998.

Lacoue-Labarthe, Philippe, and Jean-Luc Nancy. "The Nazi Myth." *Critical Inquiry* 16.2 (1990): 291–312.

Lander, Richard, and John Lander. *Journal of an Expedition to Explore the Course and Termination of the Niger; with A Narrative of a Voyage down That River to Its Termination.* Vol. 1. New York: Harper and Brothers, 1836.

Lang, Andrew. *The Secret of the Totem.* London: Longmans, Green, 1905.

Lem, Stanislaw. *Solaris.* 1961. Translated from the French by Joanna Kilmartin and Steve Cox. San Diego: Harcourt, 1970. Translated from the Polish by Jean-Michel Jasienko. N.p.: Éditions Denoël, 1966.

Lévi-Strauss, Claude. *Introduction to the Work of Marcel Mauss.* Translated by Felicity Baker. London: Routledge and Kegan Paul, 1987. Translation of "Introduction à l'oeuvre de Marcel Mauss." In *Sociologie et anthropologie,* ix–lii. Paris: Presses Universitaires de France, 1950.

———. *The Savage Mind.* Chicago: University of Chicago Press, 1966.

Lévy-Bruhl, Lucien. *How Natives Think.* Translated by Lilian A. Clare. Princeton: Princeton University Press, 1985.

Lubbock, John. *The Origin of Civilisation and the Primitive Condition of Man.* 1870. Edited by Peter Rivière. Reprint; Chicago: University of Chicago Press, 1978.

Lukács, Georg. *History and Class Consciousness: Studies in Marxist Dialectics.* Translated by Rodney Livingstone. Cambridge, MA: MIT Press, 1971.

Lyotard, Jean-François. *Libidinal Economy.* Translated by Iain Hamilton Grant. Indianapolis: Indiana University Press, 1993.

Malinowski, Bronislaw. *Magic, Science and Religion, and Other Essays.* Garden City, NJ: Doubleday, 1954.

Marett, R. R. "The Conception of Mana." In *The Threshold of Religion,* 115–41. London: Methuen, 1909.

Marx, Karl. *Capital: A Critique of Political Economy.* Vol. 1. 1867. Translated by Ben Fowkes. New York: Vintage Books, 1977. Translation of *Das Kapital. Kritik der politischen Ökonomie. Erster Band: Der Produktionsprozeß des Kapitals.* Karl Marx Friedrich Engels Werke, vol. 23. Berlin: Dietz Verlag, 1969.

———. *Capital: A Critique of Political Economy.* Vol. 2. 1885. Translated by David Fernbach. Harmondsworth: Penguin Books, 1978. Translation of *Das Kapital. Kritik der politischen Ökonomie. Zweiter Band: Der Zirkulationsprozeß des Kapitals.* Edited by Friedrich Engels. Karl Marx Friedrich Engels Werke, vol. 24. Berlin: Dietz Verlag, 1970.

———. *Capital: A Critique of Political Economy.* Vol. 3. 1894. Translated by David Fernbach. Harmondsworth: Penguin Books, 1981. Translation of *Das Kapital. Kritik der politischen Ökonomie. Dritter Band: Der Gesamtprozeß der kapitalistischen Produktion.* Edited by Friedrich Engels. Karl Marx Friedrich Engels Werke, vol. 25. Berlin: Dietz Verlag, 1969.

———. *A Contribution to the Critique of Political Economy.* Edited by Maurice Dobb. Translated by S. W. Ryazanskaya. New York: International Publishers, 1970.

———. "Critique of Hegel's Doctrine of the State." In *Early Writings,* translated by Rodney Livingstone and Gregor Benton, 57–198. London: Penguin Books, 1975.

———. "Economic and Philosophical Manuscripts." In *Early Writings,* translated by Rodney Livingstone and Gregor Benton, 279–400. London: Penguin Books, 1975. Translation of "Ökonomisch-philosophische Manuskripte aus dem Jahre 1844." In *Ergänzungsband: Schriften, Manuskripte, Briefe bis 1844,* 465–588. Karl Marx Friedrich Engels Werke, vol. 1. Berlin: Dietz Verlag, 1968.

———. "Excerpts from James Mill's *Elements of Political Economy.*" In *Early Writings,* translated by Rodney Livingstone and Gregor Benton, 259–78. London: Penguin Books, 1975. Translation of "Auszüge aus James Mills Buch *Élémens d'économie politique.*" In *Ergänzungsband: Schriften, Manuskripte, Briefe bis 1844,* 443–63. Karl Marx Friedrich Engels Werke, vol. 1. Berlin: Dietz Verlag, 1968.

———. *Grundrisse: Foundations of the Critique of Political Economy (Rough Draft).* 1939. Translated by Martin Nicolaus. London: Penguin Books, 1973. Translation of *Ökonomische Manuskripte, 1857–58.* 2 vols. In *Karl Marx Friedrich Engels Gesamtausgabe, Zweite Abteilung: "Das Kapitale" und Vorarbeiten.* Berlin: Dietz Verlag, 1976 and 1981.

Marx, Karl, and Friedrich Engels. *The German Ideology: Critique of Modern German Philosophy according to Its Representatives Feuerbach, B. Bauer and Stirner, and of German Socialism according to Its Various Prophets.* In *Collected Works of Karl Marx and Friedrich Engels: 1845–47,* 5:19–539. New York: International Publishers, 1976.

Mauss, Marcel, [and Henri Hubert]. *A General Theory of Magic.* Translated by Robert Brain. London: Routledge and Kegan Paul, 1972. Translation of *Esquisse d'une théorie générale de la magie.* In *Sociologie et anthropologie,* 1–141. Paris: Presses Universitaires de France, 1950.

McKee, Christopher. *Treaty Talks in British Columbia: Negotiating a Mutually Beneficial Future.* Vancouver: UBC Press, 1996.

Miller, Bruce. Introduction to the special issue. *BC Studies* 95 (1992): 3–6.

Miller, J. Hillis. *Versions of Pygmalion.* Cambridge, MA: Harvard University Press, 1990.

Mitchell, W. J. T. *Picture Theory.* Chicago: University of Chicago Press, 1994.

Moore, Rachel O. *Savage Theory: Cinema as Modern Magic.* Durham, NC: Duke University Press, 2000.

Müller, Max. *Comparative Mythology.* Edited by A. Smythe Palmer. London: G. Routledge, [1909].

———. *Contributions to the Science of Mythology.* Vol. 1. London: Longmans, Green, 1897.

Nancy, Jean-Luc. *The Inoperative Community.* Edited by Peter Connor. Translated by Peter Connor, Lisa Garbus, Michael Holland, and Simona Sawhney. Minneapolis: University of Minnesota Press, 1991.

Nietzsche, Friedrich. *Beyond Good and Evil: Prelude to a Philosophy of the Future.* Translated by Walter Kaufmann. New York: Vintage, 1966. Translation of *Jenseits von Gut und Böse.* In *Werke in Drei Bänden,* edited by Karl Schlechta, 2:563–759. Munich: Carl Hanser Verlag, 1955.

———. *The Birth of Tragedy.* In *"The Birth of Tragedy" and "The Case of Wagner,"* translated by Walter Kaufmann, 15–144. New York: Vintage, 1967. Translation of *Die Geburt der Tragödie.* In *Werke in Drei Bänden,* edited by Karl Schlechta, 1:7–134. Munich: Carl Hanser Verlag, 1954.

———. *The Case of Wagner.* In *"The Birth of Tragedy" and "The Case of Wagner,"* translated by Walter Kaufmann, 153–92. New York: Vintage, 1967. Translation of *Der Fall Wagner.* In *Werke in Drei Bänden,* edited by Karl Schlechta, 2:901–38. Munich: Carl Hanser Verlag, 1955.

———. *Daybreak: Thoughts on the Prejudices of Morality.* Edited by Maudemarie Clark and Brian Leiter. Translated by R. J. Hollingdale. Cambridge: Cambridge University Press, 1997. Translation of *Morgenröte.* In *Werke in Drei Bänden,* edited by Karl Schlechta, 1:1010–1279. Munich: Carl Hanser Verlag, 1954.

———. *Ecce Homo: How One Becomes What One Is.* Translated by R. J. Hollingdale. London: Penguin Books, 1979. Translation of *Ecce homo.* In *Werke in Drei Bänden,* edited by Karl Schlechta, 2:1063–1159. Munich: Carl Hanser Verlag, 1955.

———. *The Gay Science*. Translated by Walter Kaufmann. New York: Vintage, 1974. Translation of *Die fröhliche Wissenschaft*. In *Werke in Drei Bänden*, edited by Karl Schlechta, 2:7–274. Munich: Carl Hanser Verlag, 1955.

———. *Human, All Too Human: A Book for Free Spirits*. Translated by R. J. Hollingdale. Cambridge: Cambridge University Press, 1986. Translation of *Menschliches, Allzumenschliches*. In *Werke in Drei Bänden*, edited by Karl Schlechta, 1:435–1008. Munich: Carl Hanser Verlag, 1954.

———. "Nietzsche contra Wagner." In *The Portable Nietzsche*, edited and translated by Walter Kaufman, 661–83. New York: Penguin Books, 1954. Translation of *Nietzsche contra Wagner*. In *Werke in Drei Bänden*, edited by Karl Schlechta, 2:1035–61. Munich: Carl Hanser Verlag, 1955.

———. *On the Genealogy of Morality*. Edited by Keith Ansell-Pearson. Translated by Carol Diethe. Cambridge: Cambridge University Press, 1994. Translation of *Zur Genealogie der Moral*. In *Werke in Drei Bänden*. edited by Karl Schlechta, 2:761–900. Munich: Carl Hanser Verlag, 1955.

———. *Thus Spoke Zarathustra*. In *The Portable Nietzsche*, edited and translated by Walter Kaufman, 103–439. New York: Penguin Books, 1954. Translation of *Also Sprach Zarathustra*. In *Werke in Drei Bänden*, edited by Karl Schlechta, 2:275–561. Munich: Carl Hanser Verlag, 1955.

———. *Twilight of the Idols*. In *The Portable Nietzsche*, edited and translated by Walter Kaufman, 463–563. New York: Penguin Books, 1954. Translation of *Götzen-Dämmerung*. In *Werke in Drei Bänden*, edited by Karl Schlechta, 2:939–1033. Munich: Carl Hanser Verlag, 1955.

———. *Untimely Meditations*. Edited by Daniel Breazeale. Translated by R. J. Hollingdale. Cambridge: Cambridge University Press, 1997. Translation of *Unzeitgemäße Betrachtungen*. In *Werke in Drei Bänden*, edited by Karl Schlechta, 1:135–434. Munich: Carl Hanser Verlag, 1954.

———. *The Will to Power*. Translated by Walter Kaufman and R. J. Hollingdale. New York: Vintage Books, 1967. Translation of *Der Wille zur Macht: Versuch einer Umwerthung aller Werthe*. In *Gesammelte Werke*, vols. 18 and 19. Munich: Musarion Verlag, 1926.

Norman, Waerete. "The Muriwhenua Claim." In *Waitangi: Māori and Pākehā Perspectives of the Treaty of Waitangi*, edited by I. W. Kawharu. Auckland: Oxford University Press, 1989.

Novalis. *Hymns to the Night and Other Selected Writings*. Translated by Charles E. Passage. Indianapolis: Bobbs-Merrill, 1960.

———. *Philosophical Writings*. Translated and edited by Margaret Mahony Stoljar. Albany: State University of New York Press, 1997.

Orange, Claudia. *The Treaty of Waitangi*. Wellington: Allen and Unwin, 1987.

Ovid. *Metamorphoses*. Translated by Charles Martin. New York: W. W. Norton, 2004.

Owens, J. M. R. "New Zealand before Annexation." In *The Oxford History of New Zealand*, 2nd ed., edited by Geoffrey W. Rice, 28–53. Auckland: Oxford University Press, 1992.

Peirce, Charles Sanders. *The Essential Peirce: Selected Philosophical Writings, volume 1 (1867–1893)*. Edited by Nathan Houser and Christian Kloesel. Bloomington: Indiana University Press, 1992.

———. *The Essential Peirce: Selected Philosophical Writings, volume 2 (1893–1913)*. Edited by the Peirce Edition Project. Bloomington: Indiana University Press, 1998.

———. *Peirce on Signs: Writings on Semiotic by Charles Sanders Peirce*. Edited by James Hoopes. Chapel Hill: University of North Carolina Press, 1991.

———. *Reasoning and the Logic of Things: The Cambridge Conferences Lectures of 1898*. Edited by Kenneth Laine Ketner. Cambridge, MA: Harvard University Press, 1992.

Plato. *Cratylus*. In *Complete Works*, edited by John M. Cooper and D. S. Hutchinson, 101–56. Indianapolis: Hackett Publishing, 1997.

———. *The Republic*. Translated by G. M. A. Grube. Indianapolis: Hackett Publishing, 1974.

Proust, Marcel. *The Captive*. In *Remembrance of Things Past*, translated by C. K. Scott Moncrieff, Terence Kilmartin, and Andreas Mayor, 3:1–422. New York: Vintage Books, 1981. Translation of *La prisonnière*. In *À la recherche du temps perdu*, edited by Pierre Clarac and André Ferré, 3:7–415. Paris: Éditions Gallimard, 1954.

———. *Cities of the Plain*. In *Remembrance of Things Past*, translated by C. K. Scott Moncrieff and Terence Kilmartin, 2:621–1169. New York: Vintage Books, 1981. Translation of *Sodome et Gomorrhe*. In *À la recherche du temps perdu*, edited by Pierre Clarac and André Ferré, 2:599–1131. Paris: Éditions Gallimard, 1954.

———. *Swann's Way*. In *Remembrance of Things Past*, translated by C. K. Scott Moncrieff and Terence Kilmartin, 1:1–462. New York: Vintage Books, 1981. Translation of *Du côté de chez Swann*. In *À la recherche du temps perdu*, edited by Pierre Clarac and André Ferré, 1:1–427. Paris: Éditions Gallimard, 1954.

———. *Time Regained*. In *Remembrance of Things Past*, translated by C. K. Scott Moncrieff, Terence Kilmartin, and Andreas Mayor, 3:707–1107. New York: Vintage Books, 1981. Translation of *Le temps retrouvé*. In *À la recherche du temps perdu*, edited by Pierre Clarac and André Ferré, 3:689–1048. Paris: Éditions Gallimard, 1954.

———. *Within a Budding Grove*. In *Remembrance of Things Past*, translated by C. K. Scott Moncrieff and Terence Kilmartin, 1:463–1018. New York: Vintage Books, 1981. Translation of *À l'ombre des jeunes filles en fleurs*. In *À la recherche du temps perdu*, edited by Pierre Clarac and André Ferré, 1:429–955. Paris: Éditions Gallimard, 1954.

Quintilian. *The Orator's Education*. Vol. 3. Edited and translated by Donald A. Russell. Cambridge, MA: Harvard University Press, 2001.

Raunet, Daniel. *Without Surrender, without Consent: A History of the Nisga'a Land Claims.* Vancouver: Douglas and McIntyre, 1996.

Ricoeur, Paul. *The Philosophy of Paul Ricoeur: An Anthology of His Work.* Edited by Charles E. Regan and David Stewart. Boston: Beacon Press, 1978.

———. *The Rule of Metaphor: Multi-disciplinary Studies of the Creation of Meaning in Language.* Translated by Robert Czerny, with Kathleen McLaughlin and John Costello. Toronto: University of Toronto Press, 1977.

Robinson, Eden. *Monkey Beach.* Toronto: Alfred A. Knopf Canada, 2000.

Rohner, Ronald P., ed. *The Ethnography of Franz Boas: Letters and Diaries of Franz Boas Written on the Northwest Coast from 1886 to 1931.* Chicago: University of Chicago Press, 1969.

Ross, Ruth. "Te Tiriti O Waitangi: Texts and Translations." *New Zealand Journal of History* 6.2 (1972): 129–57.

———. "The Treaty on the Ground." In *The Treaty of Waitangi: Its Origins and Significance,* 16–34. University Extension Publication, no. 7. Wellington: Department of University Extension, Victoria University, 1972.

Rousseau, Jean-Jacques. "Discourse on the Origin and the Foundations of Inequality among Men or Second Discourse." 1755. In *The "Discourses" and Other Early Political Writings,* edited and translated by Victor Gourevitch, 111–222. Cambridge: Cambridge University Press, 1997.

———. "Discourse on Political Economy." 1755. In *"The Social Contract" and Other Later Political Writings,* edited and translated by Victor Gourevitch, 3–38. Cambridge: Cambridge University Press, 1997.

———. "Essay on the Origin of Languages in Which Something Is Said about Melody and Musical Imitation." In *The "Discourses" and Other Early Political Writings,* edited and translated by Victor Gourevitch, 247–99. Cambridge: Cambridge University Press, 1997.

———. "Of the Social Contract." 1762. In *"The Social Contract" and Other Later Political Writings,* edited and translated by Victor Gourevitch, 39–152. Cambridge: Cambridge University Press, 1997.

Rushdie, Salman. *Fury: A Novel.* Toronto: Vintage Canada, 2002.

Said, Edward W. *Orientalism.* New York: Vintage Books, 1979.

Sartre, Jean-Paul. *Being and Nothingness: A Phenomenological Essay on Ontology.* 1943. Translated by Hazel E. Barnes. New York: Washington Square Press, 1956.

Saussure, Ferdinand de. *Course in General Linguistics.* Translated by Roy Harris. Edited by Charles Bally and Albert Sechehaye with Albert Riedlinger. La Salle, IL: Open Court, 1983.

Schelling, F. W. J. *The Ages of the World.* Translated by Jason M. Wirth. Albany: State University of New York Press, 2000.

———. *Bruno, or, On the Natural and the Divine Principle of Things.* Translated by Michael G. Vater. Albany: State University of New York Press, 1984.

———. *Clara, or, On Nature's Connection to the Spirit World.* Translated by Fiona Steinkamp. Albany: State University of New York Press, 2002.

———. *Ideas for a Philosophy of Nature.* Translated by Errol E. Harris and Peter Heath. Cambridge: Cambridge University Press, 1988.

Schlegel, Friedrich. *Friedrich Schlegel's "Lucinde" and the Fragments.* Translated by Peter Firchow. Minneapolis: University of Minnesota Press, 1971.

Schopenhauer, Arthur. *The World as Will and Representation.* Vol. 1. Translated by E. F. J. Payne. New York: Dover, 1958.

Shakespeare, William. *The Life of Timon of Athens.* Edited by Stanley T. Williams. New Haven: Yale University Press, 1919.

Smith, Adam. *An Inquiry into the Nature and Causes of the Wealth of Nations.* Edited by Edwin Cannan. New York: Modern Library, 1994.

Smith, Crosbie. "Lord Kelvin: Scientist of Energy." *Superconductor Science and Technology* 4 (1991): 502–6.

Soderbergh, Steven, director. *Solaris.* Twentieth Century Fox, 2002.

Spencer, Baldwin, and F. J. Gillen. *The Native Tribes of Central Australia.* 1899. Reprint; New York: Dover, 1968.

Spencer, Herbert. *The Principles of Sociology.* 3rd ed. 3 vols. New York: D. Appleton, 1893.

Sterritt, Neil. "The Nisga'a Treaty: Competing Claims Ignored!" *BC Studies* 120 (1998–99): 73–97.

Tarkovsky, Andrei, director. *Solaris.* Mosfilm Studios, 1972.

Taussig, Michael. *Mimesis and Alterity: A Particular History of the Senses.* New York: Routledge, 1993.

Tennant, Paul. *Aboriginal Peoples and Politics: The Indian Land Question in British Columbia, 1849–1989.* Vancouver: UBC Press, 1990.

Titley, E. Brian. *A Narrow Vision: Duncan Campbell Scott and the Administration of Indian Affairs in Canada.* Vancouver: UBC Press, 1986.

Torgovnik, Marianna. *Gone Primitive: Savage Intellects, Modern Lives.* Chicago: University of Chicago Press, 1990.

Tylor, Edward B. *Primitive Culture: Researches into the Development of Mythology, Philosophy, Religion, Language, Art and Custom.* 2nd ed. 2 vols. New York: Henry Holt, 1874.

Vancouver Sun. February 16, 1995 to April 15, 2000.

Vico, Giambattista. *The New Science of Giambattista Vico.* 1744. Translated by Thomas Goddard Bergin and Max Harold Fisch. Ithaca, NY: Cornell University Press, 1968.

Walker, Ranginui J. *Ka Whawhai Tonu Matou/Struggle without End.* Auckland: Penguin Books, 1990.

———. "The Treaty of Waitangi as the Focus of Māori Protest." In *Waitangi: Māori and Pākehā Perspectives of the Treaty of Waitangi.* Edited by I. W. Kawharu. Auckland: Oxford University Press, 1989.

White, Hayden. *Metahistory: The Historical Imagination in Nineteenth-Century Europe.* Baltimore: Johns Hopkins University Press, 1973.

———. "The Tropics of History: The Deep Structure of the *New Science.*" In *Tropics of Discourse: Essays in Cultural Criticism,* 197–217. Baltimore: Johns Hopkins University Press, 1978.

Wilson, J. Leighton. *Western Africa: Its History, Condition, and Prospects.* New York: Harper and Brothers, 1856.

Wittgenstein, Ludwig. *Philosophical Investigations.* 2nd ed. Translated by G. E. M. Anscombe. Oxford: Blackwell, 1953.

INDEX

aboriginal people: Australia, 46–47, 52–53, 163–65; as beings without limits, 200; Boas's fieldwork with, 186; Dakota, 38; dances of, 36–40; Gitxsan, 197–98; Haisla, 170; Hegel's account of, 179–80; labor of, 38–39; Mâori, 128–34; Nisga'a, 188–202, 204–5; of the northwest coast, 202–3; residential schooling of, 36–40; rights of, 198; as specters of excess, 181, 188, 198–200, 202, 204; Spencer's account of, 184; Tsimshian, 190, 194–96; Wet'suwet'en, 197–98

aboriginal title, 190–92, 198–99, 201

accumulation: of barbarians, 59–60; of cellular energy, 50; horizon of, 34; moral evaluation of, 185; previous, 25, 31; primitive, 24–27; of stock, 31–32, 36; time of, 23, 31–34, 59

actual ideas, 134–37

actualization: Aristotle's account of, 17–18, 81–87, 108–10, 160, 211–12; dramatic, 91–92; of dreams, 68–69, 95–98, 173–74, 209; in illocutionary acts, 115–16; of impotentiality, 103–5, 108–12, 135–37, 186–87, 211–12; labor of, 67; magic as, 127; in Marx, 160; and myth, 71; in poetry, 13, 102; of sign, 12, 18, 122, 158; of spirit, 178–80. *See also* energeia; metaphor

Adorno, Theodor W.: on animism, 98; "The Concept of Enlightenment," 11; correspondence with Benjamin of, 15; on positivism, 64; on realism, 11

Aeschylus, *Prometheus Bound*, 56–57

Africa: Conrad's, 55–56; Hegel's, 180–81

Agamben, Giorgio: "On Potentiality," 103–5; "*Pardes*: The Writing of Potentiality," 211

alienation, 153–55

allegory, 177–78, 181–83, 185, 193, 195, 235n15

Ampere, André Marie, 137, 230n105

animism: Benjamin's, 17, 138–39; childhood and, 97–98; Derrida's, 186–88; Freud's definition of, 3; hermeneutics of, 17; in language, 80; Lévy-Bruhl's account of, 144–47; and monotheism, 141; and proso-popoeia, 72–73, 78, 85, 99; of Proust's narrator, 98; recourse of, 186–88; as savage world-picture, 3; without spirits, 94; survival of, in political economy, 155; survival of, in tragedy, 89; Swann's, 134–37; as theory of causality, 83, 175–76. *See also* causality; mythology; Nietzsche, Friedrich; realism; Tylor, Edward Burnett

Aristotle: on entelechy, 109–10; on metaphor, 80–86; *Metaphysics*, 105, 108; on nature, 17–18, 57; and Nietzsche, 90; *On the Soul*, 83, 103–4; *Physics*, 17, 57; *Poetics*, 80–81; on potentiality, 104–5, 108–10, 211–12; *Rhetoric*, 81–86; on skill, 57. *See also* actualization; change; nature

art: energy, 58, 67, 93; as frenzy, 91–92; life of, 16–17; savage, 68–69; as survival, 75–76; as transgression, 57

Artaud, Antonin, 19–20

Austin, J. L., *How to Do Things with Words*, 113–16, 119

autofictioning, 61–64, 94